THE DISAPPEARANCE
OF ÉMILE ZOLA

the Dis appear ance of Émile Zola

A STORY OF LOVE, LITERATURE, AND THE DREYFUS CASE

MICHAEL ROSEN

PEGASUS BOOKS
NEW YORK LONDON

The Disappearance of Émile Zola

Pegasus Books Ltd
148 West 37th Street, 13th Floor
New York, NY 10018

Copyright © 2017 by Michael Rosen

First Pegasus Books hardcover edition September 2017

ISBN: 978-1-68177-516-6

10 9 8 7 6 5 4 3 2 1

Printed in the United States of America
Distributed by W. W. Norton & Company, Inc.

33614080406001

To Emma, Elsie and Emile

In memory of Oscar, Rachel and Martin Rosen who
perished as a result of a time in France when Zola's words
on anti-semitism were rejected by those in power.

Contents

Illustrations

'J'accuse': Zola's open letter published on 13 January
1898. *Getty/SSPL*
Captain Alfred Dreyfus, before his arrest and imprisonment
in 1895 for the alleged crime of treason. *Getty/Popperfoto*
Major Ferdinand Esterhazy. *Getty/Universal Images Group*
Le Petit Journal reports Zola's departure from the trial at
Versailles, 18 July 1898. *Getty/Hulton Archive*
M. Labori, Zola's lawyer who advised him to flee the
country. *Photo: V. R. Vizetelly*
'Le Roi des Porcs': anti-semitic cartoon depicting Émile
Zola in relation to the Dreyfus Affair.
Zola with Jeanne Rozerot and their children, Denise and
Jacques, in 1899. *Alamy*
Zola's wife, Alexandrine, with Zola in the 1880s. *Bridgeman*
The front of 'Penn' in Weybridge, Surrey, with Denise,
Jacques and Violette Vizetelly, August 1898. *Photo: Émile
Zola, © Association du Musée Émile Zola*
Zola writing *Fécondité*, at 'Penn', 1898. *Photo: V. R. Vizetelly*
Ernest Vizetelly, Zola's translator and friend.
Zola in England (front cover), by Ernest Vizetelly.
Jeanne with Denise and Jacques at 'Summerfield'
in Addlestone, autumn 1898. *Photo: Émile Zola,
© Association du Musée Émile Zola*

The Queen's Hotel in Upper Norwood, where Zola moved in October 1898. *Photo: Émile Zola, © Association du Musée Émile Zola*

Alexandrine in the window of the Queen's Hotel. *Photo: Émile Zola, © Association du Musée Émile Zola*

Jasper Road off Westow Hill in Crystal Palace, south-east London. *Photo: Émile Zola, © Association du Musée Émile Zola*

Mme Zola near the bottom of Hermitage Road, Upper Norwood, November 1898. *Photo: Émile Zola, © Association du Musée Émile Zola*

Zola 'in his English garden', 1898. *Photo: V. R. Vizetelly*

Zola with his children, Denise and Jacques, not long before his death. *Getty/Corbis*

Acknowledgements

This book arose out of the collaboration between me and Emma-Louise Williams when we made a radio programme for BBC Radio 3 together about Émile Zola's time in Britain. Her work as producer selecting passages for broadcast, talking about what was poignant, affecting or striking, is an invisible hand behind many parts of the book. The details of the programme are in the bibliography. We interviewed Alain Pagès, Evelyne Bloch-Dano and Martine Le Blond-Zola and so thanks are owed to them for crystallising for us in conversation what they have edited, written or talked about elsewhere.

The fact that I can speak French is a result of my parents, Harold and Connie Rosen, taking me and my brother Brian to France many times when we were young, and encouraging us as a family to talk about France and French culture throughout our lives. Our father was still going to French classes in his late eighties and discussing his homework with me. I would like to thank my French teachers at my secondary schools, in particular Mr and Mrs Emmans who were so enthusiastic and thoughtful about French literature in the Sixth Form at Watford Grammar School.

Thanks too to the Miquel family who, since 1963, have sustained my interest in more aspects of French life, history and language than I can describe, in particular François who has been on hand literally and figuratively to offer support and expertise with this book.

Special thanks are due to Miles Deverson who carefully copied many of the contemporary newspaper and magazine sources cited in the book, and to Seema Beeri who found and translated the Yiddish newspapers of the time. Donald Sommerville has been a superb copy editor, scrutinising, questioning and correcting hundreds of details of history, language, bibliography and more.

Sarah Ardizzone translated the passage from *Fécondité* which appears on pp. 182–3.

Acknowledgements are due to the following for passages reprinted with their permission:

Éditions du Frisson Esthétique, for the message by Émile Zola from the cover of *Le Docteur Pascal* from p. 55 in *Mes étés à Brienne* by Brigitte Émile-Zola.

Les Presses de l'Université de Montréal, for use of a passage from a letter from Ernest Vizetelly to Macmillan Publishers, taken from p. 320 of *Mon cher Maître, Lettres d'Ernest Vizetelly à Émile Zola*, edited by Dorothy E. Speirs and Yannick Portebois. Les Presses de l'Université de Montréal also for use of extracts from letters from Émile Zola to Alexandrine, Jacques and Denise or letters from Alexandrine to Zola, taken from pages 225, 245–6, 250, 256, 259, 346 (Labori to Zola), 351, 369, 394, 438–9, 450, 451, 452, 460, 485i, 485ii, 488, 491, 492 of *Correspondance d'Émile Zola*, general editor B. H. Bakker, Volume IX, *Octobre 1897– Septembre 1899 (L'affaire Dreyfus)*.

Yale University Press for passages taken from pages xxvii, 73, 136–7 of *The Dreyfus Affair, 'J'accuse' and Other Writings* by Émile Zola, edited by Alain Pagès, translated by Eleanor Levieux.

University of Toronto Press for passages taken from pages 26, 27, 27–9, 43, 58, 59–60 in *Notes from Exile* by Émile Zola, edited and translated by Dorothy E. Speirs and edited by Yannick Portebois.

Éditions Gallimard for passages taken from letters on pages 200, 202, 207, 219, 221, 222, 225, 226, 234, 238, 240, 241, 241–2, 243, 245, 246, 253, 257, 263, 264, 268, 269, 274, 276, 279–80, 282, 287, 289, 290, 292, 293, 296, 297, 297–8, 298, 305, 313, 316, 318, 320, 322, 333, 334–5, 338, 340, 342, 355, 356 from *Lettres à Jeanne Rozerot, 1892–1902*, edited by Brigitte Émile-Zola and Alain Pagès.

Preface

Outside of France, people tend to know little of Émile Zola's life, so it's not surprising that they usually have heard little or nothing about his exile in London. Strictly speaking, it wasn't exile, it was flight. The world-renowned novelist – as he was even then – fled from France, having been fined and given a prison sentence. This was not due to any of the usual writers' transgressions – duels, crimes of passion, dissolution, immorality, or indecency in their writing. It was a political offence. On behalf of the disgraced army officer Captain Alfred Dreyfus, Zola took on the highest courts in the land and lost.

As many thought at the time, how odd. Wasn't this the novelist of the gutter? What was he doing siding with a rich Jewish traitor? They had an answer: arrogance, vanity and a probable secret allegiance to the 'syndicate', the mythic conspiracy that bound 'the Jews' together. Then, rather than face justice, he turned tail and escaped his due punishment. He was a coward too.

All this would be not much more than a scandal but for the fact that these events split France down the middle, brought the fundamental nature of the French state into question, and have left their marks on France ever since. Yet, at a crucial moment in their unravelling, Zola was sitting in suburban houses and hotels in South London, pottering about on his bike, and taking photos of shops and trees.

Reading a brief account of this period, it's easy to get the impression that he was in some kind of isolation ward or house arrest and that life stood still while he was in England. In actual fact, it was a time of turmoil, change and stress on three fronts: political, literary and personal. Reading what he wrote at the time in his incomplete memoir and his many letters, you can feel these three zones in his life tumble over each other.

And history didn't stand still. Zola was constantly observing what was going on around him in the incongruous surroundings of a London suburb. Meanwhile, people in Britain had a view of him. Zola as novelist, Zola as purveyor of filth, Zola as champion of justice, were all images that preceded him and surrounded him – even if he hardly acknowledged this at the time of his exile. Just occasionally, we hear from him his regrets that he is not being fêted as he had been only five years earlier when he had paid a quick visit to England as a guest of honour. There was a contrast of enormous proportions between the Zola in England of 1893 and the Zola in England of 1898.

'Coward!'

On the evening of Monday, 18 July 1898, Émile Zola disappeared.

Earlier in the day, Zola had appeared in a court in Versailles. Zola's lawyer, M. Labori, had tried to claim that the case could not be brought. The judge ruled against; Labori appealed. The judge said the case would continue. Zola and Labori met to discuss matters and then left the court and the building. Outside, the crowd shouted at Zola, 'Go back to Venice!' (his father came from Venice), 'Go back to the Jews!', 'Coward!' Zola was escorted through the crowds by soldiers and got into a coach. According to the radical journalist and politician Georges Clemenceau the crowds were: 'hurling stones, hissing, booing, shrieking for his death. If Zola had been acquitted that day, not one of us would have left the courtroom alive. This is what this man did. He braved his times. He braved his countrymen.'

As far as the world was concerned, this was his point of disappearance.

Zola had arrived at this extraordinary stage in his life as a consequence of two major events, the one sitting inside the other: the Dreyfus Affair and Zola's role in it as a campaigner for Dreyfus's innocence. The Dreyfus Affair was in its narrowest terms a question of justice. An army officer, Alfred Dreyfus, was accused of passing secrets to a foreign power, Germany. He was found guilty, stripped of his rank and sentenced to imprisonment on Devil's Island. Dreyfus was Jewish. In its widest terms, the Affair was a matter concerning the French Army, the government and powerful and very popular anti-Republican, pro-Monarchist and anti-semitic movements ranged on one side and, on the other, Republicans, liberals, socialists and pro-Jewish groups. The two sides were far from being united, unanimous, monolithic blocs, though at times it was in the interest of either side to characterise its opponents as precisely that.

Émile Zola did not immediately join the group which claimed that Dreyfus was innocent, but when he did, his intervention was decisive. He wrote – though it is probably more correct to say co-wrote – an open letter to the prime minister about Dreyfus. This was published on the front page of the newspaper *L'Aurore*, edited by Georges Clemenceau, with the headline 'J'Accuse'. In essence, the letter claimed that Dreyfus was innocent; that it was not Dreyfus who had prepared the '*bordereau*', the incriminating piece of paper on which military information to be given to the Germans had been written, but one Major Esterhazy. What's more, the accusation was that the army and the government were guilty of various crimes: illegality in the various trials, cover-ups, a campaign to mislead public opinion, and corruption. (All of these accusations were essentially true.) Zola also claimed that it was a crime to poison people's minds with anti-semitism and that liberal France would die of this disease unless she was cured of it.

This brought together in one place all the discoveries and allegations that the pro-Dreyfus camp had collected and put them before the French public. Its prime purpose was to corner the government and the army in order to secure the release of Dreyfus. Zola and his companions anticipated in 'J'Accuse' that Zola would be accused of libel. 'J'Accuse' even directed legal-minded readers to exactly which law, and which clauses of that law could be cited! And, as if in reply to himself, Zola stated that in so doing, he knew that he was voluntarily exposing himself to the justice system. This would necessitate the case against Dreyfus being heard in court and then shredded by the lawyers for the pro-Dreyfus camp. Or so they thought. After all, surely if one was accused of libel, all one needed to do was show the truth, and the libel case would fall.

In fact, the case was only allowed to proceed on the basis of the interpretation of one short passage in 'J'Accuse', the part where Zola employed the words *'par ordre'* ('by order' or 'on orders'). Any reference to the Dreyfus case itself was ruled inadmissible; it could not be brought before the court. With that expression, *'par ordre'*, Zola had accused the highest military court in the land of behaving corruptly – that is, under instruction from the General Staff. More precisely, Zola accused a first court martial of sentencing someone (Dreyfus) on the basis of a document which had been kept secret, meaning that the court had acted illegally. A second court martial, Zola claimed, had covered up the first trial's illegality and then had knowingly 'by order' acquitted a guilty man. This was Major Esterhazy. Zola claimed it was Esterhazy who had written a paper outlining French military secrets and passed it to the Germans, and it was not, as the army had alleged, Dreyfus – but this counter-accusation could not be heard in court. It was for making the specific charge that the court martial had acted in these matters 'by order' of the General Staff – and only on this specific charge – that Zola was found guilty of libel.

For a British audience at the time, perplexed as to how France could arrive at this point, there was the added question of how the French justice system could find someone guilty of libelling a public institution rather than a person, yet that was precisely how the Republic could and did defend its values in a court of law. It showed this by fining Zola 3,000 francs and sentencing him to one year's imprisonment.

Zola's sentence was news in itself but his disappearance was sensational. Over the next few days, the newspapers carried stories telling the world what had happened to this international figure. In London, on the evening of 19 July, the *Daily News* said that Zola had gone on a tour to Norway. On the 20th the same paper tried to flesh it out:

M. Zola has left Paris. What can be more natural in this torrid weather? He may have gone to Norway leaving M. Labori to deal as he thinks fit with his law affairs, or he may have only gone to stay at a friend's place in the country. He ordered some days ago four excursionist tickets for Norway. It appears that he left Paris last night, but not for Médan [Zola's country house]. The house in the Rue de Bruxelles is shut up. Anti-Dreyfusard papers announce 'Zola's Flight' in gigantic characters . . .

On the same day, the *Pall Mall Gazette* wrote: 'Zola, accompanied by Madame Zola and her maid left Paris by the 8.35 train for Lucerne.'

The Times ran a story that people were 'hinting that he is about to join his good friend Ibsen ...'

By the 21st, the story had developed. In the *Daily News* it was now:

M. Zola's flitting –
a holiday abroad – to return in October
From our correspondent

I have seen one of the counsel in the Zola case, and learnt that M. Zola left for Amsterdam and Christiania [Oslo] last evening, but by the round about way of Switzerland. Cycles for him and his two companions were sent on to the last place the train was to stop at, on this side of the frontier. They were to cycle on some distance and enter Switzerland by Neuchatel or Geneva, according to the weather.

On another page of the same newspaper we find: 'M. Zola, our Paris Correspondent says, has left Paris for Holland and Norway ... He and his family crossed the frontier on bicycles on Tuesday night.'

The *Pall Mall Gazette* on the 21st gave it a comic twist:

M. Zola has, in the language of the modern schoolboy, 'bunked'. His action in so doing is, naturally, being variously judged by his foes and friends respectively. To the former it presents itself in the light of an ignominious flight – in fact, as 'bunk' the outcome of 'funk' – to the latter it appears to be merely a judicious strategic movement to the rear. For the moment the 'funk' theory has the best of it, because retirement to the rear is never a brilliant operation to look at. On the other hand, they laugh longest who laugh last, and M. Zola is probably quite right in believing that a good many things will happen before he returns to the fray in October.

On the 22nd, *The Times* ran the story as: 'He left Paris yesterday morning for Switzerland, and intends thence to go and stay with the novelist Björnson in Norway.'

Also on the 22nd, the *Daily News* called it 'M. Zola at Hide-and-seek' and said that *L'Aurore* (the newspaper which published 'J'Accuse') which 'really knows everything about it, says nothing'. Their journalists revealed that: 'Madame Zola is at Médan, but she does not, nor do the servants, open her doors. They speak at the hall-door through a sliding panel.'

Then, in a scene typical of a Zola novel, it related how M. Mouthiers, the '*huissier*' (the official who served law papers from the court):

... knocked first at the door of one pavilion and then at that of the other without obtaining an answer. There were lights in the windows and he could see in a kitchen two women and a man servant. He went to the door nearest to the kitchen and rang and rapped till he was tired.

At last a woman came to a window and asked what he wanted.

'Are you one of the household?' he asked.

'No, I am only a neighbour. Some other neighbours are with me. We had leave to come into the garden to eat cherries, and I, seeing the kitchen open, entered the house.'

'Is M. Zola there?'

'No.'

'Madame Zola?'

'No.'

'Is there a servant?'

'No, there's nobody.'

The huissier then said who he was, and why he came. He said he was sure the woman at the window was lying, and that he would write on the original of the notice: 'Served a copy on a servant, who was looking from a window.' When he thrust it under the door, however, the others joined her, and declared she told the truth.

Mouthiers then went to the Mayor of Médan, informed him how things stood, and in the name of the law required him to send the notice next day by the rural policeman. He would be sure to know who were servants and who were not.

If nothing else, this report shows us Zola's situation: he was a fugitive, with spying journalists and officers of the state tracking him.

By the 25th the *Morning Post* gave its readers a different story altogether:

M. Zola found. – While Correspondents have been announcing the simultaneous appearance of M. Zola in Brussels, Geneva, Berlin, Rome and elsewhere, the novelist has been quietly hiding at Verneuil, a village in the environs of Paris. He is residing with friends whose garden is enclosed by a stone wall 6ft. high, over which occasional peeps of Zola have been obtained by enterprising reporters. I am told that M. Zola intends to leave Verneuil for London.

However, on the 27th the same paper said: 'It appears that at the last moment M. Émile Zola abandoned his intention of proceeding to London, and that he is still residing at Verneuil.'

Meanwhile, on the 28th the *Pall Mall Gazette* sought to amuse its readers:

A Swiss Church paper, the 'Kirchenblatt', has started a veritable press polemic about the [Zola] trial. Bâle the Protestant has been praying publicly in the churches for M. Zola ... the 'Indépendence Belge' [a Belgian newspaper] adds that Belgian and Dutch preachers are praying too.

Le Jour, one of the French papers, is reported as replying, 'It is not of the smallest importance to France whether all the curés, the rabbis, and the Protestant pastors of Holland, Belgium, and Switzerland are praying for Dreyfus.'

What's more the *Pall Mall Gazette* reported, the Volkstheater in Zurich was advertising for a 'dozen gentlemen, washed and dressed in long black coats, to represent the jury in the Zola trial. Salary one franc per night. Duties – to listen to the evidence and look wise.'

Leaving aside the pantomime element that was creeping

in, the stories about Zola's whereabouts were all wrong. Whether that was because Zola's followers were leaking false reports or that the journalists and editors invented stories to make up for what they didn't know, is not clear.

Ernest Vizetelly was one of Zola's translators and wrote a memoir, *With Zola in England*. He says that on 25 July,

... our own 'Daily Chronicle' announced M. Zola's presence at a London hotel, and on the following day the 'Morning Leader' was in a position to state that the hotel in question was the Grosvenor. Both 'Chronicle' and 'Leader' were right; but as I had received pressing instructions to contradict all rumours of M. Zola's arrival in London, I did so in this instance through the medium of the Press Association. I here frankly acknowledge that I thus deceived both the Press and the public. I acted in this way, however, for weighty reasons, which will hereafter appear.

The tales that Vizetelly claimed he fed the press include those about Zola heading to Norway, Switzerland or Hamburg. The Norway story was embroidered, he says, to include Zola trying to meet Kaiser Wilhelm of Germany, who was in Norway at the time, but that the Kaiser had refused.

What really happened on 18 and 19 July? We should start in Versailles.

Before the court's decision had been finalised, Zola and his lawyer, M. Labori, had an urgent discussion in an office in the court building. Labori put it to Zola that he should flee. Zola favoured prison. The issue was: which of these two courses of action would benefit Dreyfus the more? Then, if he didn't flee, would Zola be able to cope with imprisonment? Either way, Labori was anxious they should leave the building before the court's decision was served. The chief of police told them a coach was ready, but as they left they were spotted by the crowd. According to Zola, it took the cavalry to keep them back.

The coach took the route through Saint-Cloud and the Bois de Boulogne. After some silence and the sharing of a bit of bread that Zola had remembered to bring in the morning, Labori urged Zola to leave the country. The coach dropped them off at the house of Zola's publisher, Georges Charpentier, at 11 rue de Grenelle where participants in the discussion included Georges Clemenceau, Clemenceau's brother Albert (a lawyer, who had defended the owner of *L'Aurore*), and Fernand Desmoulin, artist and close friend of Zola. Desmoulin went off to the Zola residence at 21 *bis* rue de Bruxelles to fetch Alexandrine, Zola's wife. There was a heated discussion. The outcome was that it was thought best that Zola should flee, thereby avoiding having the sentence on him put into effect. Labori would demand a re-trial while Zola should go on the run to Britain. All this would keep the Dreyfus case in the public eye. However, clearly there were risks. If Zola were re-captured, he would bring a further charge on himself. In Britain, wouldn't he run the risk of being extradited and brought back to France – all of which would distract from the Dreyfus case, diverting attention away from the revelations that the pro-Dreyfus camp had made public? The problem was that Zola was a very recognisable figure. Even in that pre-TV era, Zola's appearance was extremely well known, his image having appeared in books, magazines, newspapers and on posters, whether to celebrate his achievements, describe scandals or to mock and caricature him for supporting Dreyfus. He was a celebrity.

Alexandrine arrived, 'very upset' says Zola, bringing a nightshirt and a few other things wrapped in a newspaper. With just these, she and Zola took a carriage to the Gare du Nord. Zola writes:

I held her hand and squeezed it hard: we spoke only a few words to each other. Charpentier, who had followed in another carriage, bought a ticket to London for me, and he and my wife came with me to the train, where they stayed for fifteen minutes, waiting for the train to leave, shielding the window of the coach, which was the first one behind the engine. What a wrenching separation! My dear wife watched me leave, with her eyes full of tears and her hands clasped and trembling.

At this point I should introduce someone else, someone who was not there to see him off: Jeanne Rozerot. Conventionally, she is called Zola's mistress. It's an expression that doesn't do the work of describing Jeanne or her relationship with Zola or indeed with Madame Zola. Jeanne was the mother of Zola's only two children and we can get a sense of how he thought of her from how he wrote to her. He opened many of his letters to her with *'Chère femme'*; the most accurate translation here is 'Dear wife', though of course she wasn't (he began his letters to Alexandrine the same way). *'Femme'* can also mean 'woman', but as his letters to Alexandrine show, in this context, in the modern era, it would usually be taken to have the legal meaning of 'wife'. Somewhere and some time in the rush and confusion of leaving the court, driving to the Charpentiers' and before Alexandrine joined him, Zola wrote a note to her, possibly slipping it to Desmoulin to take to Jeanne, on his way to fetch Alexandrine. This kind of triangular dance was how Zola, Alexandrine and Jeanne had lived their lives for the previous few years. One question concerning the three of them at this precise moment was how they would manage this arrangement in the immediate future. It would require delicate negotiations. This is the letter Jeanne received:

Dear wife, matters have taken such a turn that I am obliged to leave for England this evening. Don't worry: just wait quietly for me to send news. As soon as I've been able to make some decisions, I'll be in touch with you. I'm going to try to find a place where you and the children can come and join me. But there are things to be settled and that will take several days. Anyhow, I'll keep you informed. I'll write to you as soon as I am abroad. Don't tell a soul where I'm going.

My tenderest love to the three of you.

We can see here that Jeanne and the children are not living a life separate from Zola. They haven't been tidied away to another town. They are not living hidden from Zola's companions. In fact, wherever Zola and Alexandrine live or go, Jeanne and the children, Jacques and Denise, are not far away, whether that's in central Paris round the corner from the Zolas at 66 rue St-Lazare, at the house in Médan, or on holiday. In the meantime, it's clear that Zola has every intention of carrying on the triangular arrangement while he's in England. Quite how it would be manoeuvred into place was another matter. However or whenever that might be, Zola makes clear in this little note that he wants Jeanne to believe that he would like her and the children to come and stay with him.

In short, the delicate situation of being a fugitive had just got more delicate. The train journey gave him time to think:

All the way to Calais I was alone in the compartment. Since that morning, I had hardly had time to think. My chest was tight with anxiety, and my hands and face felt as if they were on fire. I opened the train window and pulled the shade on the lamp; in the darkness with a cool breeze coming in, I was finally able to calm down, to cool off, and to think a bit.

And what thoughts! To think that, after a lifetime of work, I would be forced to leave Paris, the city which I've loved and celebrated in my writings, in such a way! I hadn't been able to eat at Charpentier's. The day had left such a bitter taste in my mouth that even a piece of bread would have choked me. Now that I was a bit calmer, I was ravenously hungry and, luckily, at Amiens I was able to buy a roll and a chicken leg.

After that, all the way to Calais, I remained wrapped in my thoughts. I admit that they weren't particularly happy: my heart was overflowing with sadness and anger.

Part of Zola's attitude to the Dreyfus Affair was informed by a sense of outrage and despair that the French ruling class could reject reason and truth. Leaving France, running to England on his own, filled Zola with bitterness: this was a punishment being meted out on him, and not on the true criminals of the piece. It is significant that he invokes Paris in this passage. He is berating the inanimate, saying in effect, 'Paris, look what I've done for you! And yet this is how you treat me!' Both at the time, and in retrospect, Zola did indeed do a lot for Paris. His huge cast of characters throngs through its streets, dwellings and shops. Some act out their tragedies beneath the city in its sewers. He lent Paris a texture and taste to hundreds of thousands of people, in France and around the world, to many who had never been there.

In fact, Zola wasn't brought up as a Parisian. He was a provincial from Aix-en-Provence, the son of an Italian engineer who designed the town's water supply. Paris became his home when he was a late teenager and what with him being both Italian, as some said, and from the Midi (the South), enemies could portray him as an outsider and doubly so. But from that time till this point heading to England at the age of fifty-eight, Paris, with its bohemianism, its theatre, its painters and, above all, with its writers, was the milieu he belonged to, owned and adored. The consequence of his writing about it was that the world read about it in his books, serialised in newspapers, re-issued in cheap paperbacks, with many copies circulating in libraries or dramatised for the theatre. In this passage, we can hear him pointing out that this wasn't a desiccated lawyer defending Dreyfus, nor someone with a partisan interest in making the case for his innocence, it's me, Émile Zola, with nothing to gain, everything to lose by taking up this cause.

In the meantime, Zola had more pressing and mundane things to do: he got on board the ferry.

Finally, I found myself on the boat, leaving the dock. And that was that: I was no longer in France. I looked at my watch: it was half past one in the morning. The sky was clear, although there was no moon, and it was very dark. There couldn't have been more than thirty passengers on the boat, all of them English. And I stayed on the deck, watching the lights of Calais wink out in the darkness. I confess that my eyes filled with tears and that I had never in my life experienced such deep unhappiness.

Of course I didn't expect to be leaving my homeland for ever – I knew that I would be back in a few months, that my leaving was only a tactical move. But nonetheless, what a terrible situation – to have striven only for truth and justice, to have dreamed only of preserving in the eyes of her neighbours the good name of a generous and free France – and to find myself forced to flee like this, with only a nightshirt wrapped in a newspaper!

Too, certain vile newspapers had poisoned and misled France so completely that I could still hear people shouting at me, me, a man who had always worked for the glory of France and who had only wanted to be the defender who would show France's true greatness among other nations. And to think that I had to leave like this, all alone, without a friend by my side, without anyone to whom I could talk about the horrible rancour which is choking me. I have already suffered a great deal in my life, but have never undergone a more terrible experience than this one.

Even at this late stage in the Dreyfus Affair, with all its high-level corruption, Zola had not let go of the idea of 'the glory of France'. There was for him a France (the Republic) that existed over and above the people who governed at a particular moment in time. And there is no avoiding a less glorious element to this rhetoric: a superiority. France had a 'greatness' that could and should be taught to other nations. Perhaps this was not just about Republican values but there was a hint of Napoleonic ones too. However, Zola had already discovered that a certain way to lose friends and win enemies was to take Dreyfus's side. In fact, he had gone much further. Before being involved in the case, he had written a ground-breaking essay, 'Pour les Juifs' ('For the Jews' – or more strongly put by some, 'On behalf of the Jews') in which he had called for an end to anti-semitism. Then, as he joined those campaigning for Dreyfus's release, in a series of articles and open letters (especially in one called 'The syndicate'), he became increasingly forceful about what had grown into an explicitly anti-semitic movement, supported by popular newspapers and with political representatives.

It's worth remembering that what he was saying in these writings went way beyond homilies about being nice to Jews. He said that it was anti-semitism – and it alone – which had made the miscarriage of justice possible. He mocked the mind-set of the anti-Dreyfus camp: 'A Jewish traitor betraying his country: that goes without saying ... Well, he's

Jewish – isn't that enough?' What's more, he said, the trial of Dreyfus meant that 'It is anti-Semitism itself that is on trial.' In his appeal to 'Young People' he invoked Republican values in this fight for justice – namely, equality and fraternity – and foresaw, in the century to come, something terrible in the mobs demonstrating against Dreyfus: 'They will begin the century by massacring all the Jews, their fellow citizens because they are of a different race and a different faith.' In his 'Letter to France', Zola went further, 'Today it's Jews who are being persecuted, tomorrow it will be the Protestants.'

This kind of talk guaranteed that Zola was taking big risks with his reputation, his income and his life. He plunged himself into a storm of vituperation and danger. He had to resist deeply held religious suspicions of the role of Jews in the death of Jesus, a conventionally held view that it was 'the Jews' who had been responsible for the financial disaster of the Panama Canal, and who were, through Captain Dreyfus, now responsible for treason and the betrayal of France. In these terms, Zola had sided with a sinister conspiracy that was strangling the country. In his own terms, he saw an ideology that was corrupting the founding principles of the Republic. Zola travelled on:

The wind became very high, and I hadn't brought an overcoat. Nevertheless, I stayed on the deck, where the brisk, cool wind calmed me. The sea was hardly moving. During the short crossing, thin clouds covered the sky. The clouds lightened as the dawn broke. When I arrived in Dover, day was breaking, and the gas lamps in the small port paled as the skies brightened.

I don't know a word of English, and here I am in a foreign world, as if I were separated from mankind. I hate travelling. I am sedentary almost to the point of phobia, only happy in my own familiar surroundings. I don't like being abroad. I feel horribly homesick, disoriented by all these new things which I don't understand and which upset me. The first few hours of my stay in any country whatsoever outside France are especially trying for me: I experience a feeling of revolt, of distress at understanding nothing. It's curious that when my enemies insult me, they call me the 'foreigner'. Oh God! how foolish these people are and how little they understand what they're saying!

So here I am in Dover, where I can't even ask for a glass of milk. I take refuge in a compartment of the train which will take me to Victoria Station. And I wait there. Half an hour, three-quarters of an hour passes, a horrible wait! I don't know the reason for the delay. The dull day clears up, and, on the dock, the workers pass, dragging their feet. And not another sound – I feel as if I am alone in the train. An overwhelming feeling of being abandoned.

Finally the train leaves, and I doze during the trip, overcome by a crushing fatigue. It's almost eight o'clock when I arrive in London. It's pouring rain; the city seems to be still asleep in a ghastly fog. Paris was so warm and sunny when I left.

I remember my short trip to London four years ago, when I was invited by the English press with a group of other French journalists. What a splendid, brotherly welcome we received – a reception and speeches at the station, a party laid on by the lord mayor, a gala at Covent Garden, a banquet at the Crystal Palace, not to mention all the private lunch- and dinner-parties. And here I am, getting off the train alone at Victoria, with my nightshirt in a newspaper and walking in the rain to the nearby Grosvenor Hotel, where I have to wait for a quarter of an hour before they find a waiter who can speak French. In the huge entrance hall, a group of English chambermaids, clean and attractive in their bright uniforms, were cleaning the white tiles with sawdust, all on their knees like busy blonde ants.

The fact that I have no bags embarrassed me. They checked me in anyway, taking a pound for a deposit and telling me that this is what they do for people who arrive without luggage. I registered in the name of M. Pascal from Paris, and was given a room on the fifth floor, whose window was blocked by the fretwork frieze which adorns the huge building: a foretaste of prison. What an odd building this hotel is, a huge rectangle whose decorations are so bizarre that there isn't a single window that looks like a window. The air and light vents in the rooms, especially on the top floors, look like basement windows, or port-holes, or fanlights in a closet! Nonetheless, I was relieved to be there and to be able to clean up a bit and rest in the calm I felt around me.

No one in the world knew I was there, except for a few good friends whom I had told before I left which hotel I was going to. What a change that would be from Paris where, for the last five months, I couldn't move without being recognised and insulted.

THE DISAPPEARANCE OF ÉMILE ZOLA

A first day of confused drowsiness. I had to buy a few things to wear and some odds and ends. God knows the trouble I had making myself understood in the stores! As we'd arranged, I sent my wife a telegram to reassure her, and I wrote a few letters to friends, taking the precautionary measures we'd agreed upon.

In the stress of the experience, Zola's writing here moves between witnessing, contemplating, recollecting, arguing and recounting actions. It takes us from Monday through to Tuesday. It may not seem like a particularly modern or modernist piece of writing to us now but, in its time, this kind of language explores similar territory to Proust: in which past, present and future flow into each other, whilst he looks inside and out, one moment figurative, the next topographical, the next polemical. In the word of modern theory, it also expresses 'liminality': transition, the moment of being on the border, neither here nor there, but in-between, in the moment of change. In spite of his distress, though, Zola is already anticipating here that in one respect at least, there will be something to enjoy: he will be relieved of that situation where he 'couldn't move without being recognised and insulted'.

But Zola was someone who had spent his whole life surrounding himself with friends and companions. Long glorious evenings in the company of the group of writers of the school of 'Naturalisme' were legendary. However long he was going to stay in England, there wouldn't be any of that. How would he cope?

2

Grey Suit and a Légion d'Honneur Rosette

According to Ernest Vizetelly, Zola's problems in coping with England began immediately. Far from progressing smoothly to his hotel, as Zola implied in his *Notes*, he stepped down from the train at 'forty minutes past five o'clock' on the morning of 19 July with the name of a hotel on his lips, having been given it by Clemenceau. He walked across Victoria Station to the hansom cabs, and secured one. He asked the 'Jehu' to drive him to the Grosvenor Hotel.

[The] cabby looked down from his perch in sheer astonishment. Then, doubtless, in a considerate and honest spirit . . . he tried to explain matters. At all events he spoke at length. But M. Zola failed to understand him.

'Grosvenor Hotel', repeated the novelist and then, seeing that the cabby seemed bent on further expostulation, he resolutely took his seat in the vehicle . . .

However, cabby said no more, or if he did his words failed to reach M. Zola. The reins were jerked, the scraggy night-horse broke into a spasmodic trot, turned out of the station, and pulled up in front of [the hotel].

The Grosvenor was – and still is – adjacent to the station. The furthest possible the cabby would have driven is about 150 metres.

One of Zola's first acts was to write to Vizetelly:

My dear confrère,
  Tell nobody in the world, and particularly no newspaper, that I am in London. And oblige me by coming to see me tomorrow, Wednesday, at eleven o'clock, at the Grosvenor Hotel. You will ask for M. Pascal. And above all, absolute silence, for the most serious interests are at stake.

Cordially,
Émile Zola

Cloak and dagger was the order in this first part of Zola's stay. At least, that was the intention. As the day proceeded, Zola went out into London on his own, bought himself a shirt, a collar and a pair of socks in the area of Buckingham Palace Road, explaining his requirements 'by pantomime', before wandering past Buckingham Palace, musing on its 'gaunt, clumsy and mournful aspect'. Given the repeated pleas to his nearest and dearest that we can read in his letters, Zola doesn't seem, though, to have used his pantomime skills to equip himself with a pair of underpants. Back at the hotel, he sat in the garden, then later in his room he worked on an important article for editor Clemenceau to put in *L'Aurore* explaining why he had fled France.

The next day (20 July) Zola had visitors: Vizetelly, and his friends Desmoulin and Bernard-Lazare who had followed him from Paris. Bernard-Lazare was the figure who had done the most to convince Zola that he should take sides and play a leading role in the Dreyfus case. The two of them repeated Clemenceau's wish that Zola write an article for the French public giving reasons for his flight. Zola was pleased to pass over the newly written article. Later, they would learn that Clemenceau didn't wait to receive it, wrote the article himself, published it in *L'Aurore*, and signed it 'Zola'. Many years later, Zola's daughter reflected in her memoir on the reaction: 'It's easy to imagine Zola's rage, he who wouldn't ever tolerate that someone moved a comma in one of his novels. And here was someone who had brought out an article that he hadn't written a word of.'

The Times published it too. Clemenceau made a good job of imitating Zola's style, with its grand rhetorical questions and escalating statements. 'But what had I wished for? To provoke a great debate on a question which was troubling all consciences, to produce the proofs of the monstrous illegality which resulted in the abominable judicial error.'

Clemenceau-as-Zola pleaded for the right to prove his case in court – that he had not libelled the court martial, that he had been stating the truth. Further, he called for an inquiry into the activities of Major Esterhazy who, the pro-Dreyfus camp claimed, was the real author of the document that had incriminated Dreyfus. But, again, as with 'J'Accuse', Clemenceau-as-Zola recalled the involvement of the government in what should have been a purely legal affair: he accused the prime minister, Henri Brisson, of being 'afraid' of the truth. As for Zola fleeing from prison, this was a 'question of using the necessary means to enable a full disclosure of all the facts to be made in a trial which is to come later'. This was the explanation that the French public understood at the time to be Zola's impassioned words.

This issue of *The Times* also surveyed the French press's reaction: Zola's enemies 'exclaim' that Zola has fled from justice and that he is a coward; *Le Figaro* claims that 'the mind of the multitude will not comprehend this determination'; the *République Française* describes Zola's flight as 'a crime against the country, whose tranquillity and interests cannot be allowed to remain at the mercy of a man whose insane pride would not hesitate, were it in his power, to sacrifice everything to the triumph of his delirious *ego*' (italics in original). Both sides in the Dreyfus case eagerly engaged in adjective wars.

The next tasks for Zola, however, were to sort out what exactly was his legal status in Britain and to find more secure accommodation. He, Desmoulin and Bernard-Lazare lunched on omelette, fried sole, fillet of beef and potato, washed down with a Sauternes and Apollinaris, though Zola stuck to the water. They were cautious about discussing plans while waiters moved to and fro around them but up in Zola's dingy room it felt easier to get down to business. They would have to ignore the fact that all they could see from the room was a tiny strip of sky above a high parapet positioned outside. The main view was of the stained and cracked balustrade wall immediately outside the window.

There were two chairs, so one of the party sat on the bed. They ordered coffee, though this was regarded by the staff as unusual for the time of day. The meeting began: What would Zola do in England? Where should he go? The country or the seaside? Or what about the London suburbs? It was vital that he should avoid being recognised so it was out of the question that he should stay in central London. Then for the legalities: could the French government serve the court's judgment on Zola whilst he was in England? If not, the necessity that he keep out of sight would be less pressing.

Desmoulin, who spoke some English, said that he would drive straight away to one Fletcher Moulton, QC, whose house was in Onslow Square. Moulton had been recommended to them by Zola's lawyer, M. Labori, and Desmoulin left. Bernard-Lazare headed back to Paris. Vizetelly and Zola on their own in the room chatted about the Dreyfus Affair and talked about the probable length of Zola's stay in England. October was the likely end point, he thought. Then the discussion turned to Zola's excursion to the clothes shops and he recounted acting out his requirements. Zola had tried the old way of indicating foot size for a pair of socks, by making a fist with his hand, so that the circumference could be measured, this being the length of a person's foot – a little procedure much used in Paris stores at the time. It seems as if London haberdasheries of the 1890s did not use this system and confusion reigned until Zola indicated that the socks they were offering him were twice as long as his feet.

Desmoulin returned only to reveal that Fletcher Moulton was out of town electioneering for the constituency of Launceston, Cornwall. Plan B was brought into action: a 'discreet and reliable' friend of Vizetelly would be consulted. The group already understood that extradition was not a route the French government could take. It was the possible serving of the judgment that concerned them. Vizetelly pointed out that it would have been fine for Zola to stay with him at his home, but his position as Zola's translator was widely known and journalists would be certain to come prying. Desmoulin suggested Brighton or Hastings but Vizetelly thought that, what with these towns being crowded with holiday-makers, they were not a good choice.

The three men then decided to take a walk. It was warm, the sun was out, Buckingham Palace Road was full of people. A couple of ladies passed and one of them turned her head to look at them and said something in French. Vizetelly didn't quite catch it and asked Desmoulin to translate. 'She said, "Why! There's M. Zola!"'

The three were stunned: 'Our secret is as good as gone, now! It will be all over London by to-morrow.'

They quickly discussed who the ladies were. French actresses in Sarah Bernhardt's company who were in town doing a show? The absolute necessity to leave London became immediately more pressing. Vizetelly conjured up the picture of a quiet, retired country village where Zola's glasses and light grey suit with its red Légion d'Honneur rosette would be less conspicuous. In fact, hadn't they better get to work on anglicising his appearance right away? Zola was having none of it.

Meanwhile, Desmoulin was cursing Clemenceau for sending Zola to such a fashionable neighbourhood, where it was so likely he would be spotted. And hadn't he heard some French being spoken in the hotel earlier? Zola was getting anxious. They walked on to St James's Park and sat on some chairs beside the ornamental lake. Vizetelly produced the evening papers and translated them, with their stories of Zola on his way to Norway and Switzerland. The ducks paddled in the lake, the leaves stirred in the breeze. A couple of vagrants dozed on a bench nearby. A soldier and his lover strolled past. Up above were the windows and roofs of St Anne's Mansions, further off, the clock tower of Westminster . . .

Vizetelly rambled on about another French exile, St Evremond, who was given succour by Charles II, who found him a salary of £300 a year for taking on the governorship of Duck Island there right in the middle of the ornamental lake that they were looking at. Big Ben struck six and they separated, Vizetelly heading off to see his legal friend, Zola and Desmoulin to their rooms in the Grosvenor. The friend was F. W. Wareham of Ethelburge House, 70 Bishopsgate Street, E.C., who had a home in Wimbledon. The arrangement would be for Vizetelly to meet him on the following day. Zola moved to another room in the Grosvenor.

The following day (21 July), Vizetelly arrived at the Grosvenor only to find that Zola and Desmoulin were extremely depressed. Desmoulin had bought several papers to see if the ladies who had spotted Zola had told their story to the press but they were all glad to see that the Norway and Holland saga was the one the papers were putting out. Vizetelly tried to reassure them and told them that he was going to visit his (and Zola's) publisher, Chatto & Windus, on the way to see Wareham. Zola, in the meantime, should stay out of sight indoors. Desmoulin was pessimistic: 'These actresses are certain to tell people . . .'

At Chatto's in St Martin's Lane, Vizetelly was greeted by Mr Chatto's partner, Percy Spalding, with, 'So our friend Zola is in London!' The cloak and dagger precautions had come to nothing. All was lost. How could Mr Spalding possibly know that Zola was there? 'My wife saw him yesterday in

Buckingham Palace Road,' Spalding said. Vizetelly begged for secrecy and Spalding assured him that he would telegraph his wife at once. 'We certainly had a hearty laugh at breakfast this morning when we read in the "Telegraph" of Zola bicycling over the Swiss frontier . . .'

Vizetelly needed to know more about the friend. Was she reliable? Spalding told him that she was going to Hastings later. Hastings? 'Zola does nothing but talk of Hastings,' Vizetelly said. It immediately confirmed for him his urgent need to divert Zola. 'Hastings is barred,' he decided.

Mrs Spalding and her friend were warned and didn't ever breathe a word of it. Vizetelly mused on the happenstance of dropping into the Chatto & Windus office and the certain disaster that would have ensued had he not. On he proceeded to see Wareham in Bishopsgate, where they discussed the possibility of getting Zola out of the Grosvenor that very night. Wareham suggested that Zola might stay at his house, while Desmoulin could sleep close by in the house of the firm's managing clerk: all to be discussed back at the Grosvenor, where Vizetelly headed next. Zola and Desmoulin seemed much amused by the Mrs Spalding story and decided that it was almost too coincidental for real life, and was the kind of thing which occasionally occurs in novels. 'Another instance of my good luck,' Zola added, 'which still attends me in spite of all the striving of those who bear me grudges.' .

Vizetelly was becoming increasingly nervous about guests and staff at the Grosvenor, who appeared to be watching all this toing and froing. He had noticed significant glances in the dining-room. For that reason, he took Zola to a restaurant across the road from Victoria Station – a deep, narrow place, crowded with little tables. Vizetelly observed others observing Zola, who was still wearing his light grey suit and Légion d'Honneur rosette. Hadn't the newspapers printed pictures of Zola countless times? Weren't there photographs of him in shop windows? How come he wasn't being recognised all the time? It may be that many did recognise him, Vizetelly thought, but held their tongues.

At two, Wareham arrived and all four men met in the Grosvenor's smoking room, a hot, gloomy place overlooking the station. Wareham reassured Zola that he could not be extradited, and that there was no diplomatic channel through which a French criminal libel judgment could be registered in England. But what about the question of serving the judgment? Supposing French detectives discovered M. Zola's whereabouts, following which a *huissier* quietly dropped into England and, accompanied by a couple of witnesses, succeeded in placing a copy of the Versailles judgment into Zola's hands?

Wareham was of the view that, in such circumstances, the English authorities would find it difficult to interfere, though there was no precedent for this. Consequently, judgment would be deemed to have been served and Zola would be called upon to appear at Versailles. However, Wareham wasn't absolutely certain that French law allowed such actions to be taken outside French territory, so, in the meantime, Zola ought to remain in 'close retirement'. Zola said he would write to his counsel on the matter of the service of the judgment.

Out of the corner of his eye, Desmoulin noticed that two gentlemen had entered the smoking room. One was an elderly, florid-faced man, with mutton-chop whiskers and a buff waistcoat, who took up a position by the fireplace and puffed on a big cigar. He didn't appear to be interested in the group. The other was middle-aged, tall and slim with a military moustache; he eyed them closely, changed his position several times and finally sat down on a chair which gave him a good view of Zola's face. Desmoulin signed to Zola, indicating what was unfolding here. Zola shifted his position so that he in turn could get a sight of Mr Moustachio's face. They exchanged looks. Moustachio left, making a comprehensive survey of the party on the way out.

When Vizetelly read in two of the London papers a day or so later that Zola was staying at the Grosvenor, he was in no doubt that the source of the story was this man. He also figured out how the tale that Zola had been joined by Madame Zola got into the press later: he had arranged for Mrs Vizetelly to pick up mail addressed to 'M. Pascal', Zola's pseudonym, from the Grosvenor reception.

In the meantime, the Zola party decided that they needed to leave and leave quickly. It was even too dangerous to kill time at the hotel until Wareham reached his home in Wimbledon. They gathered themselves together. Desmoulin had only one small case; Zola had his few belongings with him, including now a small bottle of ink which he refused to part with. Most of these bits and pieces were stuffed into his pockets or in a newspaper parcel, tied up with string. The staff at the hotel smiled on the tattiness of it all, perhaps knowing much more than they let on. Zola, with his gold pince-nez, gold watch-chain, Légion d'Honneur and diamond ring on his little finger, looked remarkably respectable for someone carrying such unrespectable luggage.

'Where to?' the hotel porter asked.

'Charing Cross Station,' Vizetelly replied.

Once they were beyond Buckingham Palace Road, Vizetelly tapped the cab roof with his walking stick. 'Did I tell you Charing Cross just now, driver? Ah! Well, I made a mistake. I meant Waterloo.' Vizetelly for one, was still enjoying the novelistic quality of all this.

At Waterloo, bearing in mind that Wareham would not be at home till half past six, the three men sauntered towards the New Cut and Zola was quick to note the difference between the stylish shops and roads around Buckingham Palace Road and the dingy buildings here. Vizetelly suggested strolling off to Waterloo Bridge. They stood in the middle of the bridge looking down at the Thames reflecting the summer sky. Zola gazed at the scene. He didn't like Hungerford Bridge, thought it hideous and unworthy of the city. Paris wouldn't allow such a construction to be built. Yes, it was necessary to build a bridge to take the railway across, but there was no reason for it to be so ugly. 'It seems evident,' Zola added, 'you English are very much in the habit of sacrificing beauty for utility, forgetting that with a little artistic sense, it's easy to combine the two.'

They looked the other way, down-stream, where the Victoria Embankment stretches past Temple and Blackfriars. Somerset House, with its colonnades, showed itself rather grandly while beyond that stood the grey dome of St Paul's. Zola found this much more pleasing. On the bridge was a curved viewing-point with a seat where a pitiful-looking vagrant had spread himself. Zola wasn't bothered and sat down, drawing Vizetelly and Desmoulin to join him.

Desmoulin was beginning to enjoy the element of '*nostalgie de la boue*' ('yearning for degradation', or perhaps 'slumming it') that was going on here. 'We are homeless wanderers, stranded on the bridges of London,' he said.

Zola tried to locate the Savoy where he had stayed with such acclaim in 1893. Vizetelly pointed it out to him. Zola was astonished. It seemed so small when before it had seemed so big. And what was the huge building next to it? The Hotel Cecil. More evidence for Zola that the English had got it wrong, pretension and giantism dwarfing and spoiling everything else. 'You had such a site here,' he said, 'along the river, and allowed it to be used for hotels and clubs . . . There was room for a Louvre here, and you need one badly. Your National Gallery, which I well remember from '93 is a most wretched affair architecturally.'

Now Zola wanted to find 'his lion'. In '93 while staying at the Savoy, he had had what was almost a vision, looking out of the window of his room, noticing the mist parting, one mass of vapour rising while the other hovered over the river. Between the two, he had spotted a lion, poised in mid-air. He recalled how he had called for Madame Zola, 'Come and see. Here's the British lion waiting to bid us good-day.'

The group found it atop the Lion Brewery. Desmoulin suggested that they should walk down the Strand but Vizetelly was worried. It would be 'the most dangerous thoroughfare in all London for those who wished to escape recognition'. Instead, Zola said that he wanted to send a line to Paris to stop letters going to the Grosvenor. Vizetelly suggested, albeit none too hopefully, the saloon bar of the York Hotel, next door to the then notorious 'Poverty Corner', much frequented by the ladies and gentlemen of the music-hall, when they were 'resting'.

In the bar, there were a dozen or so 'loudly dressed' men and women. Zola ordered a drink. However, there was no stamp, no paper, no envelope to be found here. Vizetelly recalled a little stationer's shop on York Road and went off on his own. By the time he returned, Zola was the object of everyone's attention. With his prosperous appearance, and the sound of conversation in French with Desmoulin, the artistes in the bar had assumed that Zola was a Parisian music-hall director on the lookout for talent. Vizetelly took Zola over to a corner where he could write his note, but it wasn't long before a gentleman, a little worse for wear, dressed in a check suit, invited himself to join them.

'I know Paree and the bouleyvards well enough,' he said. 'I was on at the Follee Bergey only a few years ago myself. A good place that – pays well, eh? I shouldn't at all mind taking a trip across the water again ...'

Vizetelly stepped in, 'You've applied to the wrong shop. My friend has all the talent he requires. He's quite full up.'

The check-suited chap switched tack, 'I say, guv'nor, you haven't got a tanner you could spare, have you?'

The party then made its way to Waterloo Station and caught the train to Wimbledon. Zola carried on with his close observations of the buildings, at first the humble dwellings of Lambeth, Vauxhall and Queen's Road, then at Clapham Junction, looking across the sea of roofs stretching away through Battersea, and the wave of houses rising up to

Lavender Hill. Zola exploded. 'It's awful!' He was appalled at the sight of the dusty streets, each house with its uniform pattern, each pressed close to the other, one moment a picture of squalor, the next of shabby gentility. Ever the novelist '*naturaliste*', he plied Vizetelly with questions: Why were the houses so small? Why were they so ugly? Why were they so alike? What classes of people lived in them? Why were the roads so dusty? Why was there so much litter? Were the streets ever watered?

'You see that house,' Zola said, 'it looks fairly clean and neat in front. But there! Look at that back-yard – all rubbish and poverty!'

After Wandsworth Common, Vizetelly told him that, apart from the matter of postal districts, they were out of London proper. There were fields on either side. At Earlsfield, Zola's attention was caught by a long row of low-lying houses whose yards and gardens extended to the railway line. In some there was a little greenhouse, while in another an attempt at an arbour. But again, litter and rubbish everywhere.

'This, I suppose,' Zola said,

is what you call a London slum invading the country? You tell me that only a part of the bourgeoisie cares for flats, and that among the middle class and the working class each family prefers to rent its own little house. Is this for the sake of privacy? If so, I see no privacy here. Leaving out the question of being overlooked from passing trains, observe the four-foot fences which separate one garden or yard from the other. There is no privacy at all! To me the manner in which your poorer classes are housed in the suburbs, packed closely together in flimsy buildings, where every sound can be heard, suggests a form of socialism – communism, or, perhaps rather the phalansterian system.*

This was food for a novel that Zola was thinking of writing . . .

At Wimbledon, Vizetelly 'spared' Zola the houses built by the speculative builders of the area north of Merton High Street and Zola found the shops and houses around the Broadway very pleasing. He paid close attention to the displays of fish, fruit and poultry. He looked in the drapers' and jewellers' windows, and wondered about public houses that could be called hotels but took in no guests. Banks, furniture shops, stationers, pastry-cooks, hairdressers, ironmongers all fascinated him. These, said Zola, were much superior to the kinds of shops you'd find in a place at a similar distance from Paris. They spent a few moments by the 'Free Library' on Hill Road.

The plan was to avoid falling on the hospitality of the Warehams by dining at Wimbledon's only restaurant, run by a Mr Genoni, who, Wareham assured them, would be utterly discreet, if by chance he should recognise the writer. After the meal, Vizetelly escorted Zola to the Warehams', where the conversation turned to where Zola might rent a furnished house. Zola made it very clear that he had taken a fancy to Wimbledon. Vizetelly and Wareham thought

---

* A form of communal living and working proposed by Charles Fourier (1772–1837).

this was dangerous, Zola disagreed. Wimbledon it would be. Wareham would hire a landau and arrange to see house agents and drive round to visit suitable places. Then at 11.30, Vizetelly took Desmoulin off to the other house, and hurried off down Lover's Walk, to his own home a mile off.

No matter how isolated and rejected Zola may have felt, on these first two days at least, Bernard-Lazare, Desmoulin, Vizetelly, Mrs Vizetelly, Wareham, Mrs Wareham and various house servants had all found themselves preoccupied with the fate of Émile Zola.

Had Zola looked closely at *The Times* of that day (21 July) – and perhaps Vizetelly did point it out to him – the paper followed the latest events in yet another legal case that had been distracting Zola since May. One of his foes, one Ernest Judet, had ferreted around in army history from sixty-six years earlier and accused Zola's long dead father of desertion. The Zola family narrative, according to the anti-Dreyfus camp, now ran that Zola was not only 'a fool, a peacock, a vice-monger' and 'smut-fancier' but that there was some deep blemish, a hitherto undetected flaw and corrupting shame that had 'sway over his infamous life and impure work'. Straight away, the dishonoured and outraged Zola had served Judet with a writ for defamation of character. Now, three months later, on this particular morning in July, *The Times* reported that the prosecution was postponed. Not that Zola could follow this properly from London. News of this case as it unfolded would have to filter through to him slowly, care of friends bringing French newspapers, letters taking several days to arrive, or Zola's own lengthy struggles with the English language in the London papers – another reason for him to feel detached from the core concerns of his life. Even on the morning of his flight, there had been developments in the case, which, had he known of them, would have given him strength to insist on staying in France. This was certainly Zola's daughter's theory and it added to her view that Zola, by fleeing, was a 'victim of his friends' who back at Charpentier's had worked so hard on convincing him of the need to disappear.

And in the back of Zola's mind was the desperately complicated matter of his two *chères femmes*.

3

'Other affections'

From the moment Zola arrived in London, he started firing off letters to Alexandrine and Jeanne. What he didn't know, though, was which of the two would come to England, or if both were to come, in what order they should arrive, nor indeed how any of this would be negotiated. In his first letter to Jeanne from London, written on the Tuesday, the same day that he arrived at Victoria and the Grosvenor, he says that 'one' is going to join him in two or three days' time, bringing Zola's books and papers. Perhaps Jeanne could interpret that 'one' as referring to Zola's friends. Perhaps not. In which case it was a discreet signal to her that he was talking about his wife. More directly, he said that he didn't know whether he and Jeanne would be alone or not alone. But, he continues, 'I know that you love me, that you are very good and very reasonable and that you will accept what destiny imposes on me. I've had to disappear in order to remain master of the Affair.'

The following day, Wednesday, he pleaded that he couldn't say anything 'decisive' yet. On the next, he informed Jeanne that it was becoming 'certain' that he would not be able to bring her to England, without them all being 'tormented'. He conjured up the picture of Jeanne arriving with the children and being forced to go off who knows where, and followed this with his concerns about being captured: '. . . for anyone in the world wanting to know, you don't know where I am. When you come, I will give you instructions so that no one can follow you. One indiscretion on your part would be disastrous.'

But he was optimistic too: 'I'm hoping that we're going to spend two happy months together, when all the annoying details have been sorted out. I kiss my two darlings and you, dear wife, with all my heart.'

Hitherto, Jeanne's letters in reply have not come to light, so the full sense of what kind of person she was and how she thought are hard to discern. Through the curtain of silence, a picture emerges of Zola talking to her as if she was a teenager.

Meanwhile, he and Alexandrine were also writing to each other. On the Thursday, in reply to a letter that hasn't survived, she wrote that she had received two 'dear' letters from Zola: 'I'm much calmer, I'm even excessively calm, as I have a sense that everything's going well.'

The following day, she wrote with a passion that regularly boils up in the midst of a correspondence that was, needless to say, full of arrangements and references to the ongoing legal situations:

You tell me to come. How do you expect me to move from here? I can't take a step – either in Paris or in the country, without everyone knowing what I'm doing minute by minute. The secret police and reporters are at our door. Yesterday, your lawyer told me not to move. I am caught sadly between your appeals and the advice of others to stay. All the stations are guarded and under surveillance and you think I should flee . . .

We can deduce, then, that Zola was asking both 'wives' to come to England. This raises the question of how the relationship stood between the three of them.

Zola was born in Paris on 2 April 1840 but at the age of three went with his French mother and Venetian father to live in Aix-en-Provence. Four years later, at his moment of glory, Zola's father died. He had masterminded the fresh water supply for Aix. Zola and his mother moved permanently to Paris in 1858 and he lived with her or very nearby till the day she died in 1880. Zola met Gabrielle Alexandrine Meley in 1864 and they lived a full bohemian – and poverty-stricken – life together in Paris, fraternising with the painters who one day would become the Impressionists.

Alexandrine, as she was known, was a year older than Zola. At the time of her birth, her father was eighteen and her mother seventeen. They weren't married. He was a hatter and she was a florist. When Alexandrine was eight or nine, her father married another woman while her mother had previously set up house with a riding instructor. Within months, her mother died of cholera, the riding instructor found someone else, and young Alexandrine found herself bereft of close and loving care. Yet, she was a survivor and managed to train to be a '*lingère*', someone who knew how to make, repair and maintain household linen and a woman's under-garments, the kind of seamstress who could, if asked, be a chambermaid to a '*femme bourgeoise*'.

Through the 1870s, Zola's novels became massively popular both in France and abroad and the couple prospered. They bought a house in Médan to the west of Paris and renovated and expanded it extravagantly, whilst keeping on an apartment in the centre of Paris. Zola and Alexandrine had no children by this point nor would they ever.

In May 1888, Alexandrine hired Jeanne Rozerot to be her *lingère*. Jeanne was born in 1867, so she was twenty-seven years younger than the 48-year-old Zola. She came from Burgundy, where her father was a miller. Her mother died when she was three, so she was brought up by her mother's parents who put her through convent school where she trained to take on the very same job that Alexandrine had trained for, seamstress chambermaid.

In October 1888, the Zolas and Jeanne went on holiday to Royan. One aspect of Jeanne's job was to attend to the *femme bourgeoise* that Alexandrine had become, sewing and repairing her most intimate clothing and, when asked, helping her mistress dress, particularly in the elaborate matter of getting in and out of nineteenth-century corsets. Though Alexandrine was pleased with her new servant, on their return from the holiday in Royan, Jeanne resigned her post. Zola and Jeanne had exchanged thoughts, feelings and intentions and the bourgeois stability of the marriage was on the verge of falling apart. The question now was whether this rupture would fit into the conventional bourgeois pattern of married-man-plus-mistress, or take on some other shape? This was answered at first by the fact that, straight after Jeanne resigned her post, Zola arranged for her to have an apartment not far from the marital home. By December, the relationship reached a new level of intimacy: a daughter, Denise, was born in September 1889, a son, Jacques, in September 1891 and, unusually for the time, Jeanne kept the children. They were not given to nuns or handed over to the Parisian version of the foundling hospital. This was not the customary mistress situation. Then, in November 1891, Alexandrine was tipped off in an anonymous letter that Jeanne and Zola were lovers and had children. What took place next is described in all sources as 'violent'. With a telegram to his old friend Paul Céard saying, 'My wife is behaving like a lunatic', Zola was able to warn Jeanne to vacate the flat. It's possible that if she had stayed, Jeanne might have been in physical danger. When Alexandrine gained access to Jeanne's home, she smashed up the furniture and grabbed Zola's letters to Jeanne from a bureau. Everything was revealed.

For Alexandrine, there was not only a terrible sense of betrayal and loss, she also had to bear the public shame of knowing that the couple's intimate friends would have known everything, acting at times as witnesses and deceivers. And there were children, something that Zola and Alexandrine had not – for reasons we do not know – been able to produce. The set-up with Jeanne, then, was like a parallel marriage with the added potency and authenticity that had come with the birth of the two children. Where Zola and Alexandrine were a couple, Zola, Jeanne and the children were a family. Only someone who had become utterly indifferent to her partner would find any of this bearable, and it's clear from all that comes before and after that Alexandrine was in no way emotionally detached from her husband. Quite the contrary. This was a bitter and painful crisis for her – a trauma. All the more reason to say that what unfolded over the next few years is quite remarkable.

Between this moment in November 1891 and Zola's arrival in London in July 1898, Zola, Alexandrine, Jeanne and the children slowly constructed a way of life. No matter what feelings of despair or joy, loss or desire passed between them, by the time Zola left on that train at the Gare du Nord, they had all come to an arrangement. In broad outline, it worked like this: wherever Zola and Alexandrine lived – Paris, Médan or on some of their holidays together – Jeanne, Denise and Jacques were found a place nearby. Zola spent his nights and mornings with Alexandrine, but went almost every afternoon to see Jeanne and the children. None of this was secret. It was understood. However, the really remarkable part came when Alexandrine took control of the situation. Here is daughter Denise's view of what took place:

> Madame Émile Zola, who had wanted to get to know us, took us on with affection and asked for news of us. Once or twice a month, on a Thursday, Jacques and I would go out for walks with her to the Tuileries, the Palais-Royal, the Champs-Elysées in winter then to the 'Bois' [de Boulogne] as soon as the good weather began. We were a bit intimidated by 'la dame', as we called her, and she watched us playing with a nice smile and laughed at our childish talk, but our father was there and we felt reassured. An air of mystery floated around us, as our mother wasn't there, and there was no talk of her and also because we were never warned of these walks in advance. We didn't go home empty-handed, 'la dame' always gave us presents, especially when she came back from her annual stay in Italy.

Since this time until nearly a hundred years later, the story of Zola's childless marriage, his transformation into a delighted and devoted lover and then '*père de famille*', has been pieced together from letters and the reported comments of friends and family. However, in 1997, the biographer Evelyne Bloch-Dano sensationally revealed that in 1859, some five years before she met Zola, Alexandrine had given birth to a girl. She was nearly twenty years old and named the baby after her mother, calling her Caroline. When the baby was four days old, Alexandrine took her to the Hôpital des Enfants-Trouvés (literally 'Hospital for Found Children'), one of many foundling hospitals, and never saw her again. The baby was wet-nursed, baptised and then picked up by another wet-nurse and taken to Brittany. Eleven days later, baby Caroline died. On that same day, Alexandrine celebrated her twentieth birthday. Needless to say, Alexandrine and Caroline were not the only mother and child to experience this sequence of events. The story of widespread urban and rural poverty is riven through with abandonment, wet-nursing and death, drawing into its net tens of thousands of women, babies and children. Bloch-Dano, commenting on Alexandrine's part in this social disaster, writes, 'Even Zola wouldn't have dared to invent it.'

Alexandrine did not ever put in writing any of her thoughts about what happened to her, and we do not know if Zola knew anything about it. What we are left with is a view of a childless marriage seen now through the prism of a woman who once gave birth. So, whatever pain we might imagine that Alexandrine experienced in relation to Jeanne and Zola's children, the experience of the foundling hospital and her dead child must have made the affair even harder to bear.

When trying to envisage how Zola, Jeanne and Alexandrine felt about each other, biographers have combed through the novels for analogous encounters, older man with younger woman, or man and wife in childless marriage. In *Doctor Pascal*, written and published in 1893, little less than five years after the affair with Jeanne began, there are erotic awakenings by a middle-aged doctor disturbed by a growing passion for his niece, Clotilde, followed by loving accounts of her hair, neck and breasts, leading to passages detailing their nights of loving passion. By casting Clotilde as Dr Pascal's niece, the novel is shot through with a sense of forbidden love, which the lovers recklessly and delightedly disregard. Pascal himself is cast as a self-obsessed workaholic who imagines that he has made a break-through in the study and curing of inherited disease – inherited defects being a theme that runs through Zola's *Rougon-Macquart* novels. Pascal's scientific materialism is contrasted with Clotilde's religiosity. Part of the erotic charge between them is the ideological confrontation and mutual anger, expressed at one point with violence, but which is overcome through passionate acts of sinful love-making.

What Alexandrine made of all this is not known – Zola usually read his latest writings to her. If he followed their usual custom, or even if Alexandrine read *Doctor Pascal* to herself, it would have been an experience full of regret and humiliation. Opposite the title page, the book reads: 'I dedicate this book, which is the recapitulation and conclusion of all my labours [it was the last novel in his great *Rougon-Macquart* sequence], to the memory of my mother and to my dear wife.' It's hard to imagine that this public display of devotion would have appeased Alexandrine's feelings. Zola also gave a copy of the book to Jeanne and this copy has survived. On the cover, he wrote:

> To my beloved Jeanne, to my Clotilde, who has given me the royal feast of her youth and taken thirty years off my life, giving me the present of my Denise and my Jacques, the dear children for whom I have written this book, so that they might know, when reading it one day, how much I adored their mother and how tenderly they should repay her the happiness with which she consoled me in my times of great unhappiness.

Even if it feels dubious when biographers blur fiction with reality, clearly Zola himself had no reservations about merging the two when it came to talking to Jeanne. Queen Clotilde of French history, it should be said, was, like Jeanne, a Burgundian.

With that dedication in mind, we don't know what Jeanne made of passages like this:

> They took each other in a mad whirl of happiness. The warm room, with its antique furniture, seemed to be encouraging them and to be filled with light. There was no more fear, no suffering, no scruples; she gave herself, knowingly, willingly, and he accepted the sovereign gift of her body ... She, in a daze of delight, surrendered herself to him in silence, except for a soft faint cry as her virginity left her; and he, with a sob of rapture, was crushing her, enveloping her, straining to make

her understand his immeasurable gratitude to her for restoring his manhood.

Meanwhile, Alexandrine would read passages like this:

Martine . . . had been in the doctor's service for more than thirty years and had become the real mistress of the household. She too had retained an air of youthfulness, though she was over sixty. Soft-footed and silent, she was constantly scurrying from task to task. In her eternal black dress and white cap she looked like a nun. The grey eyes in her small face, which was pale and serene, were like the ashes of an extinguished fire.

Zola cast the doctor in the novel, as having a 'longing for a child . . . his eyes were often wet with tears . . . What he longed for now that he was in his declining years was the continuity, the child who would perpetuate him.'

To Jeanne, Zola suggests that the book was a kind of prolonged love letter and if, in the future, their children should doubt the depth of Zola's feelings for her, they could refer to the novel. Zola would be able to speak to them from beyond the grave as if he were saying, 'This is how I loved your mother, like this, like this and like this.' Bearing in mind that he was seen by his religious critics as a novelist who had spent years purveying pornography and filth, one can sense in the book Zola's urge to portray Clotilde-Jeanne as a good, pure and devoted virgin — albeit, as a niece. Because the love between Pascal and Clotilde is full and honest and sincere, the novel pleads for them to be entitled to have that love in all its glorious, passionate wholeness, no matter what others might say or think. The stress lines of fiction and the reality of the past reached forward to Zola's stay in England. While he signed in to the Grosvenor Hotel as 'Pascal', Alexandrine was signing her letters to him as 'Caroline'.

But it wasn't only through his fiction that Zola played out his feelings for the two women. He used the camera. By the time he came to England, he was a proficient and experienced photographer, who liked to capture what looks like a happy social life with Alexandrine; a family life with Jeanne with the children running about and playing; and – much more intimately – Jeanne appearing in studio shots wearing nothing but a shift or dressed up 'in character'. One picture shows Zola and Jeanne standing on a gravel path staring into each other's eyes, he dressed in plus fours and flat cap, she in a white full-length dress with puffed shoulders. At times he dressed her like Carmen, at others more like Sarah Bernhardt with fan, feather boa and extravagant flowery hat. In some, he hugs the children to him while looking wistfully straight into the lens. With Alexandrine, they take up amusing poses with a mandolin here, a great carved face there, surrounded by publishers and composers with their wives, inventing, perhaps, new versions of 'Le Déjeuner sur l'Herbe'. To look at the pictures is to be invited into a private gallery, telling the story of these people's decade of pleasure. They are a display of the things and people Zola loves most: his social life with his wife, his lover's face and body, and his thoughtful children. They are of course the filtered-out good bits of life, betraying only occasionally looks of sadness, worry and regret. We get glimpses of meetings and departures, a daily feature of all their lives, shown in the photos as people caught in the middle distance on long roads, or underneath sign-posts. In the published sources, there is no picture of Alexandrine with the children. If we assumed that Zola never took a photo of this particular combination of people, we might speculate that this extraordinary arrangement was acknowledged by all parties as inappropriate to be recorded so permanently. In England, Zola's camera would have more work to do.

So, in Wimbledon, with Zola looking for somewhere to live, we can see from the urgent letters that his mind was not only full of how to evade the police, and of how the Dreyfus Affair was proceeding, but also of how he could manage his complex network of relationships.

Wareham the lawyer was well equipped to find places for Zola to stay, and suggested that, until a house could be found, it would be a good idea to stay in a nearby country hotel. The Oatlands Park Hotel fitted the bill, so Vizetelly, Desmoulin and Zola headed off to Walton Station and from there to Oatlands Park. It's still there, on the site of the grand Tudor palace which Henry VIII had built for Anne of Cleves and which was also occupied by Anne's lady-in-waiting and Henry's next queen, Catherine Howard. It burnt down in 1794 and was rebuilt several times since. By the time Zola arrived, signing in as M. Beauchamp, it had grown into a slightly bizarre mix of Palladian, Gothic and Byzantine but still surrounded by lavish landscaped grounds, including an aristocratic dog and monkey cemetery which Zola found very pleasing. Zola was after all the owner of a tiny island on the Seine below his house at Médan where he buried his own pets. Zola's room was up in the hotel's tower and he was glad now to have bought some more shirts, but not without complaining to Vizetelly that English shirts were too short.

The chilly receptionist and the indifference of the hotel guests suited the need to be incognito. There was a mix of honeymoon couples, Fritz the German who spoke French, families and a few old folks. Desmoulin had brought Zola one of his cameras and he was soon out snapping views of the Thames and the long tree-lined roads near the hotel. Vizetelly supplied them with English newspapers and they amused themselves with the 'news' of where Zola was supposed to have fled.

On the Saturday (23 July), Zola went out house-hunting in Weybridge and was pleased to find 'Penn', 'a charming house surrounded by trees. Five guineas a week.' The following day, he went with Vizetelly and his wife to take a second look. Desmoulin agreed to go back to Paris. It was decided that he would 'organise things' with Alexandrine. It was becoming clear that Alexandrine would have to run Zola's affairs by herself from Paris.

On the Monday, Vizetelly brought Zola some books to read: *Le Rouge et le Noir* and *La Chartreuse de Parme*, and in the evening he had a brief chat with Fritz the German, and sat out in the gardens under a giant elm tree. On Tuesday, came the alarming news that Zola had been spotted in London and Vizetelly showed Zola one or two of the papers carrying the story. Zola fretted that the *huissier* would find him out and serve notice on him. 'I'm told that my picture is in a number of shop windows in London,' he wrote but he fraternised with the hotel manager and did some dog-spotting, pondering on the fact that English dogs in the main were muzzled. By Wednesday, it was agreed he would take 'Penn'. That left a few more days to get through at Oatlands Park, reading his novels, sitting in a rustic cabin overlooking the hotel grounds, noting down the difference between French and English windows and watching a strange game called cricket.

By Friday, Desmoulin was back, bringing some of Zola's treasured nick-nacks, manuscripts, notes, books, newspaper cuttings, underwear and news of his loved ones. The books, notes and cuttings made up the essential research material for Zola's great new writing project that he was desperate to start work on. Desmoulin reassured Zola that the Dreyfus case was proceeding well and that there was an 'ever-faster movement towards the truth'. Even so, there were worries about his mail being opened and impatience about getting in to 'Penn'. Desmoulin was sent off to London to buy some photographic plates and everyone became agitated that it took him so long to get back. By the Sunday, there was some good news from the French papers that the evidence that had been used to defame Zola's father now looked like being a forgery. Monday was the day Zola could move into 'Penn'.

These ten days in limbo in an English country hotel gave Zola plenty of time to write to Alexandrine and Jeanne simultaneously, even if the letters, for safety's sake, had to be delivered by hand by the long-suffering Desmoulin. Zola told Jeanne and the children that he adored them, but he was devastated that their 'beautiful projects were for the moment, *par terre*' (literally, 'grounded'). To Alexandrine, he said that he was in a state of 'extreme anxiety' and that he was making her the 'absolute mistress of the situation' in Paris. He invoked their thirty years together, in which her happiness had been his sole concern, as if he himself did not exist. Alexandrine, we might suppose, could be forgiven for not seeing it that way. Zola closed, embracing her with all his 'ulcerated' heart. Jeanne, meanwhile, was telling Zola that she was very sad and in despair so Zola reassured her that these were just sorrows of the moment. 'Be as gay as you can,' he wrote, 'lead your usual life, laugh, sing, play the piano as if nothing sad has happened to the three of you. . . Tell the two darlings that their father hasn't forgotten them and that if they come here, he will apply himself to amusing them as much as possible.'

So how was the matter of who would or would not come to be settled? Unsurprisingly, it was Alexandrine who managed the whole thing. She sent Zola a letter that included a phrase which defines the situation they were all in, conjuring up a picture of coming to England while Jeanne was there, but then having to return soon after, in order to fix legal and household matters. 'I would be with you very little, on account of *other affections that you would want to have, and which seem to me quite natural . . .*' A few days later she wrote, 'To stay with you . . . would be to deprive you of *other affections* which are useless here', and a day or so later, 'I very much feel that after eight days of my presence with you, if I did not agree to leave until your return [to France], I would see in you a sadness, remorse perhaps, that my stay was too long, depriving you of *affections that are more consoling and gayer than mine.*' (All italics mine.)

No doubt other messages were sent to and fro care of Desmoulin, but through these letters we can make out the heartfelt mixture of empathy and self-sacrifice that Alexandrine put herself through, stepping aside to enable Jeanne to come to England with the children without her being there too. Not that she didn't also give full vent to her own feelings:

> You say that you would like to see me happy. Alas, my poor friend, you who know me better than anyone, still don't know me very well, if even now you can still keep on hoping to see me happy, with all the sadness and bitterness that has overwhelmed me for nearly ten years. I told you, two years after, that I was finished, that I had little more to do with my sad existence than to do good things for those I love. I am trying to do that and I will carry on doing so, as much as I can.

As Zola settled in to his home in England, surrounded by his books and papers, on the verge of starting a new sequence of novels, with the glorious prospect of living with Jeanne and his children for the first time, his ears were ringing with what his wife, legal representative, and manager in all things really thought. Without mentioning any names, Madame Zola had even managed matters so that Jeanne and the children could join him.

4

'I don't bloody care!'

'Penn' was – and still is – a detached, double-fronted, two-storey house set back from a long, straight road. The front gable was half-timbered in suburban, neo-Elizabethan style and, at the back, two rooms on either side of the back door overlooked the garden. Monday 1 August, the day of moving in, was a Bank Holiday, 'Isn't it a good omen that I have moved in on the day of a holiday?' Zola asked himself. This was the Zola who had a good few superstitious beliefs, which, according to his daughter, derived from his Italian background. He wouldn't start anything new on the 17th of any month, as this was the day his mother died; he counted the numbers on vehicles, added them up, and only took a taxi if he was happy with the number, while the number 7 seemed to him to be a lucky one.

Zola took a liking to what he thought of as a small house, with its bright paint, quirky furniture, funny little ornaments and its airy windows, though all this reminded him of how far he was from France. One of Vizetelly's photos shows Zola, pen in hand, sitting in one of the back rooms with piles of papers and books neatly stacked in front of him. This was the dossier of materials that Zola had asked Desmoulin to bring from Paris, a collection for a great new writing project that he had been preparing since the end of December 1897. The Dreyfus case and Zola's trials had interrupted the flow of what he saw as his real writing but now he was ready to pick up from where he had left off. Not that he was in a good state of mind to do so. He felt waves of anxiety washing over him and, after several hours of calm, he would be overcome with despair. He could hardly believe he was hiding away in this backwater. 'So this is where forty years of work have led me, with a whole wretched country at my back, shouting me down and threatening me.'

His country, he thought, had been taken over by a gang of despicable rogues, and he was paying the price for having taken a stand against the anti-semites, the government and the army high command. Not that he regretted it. He declared to his friends and to Jeanne and Alexandrine that, if necessary, he would take up the struggle for truth and justice again. He might be just a dull, plodding, deskbound writer, but he could and would again wage battle with the pen. It was taking its toll, though. He feared that he would slide into deep hypochondria. Relief came in work. He spent the afternoon of 3 August re-reading his notes and he urged himself to get back to his schedule of never letting a day go by without writing at least a line: '*nulla dies sine linea*' as he would say to himself over and over again. After an eleven-month gap of not writing any fiction, on Thursday 4 August he picked up his pen to write the first page of the novel *Fécondité*, which would be translated later, by Vizetelly, as *Fruitfulness*.

There is an incongruity between Zola sitting in the back room of a suburban house in Weybridge, writing a novel that was minutely concerned with the intimate – shockingly intimate – lives of the French. The fruitfulness at the heart of the novel was to be children, well-being and material comfort, but this was only the first part of the grand project. As Zola wrote in his notes for the novel, his intention was to write *Three Gospels* ('*Évangiles*') – *Fruitfulness, Work* and *Justice*. This would match the trilogy he had finished eleven months earlier, *Les Trois Villes* (*Three Cities*) – *Lourdes, Rome* and *Paris*. With *Fécondité*, he would cover a subject which had haunted him first under the provisional title *Le Déchet* (*Waste*). On one side, there would be a fecund woman who would breast-feed her many children, but whose life would be contrasted with virginity and the 'religion of death'. The book would take a stand for the country as a whole to be more fecund, as it would call for an increased birth-rate in France, an idea which would then be spread to the whole of the rest of humanity.

The second novel, *Travail* (*Work*), would take up the ideas of the eighteenth-century utopian thinker Charles Fourier. Zola's heroes would create the city of the future, made up of Fourier's 'phalansteries' – work–life communes. The book would show the dignity of labour, how work was necessary for health, how happiness would flow from the 'human hive'. The third, *Justice*, would show a humanity existing over and above national borders, an alliance of all nations. He would tackle the question of human races and show the great joy of peace.

The hero-narrator in the trilogy would be Jean Froment, the son of characters who had appeared in previous novels. In *Fruitfulness*, Jean and his wife would make babies through making love in a loving way, while others would be shown using 'trickery' to avoid conception, sperm lost – voluntarily or not. Then, as Jean and his wife have many babies, others like the egotistical bourgeois couples of French society would be shown trying to restrict the size of their families. Other women would be shown having abortions, killing babies just before and after they were born, along with surgeons performing hysterectomies or handing babies over to foundling hospitals. While Jean's wife breast-fed her children, he would show others farming out their babies to wet-nurses. By the end of the book, Jean and his wife would sit in a prosperous heaven-on-earth surrounded by their adoring children and grand-children. 'I see "Fécondité" set in a house with a garden,' he wrote in these preparatory notes. The purpose of the trilogy would be to save France from the dangers of it becoming a monarchist, Catholic, war-mongering state. Instead he would show that it should be Republican, free-thinking and war-hating; he would instate a new kind of chivalry, one that stood in defence of the Rights of Man, law and liberty. This was the real role for France, her greatness shared with the peoples of the world, her mission and her victory in the future.

In time, with the addition of *Vérité* (*Truth*), this grand utopian schema would turn into *Les Quatre Évangiles* (*Four Gospels*) and envisaging this major project drove Zola to his writing-table almost every day of his stay in England. While he sat cooped up in hotels and rented houses in south London, in his mind's eye he was saving France from itself. At the outset, on that day in August, in front of him sat his prime sources: recent sociological and socio-medical texts about the declining birth-rate and depopulation of France, contraceptive methods, sterilisation of women and investigations into foundling hospitals and baby-farming.

For the last section of *Fruitfulness*, Zola had ferreted out books such as *Timbuctoo*, *The Mysterious* and *Four Years in the Congo*, as he was planning on having his hero take the ideology of fruitfulness to the colonies.

It's possible to trace several strands in Zola's thinking at this time: a nationalist worry in France as a whole that its declining birth-rate was in stark contrast to the rising birth-rate of its rival, Germany. Great Britain had conquered the world while crazy France (in Zola's eyes) was – with the Dreyfus case – giving up on the one virtue that it had, its love of freedom and justice. France should be an enlightened coloniser, spreading this virtue to all parts of the globe and she should lead the way in enlightened work practices, a kind of guild socialism organised in co-operative communes. By defying Malthusian ideas of ending poverty through depopulation, France could find a new wealth through fecundity – having many babies. That was the theory. There's an irony here in that just a suburban train-ride from where Zola was reading, thinking and writing about such matters, his equivalents, amongst them many British Fabians and enlightened intellectuals, were envisaging a future in which poverty would be eradicated through a mix of socialism, birth control and sterilisation.

From a literary point of view, at first glance there doesn't seem to be much of a correspondence between the Zola of *Thérèse Raquin* and *Germinal*, and this new Zola. The old Zola didn't try to right the wrongs of the world in his novels: he exposed the plight of the poor and downtrodden. His method had been '*Naturalisme*' – not in the sense that he wrote in a realistic way, but that the subject-matter of the novels came out of lengthy immersion in empirical research. The food, the clothes, the buildings and rooms would all be accurate; the language and expressions of the speakers would be observed correctly; the sex, births and deaths would appear as noted down – if not by Zola, then by the many scientific studies that he acquired and devoured. In Zola's hands, though this did indeed produce scenes and images of stark realism, we can see that they were manipulated symbolically. It's not a coincidence that *Germinal*, for all its minute accuracy in depicting a coal-mining community, shows a working-class hacking out survival below ground, in the dark. But now, in this new way of writing, these *Gospels* would include scenes and ideas of the future, moments that would not be typical, or accurate as *Naturalisme* would have it, scenes that would not happen unless France woke up and took the right path. As Zola himself put it: 'All this is quite utopian, but what do you want? I've been dissecting for forty years; let me dream a little in my old age.'

In fact, as can be seen from the list of documentary texts sitting in front of Zola in the back room at 'Penn', the negative side of *Fécondité*, the 'religion of death' as he called it, would inform Zola's writing in his old Naturalist way. In the summer of 1898 from Weybridge, Zola was planning on giving the fiction-reading public graphic depictions of abortion, sterilisation, contraception, baby-abandonment, baby-farming, wet-nursing and infanticide, the like of which, outside of academic circles, had never been read before. If people had found his *L'Assommoir* and *Nana* shocking, *Fécondité* would, he hoped, create an outcry and the outrage would help transform France. But whatever Zola's grand utopian intentions, it's not difficult to see, lying behind this project, the outlines of something more personal. The pen he used to write that first page of the *Four Gospels*, on 4 August, was the same pen that was writing urgent, anxious letters to Jeanne the fertile mother and Alexandrine, the mother who had given her baby to a foundling hospital and who hadn't produced a baby since. The sources taken from real life to write *Doctor Pascal* were helping to provide ideas for this novel too.

So Zola established a routine: he would write all morning; in the afternoons, which he described as 'difficult', he might walk round the garden. He was amused to see that this one at 'Penn' was like a French *potager* with squares of cabbages, potatoes and peas. The robins hopped about right up close to him, as if he were their friend. But thinking that reminded him of his own dear pet dog, Pinpin. He deluded himself that he was brushing past his legs, only to discover, sadly, that he wasn't. He figured out why England was so green – the mild wet weather. The haze over the fields produced a dream of never-ending gentleness and melancholy.

Another addition to Zola's life was a bike, and soon he was off cycling round the roads which, he found, weren't as good as French ones. On either side were parks and thick, shiny holly-bushes, so thick that even a skinny cat couldn't get through them. If only the holly at Médan would grow like that. These bike rides took him as far off as Walton, which was so perfectly neat that Zola wondered where the English hid their poor people. He snapped away on the camera that Alexandrine had been so kind as to give to Desmoulin to bring over to England. Out in the garden, amongst the cabbages and robins, he wondered what was going on in France. He would suddenly lift up his head, as if to catch what people were saying over there. Where had they got to in the frightful Dreyfus case? Would truth and justice prevail? Then it was back to the cabbages and robins. Some French newspapers were getting through to him, thanks to his friends, and he was appalled to see that Esterhazy, whom Zola had accused of having written the document which had incriminated Dreyfus, had been set free, while the good Colonel Picquart, who had done so much to prove Dreyfus's innocence, was still behind bars.

The matter of whether it would be Alexandrine or Jeanne who would come out to join him was confirmed when he received a letter from Desmoulin, dated 5 August, telling him that Alexandrine had decided to stay in Paris to deal with the many letters and with household affairs. Apart from anything else, there were the court fines to pay. Desmoulin revealed that Zola's 'poor wife' had given him, Desmoulin, the job of asking Zola to call for the children to come and stay with him in London. In this one tortuous sentence, Desmoulin was passing on the news that the shape of the relationships between Zola, Alexandrine and Jeanne was about to take a new turn. Madame Zola understood very well, Desmoulin reported, that Zola wouldn't be able to stand being alone for very long. Alexandrine was in effect administering Jeanne and the children as prophylaxis.

In his reply, Zola modified his delight by sharing with Desmoulin his thoughts of not wanting to cause his 'poor wife' pain, adding that he couldn't be happy unless he knew that she was happy. As for himself, he was suffering from being in a state of 'total moral distress'. Maybe, when the children came, he would calm down a little.

On consecutive days, he ran off brusque instructions to Jeanne: bring warm clothes, bring me my cycling outfit, don't bring culottes for yourself, bring a skirt. (Zola used his powers of observation to scrutinise young women cyclists in England and was very interested to see that they wore skirts not culottes as they cycled past, looking, he thought, very gracious and sure of themselves, not at all like the big-hipped French women he had seen on bikes in the Bois de Boulogne.) Detail was important to Zola. He had already mislaid his umbrella and walking-cane. The umbrella he could cope with, but the loss of the cane, which had been his companion for ten years, pierced his heart. But then it turned up. Vizetelly spotted it sitting in the corner a few feet away from Zola's work-table. Perhaps, Zola wondered, objects deliberately hide from us in order to test us. He gave Jeanne a list of instructions on how to negotiate the Gare du Nord and Victoria Station and how to take precautions to avoid being followed. 'Disappear,' he urged.

In the subsequent note, he carried on: '... bring some music, there's a piano. Don't trust the servants. Don't forget to take food for the journey. After Dover, they don't take French money, only get off the train after it stops at the end of the line in London.'

This fatherly tone breaks through Zola's letters to Jeanne but he also wrote to her with a sense of their destiny within the epoch they were living through. Just prior to hearing that Jeanne and the children would be able to join him, he tried to reassure her:

It's only an awful moment in time that we're going through, I am more and more convinced that we will come out of the struggle triumphant, as it seems to me that things are moving very quickly in Paris. Later, I will be so happy that our dear children will be proud of their father and that my beloved Jeanne will tell them one day of all that we will have suffered for truth and justice . . . We are doing something very beautiful, for which history will hold us to account . . . Be hopeful, confident and strong, my beloved Jeanne.

No matter how self-important this may read to a modern reader, Zola was right. The point is he had had no need to take sides in the Dreyfus Affair, and prior to that, he had had no need to produce two highly partisan articles decrying anti-semitism. He was a novelist and cultural critic, not a politician. He continued: 'Our life will pick up again and be greater and more magnificent. Have hope, be confident and brave, my beloved Jeanne. I kiss you with all my heart, my three darlings, love me well.'

Love, destiny and the fight for truth and justice had become intermingled in his mind. Seen from some other people's perspective though, they were intermingled in an undesirable way: Vizetelly and Desmoulin confronted Zola with their view that he was taking unnecessary and dangerous risks by bringing Jeanne and the children to stay with him. Vizetelly had no reservations about warning him that if the French spooks ('*mouchards*') were to spot Zola with Jeanne in 'Penn', they wouldn't hesitate in telling the world that he was accompanied by a lady who was not his wife. In which case a huge scandal and an explosion in the British press would follow. Desmoulin admitted to being perplexed. He asked Zola, wasn't he fearful that, what with the house being peopled with restless, noisy little beings, it would attract more attention? Didn't he think that in this country of 'cant', France, he would attract antipathy and hate? Their friends, the Protestants, who represented a great regiment of support for the Dreyfus cause, would change their attitude towards Zola, all because of the 'irregularity' of his situation. It would, quite clearly, be very, very bad, Desmoulin said.

Zola must have felt even more isolated. The two companions who were making his exile possible had turned on him. Zola's reply to Desmoulin was furious:

. . . for some time now, everything you've said to yourself, I've been saying to myself too. And yet you don't know why I am carrying on regardless! Because I don't bloody care! [*je m'en fous*] I've had enough, I've had enough, I've had enough! I've done my duty and all I ask for is to be left in peace. And this peace, I know very well how to get it myself. I don't care what people will say, what people will think. When I've done what's necessary for me and my loved ones, we will be as happy as is possible and the world can come tumbling down without me turning my head to notice. Rest assured, I'm not coming back to France till justice has been done . . .

I have thought of others, my good friend, and I'm telling you again, I regard my public role to be over and I've made up my mind to think only of my family and me. There you go. Even so, I will take all possible precautions, but without tormenting myself about it any more, as I have come to the end of all the struggle and sorrow.

The anger is palpable. Yet in the midst of batting to one side those who would disapprove of his family arrangements, is an announcement, from Weybridge, that the public face of Zola, the fighter for justice in France, was no more. With Jeanne and the children coming to live with him for the first time in their lives, the exile in England was proving to be a moment in which three corners were being turned simultaneously: in his personal relationships, in the nature of his literary output and in his political profile. To look at the suburban solidity and quiet of 'Penn' today – and indeed as it was then – it is hard to imagine the emotional, cultural and historical turmoil taking place inside.

But there was joy to come too.

In Verneuil, in the house not far from Médan that Zola had acquired for Jeanne and the children, conspiratorial whispers signalled to Denise that something was afoot with her mother's plans. Why wasn't the family guest his usual playful self? Why were they, the children, being instructed to be good and say nothing? Why were they being told to sleep a little on the divan in preparation for a journey? Tension was already high, as only a day or two earlier, Denise had been sent a bar of Félix Potin chocolate, opened it, took out the little celebrity photograph only to find a picture of Papa. How nice! She rushed to show Jeanne, who, on seeing it, screamed, 'They've ripped out his eyes! Those awful people, doing that to a child!' At the same time, a neighbour had lent a ladder to journalists so that they could peep over the garden wall to spy on Jeanne and the children.

The party left at ten in the morning, with the house-guest, M. Triouleyre, carrying the case. They took a detour through the woods of Verneuil where people of ill-repute were known to hang out. Triouleyre nursed a revolver. If anyone asked, the children were to say that their father was in Russia. They stayed the night with the Triouleyres. The next day, they arrived in Calais. On the boat, the children were tired and sick, and had no idea where they were. They weren't used to travel. Victoria Station was frightening; they felt as if they were being pushed about by the crowd and deafened by the shouting. A porter seized their heavy case along with Jeanne's personal bag, shouting things that none of the three of them understood. And where was Vizetelly? He was supposed to have been there to meet them. Jeanne tried to keep hold of the bags. For a moment, it was all confusion. Someone tried to help them by translating for them, but then Vizetelly appeared at the end of the platform. He took the little party to Weybridge.

'I can still see Penn, the white door of the house opening and my father holding out his arms to us, with Violette Vizetelly smiling at us,' Denise would write some thirty years or so later.

Violette was Vizetelly's nearly sixteen-year-old daughter who would act as maid and interpreter for the family. One of Zola's photos shows Jacques sitting on the front gate at 'Penn', with Denise on one side and Violette on the other, Jacques in a sailor's hat, Denise in a straw one and Violette in a boater. It has all the air of a holiday picture.

In the morning Zola told Desmoulin that the children had slept well, and were now as happy as larks (in French, it's chaffinches). They would be, Zola told him, a great consolation – exactly the same word that Alexandrine had used – as his poor heart still felt torn apart. A day or so later, he put Alexandrine in the picture too, filling her in with details of the children's journey, their trip from the station where the man used to play the tin-whistle, and the children's sea-sickness. As expected they were cheering him up and he hoped that they wouldn't get too bored – after all there weren't any toys for them. There was no mention of Jeanne or 'Jean', the French man's name, as Zola's followers had asked him to call her in all his letters. In true literary fashion, the weather got better with the arrival of the children. The sun was doing what it did in England, full on during the day, thick mist evening and morning. He was suffering with the heat. Nevertheless, he was turning out his five pages a day; he hoped to finish the second chapter by the next day.

Back in Paris, Alexandrine was now handling the Dreyfus case, the Zola case, and the libel suit against Judet, who had defamed Zola's father.

5

The Haunted House

The next few weeks in Zola's life tested him with great contrasts. For the very first time in his life, he lived twenty-four hours a day with Jeanne and the children. With full permission and blessing from Alexandrine, he could take on the role of being the type of husband who was at the same time a father. In the mornings, undisturbed, he could pursue his other great love, writing. In the afternoons, he and Jeanne could go out on their bikes exploring the villages of Norwood, Weybridge, Walton-on-Thames and beyond, experimenting with photography. He captured the summer sunlight falling on the still water of the River Wey and Virginia Water. He captured the local churches, bridges over the Thames, deserted lanes and the landscape of Chatham Heath. From the outside, it looks idyllic.

In his diary and letters, Zola struck a different note. The core feelings are rage and despair: France has turned on him while descending to a shameful level of existence; he was being persecuted. It was announced that his Légion d'Honneur was to be taken from him and the three 'experts', who had determined that the *bordereau* incriminating Dreyfus was indeed written by Dreyfus, successfully sued Zola for libel costing him, he predicted, 40,000 francs. 'They think I'm rich,' he wailed in his notes, 'I'm financially ruined.'

He knew that as a result of his stand on the Dreyfus case and of the anti-semites' campaign against him, his sales had plummeted. In Paris, Alexandrine had to arrange for a sale of furniture and effects. There was also the nagging anxiety of being spotted. One of the papers revealed that he was staying at the Oatlands Park Hotel under the name 'Beauchamp'. This confirmed his sense of being a fugitive from the country that he loved: 'My whole being protests furiously against this ferocious, idiotic persecution.' If necessary, he would take himself off somewhere else, to some quiet corner of the world where he would continue to work and serve a country which was being dishonoured by a bunch of despicable rogues.

One way he could distract himself from these thoughts was to read novels – though he was beginning to find Stendhal irritating – and then, just as we might expect, English food irritated him even more. Why didn't they put any salt in the food? The vegetables were cooked without any butter or oil; the cutlets and steaks were uneatable; the sauces were so bad they had to be avoided altogether; English bread was like a sponge. Plain, boiled, watery potato and greens were abominations. He found the roasts palatable, and these could be supplemented with ham, eggs and salad. Plum tart was bearable but why did the English insist on eating it hot, when everyone knew that *tarte* should be served cold? Apple pudding was a disgusting invention and who could have thought up the appalling idea of making 'gravy' by pouring water on steak instead of garnishing it with butter and parsley? A small pleasure could be found making visits to the fishmonger where he discovered the delights of the British kipper and bloater.

The summer of 1898 was particularly hot, and Zola fulminated against the English habit of building houses without shutters, but he still managed to fit in his afternoon siesta. Thinking ahead to his next novel, *Work*, and of Charles Fourier's phalanstery, Zola spent time observing and making notes on housing. Even as he was doing this, a huge report on housing and poverty (*Life and Labour of the People in London*, 1889–1903) conducted by the philanthropist Charles Booth was coming to fruition. In the time Zola was living in England, Booth was publishing the most graphic and accessible part of the report, 'Maps Descriptive of London Poverty', each with colour-coding showing the various levels of prosperity and want. Though poor people quite obviously know that they are poor and that usually they are surrounded by other poor people, for some, especially the professional classes, Booth 'discovered' something important and it was a shock. Even the left-wing movement, which was agitating for a new society that would end poverty, put poverty levels in London at this time at around 20 per cent. Booth – no radical himself – showed that they were nearer to 35 per cent.

Zola, who was almost certainly unaware of Booth, but who had spent his literary life reading, absorbing and recycling modern research and analysis such as Booth's, was conducting his own impressionistic studies. As we've seen, he had identified some London housing as a phalanstery come to life and he carried on comparing London housing with Parisian.

This drew him back to looking closely at 'Penn' itself. He was surprised by the fact that the rooms were painted in light colours – soft green, pink and yellow – while the woodwork was painted much more brightly. It seemed odd that the place was fully carpeted, even the stairs, while the furniture, he thought, was disgraceful and the ornaments ugly and childish. The engravings on the walls – mostly of animals – were sentimental. Though he loved dogs, there was no need to overdo it: dog with child, dog with grandfather, dog with beggarwoman ... And horses expressing human feelings! Squirrels nibbling hazelnuts, sparrows in the snow, butterflies on roses – all sentimental. The children, meanwhile, were amazed and delighted that in one of the drawers in their bedroom was a collection of butterflies.

In his letters to Alexandrine, he spent a few moments describing the children's state of mind and health: Jacques was a little homesick. 'I think of you when I kiss the children', he added (did he forget for a moment that Alexandrine wasn't their mother?). In reply, Alexandrine said that she wasn't surprised that 'Ma' (her nickname for Jacques) was feeling like this as he was by nature more reflective than 'Poulet' ('chicken', for Denise). Alexandrine told him that she was happy that he had the children close to him, as this must certainly be making the exile easier.

Occasionally, she painted a picture of her existence. In one striking piece, with the qualities of a prose poem, she wrote:

Nothing here has been disturbed. The moment you come back you would have the illusion that your absence had only been a dream. I have put flowers in the *jardinières* in your study, I have put flowers on your desk in your green vase and I go up there each day to see that everything is in place just as you left it. Letters, magazines, everything that is addressed to you is placed on the table by your chair downstairs; in the evening, before I go up to bed, I arrange them, I put them in order, I put the paper knives on top.

A further distraction came from a derelict house close to 'Penn'. Zola became interested in this old neo-Georgian mansion called 'The Castle', situated in the midst of deserted grounds, overrun with weeds. It was a mournful-looking place, with a broken iron gate at the front which he liked to peep through, looking in to the ground-floor windows. Violette Vizetelly started to make enquiries while Zola took pictures of the house, with its rather grand 'pepper-pot' tower on one side.

Violette discovered that a story surrounded it: a murder had been committed there, many years earlier. A little girl had been killed by her stepmother and her remains buried beneath the scullery floor. There was also talk of the child's father, who at night drove up to the house in a phantom carriage drawn by ghostly horses and hammered at the door of the mansion, shouting aloud for his dead child. The story was well-known in the area and not a girl from Chertsey to Esher, or from Walton to Byfleet, dared to pass the house after nightfall, when terrible voices rang out through the trees and the shadowy horses of the ghostly carriage trotted silently over the gravel.

Violette told the story to Zola and it aroused his interest. Vizetelly questioned neighbours and put together another account. The house had been built some forty years earlier by a retired pawnbroker who was, of course, a 'gaunt, shrivelled old man'. In his old age, he rode a white mare and was well-known for appearing on the roads round about. He furnished the house with unredeemed articles from his pawnshop so that nothing matched anything else. He filled the rooms with tables, sideboards and sofas and covered the walls with supposed Old Masters and assorted Wardour Street bric-a-brac.

The old man had three daughters, whom he kept more or less imprisoned in the house. Three army officers staying in the area had tried courting them but, in response, he simply made their confinement even more strict. Eventually, the officers were successful and three weddings all took place on the same day. The old pawnbroker then married again but after his death his will was contested and an interminable lawsuit followed. As a result, the property was left unoccupied and before long would probably be cut up into building plots.

Zola heard these local stories during the hot, light evenings in 'Penn' and Vizetelly coaxed him to set a short story in 'The Castle', but before he did so, his attention was taken up with several other matters. The lease expired on 'Penn', so on 27 August the little household transferred to a house called 'Summerfield' in Addlestone, which he described as 'taking refuge further from the capital'. Here, he was pleased that the garden was much bigger so the children had more space to play and hide in. He wrote of it being 'half-wild', with a big disused sandpit in it, which had been turned into a flower bed.

Denise recalled a scene of her mother sitting in the garden reading or doing her embroidery; from his table, Zola would watch, keeping an eye on them, preventing them from getting too close to the windows, making a noise or disturbing his work. For hours on end the children played on a hammock, in the sandpit or 'hole' as they called it, with the long grass, oak and acacia trees giving shade. You could imagine you were a hundred miles from the next house, Zola thought. Nearly every day, he sat in a wicker chair on the old tennis court struggling, with the help of the English grammar book that Vizetelly gave him, to read the *Daily Telegraph* or the *Standard*. At first the news looked bad with the anti-Dreyfusards consolidating their power at the helm of French government. Protracted, long-distance, much delayed, and occasionally quite irritated correspondence with Alexandrine dwelled on when Zola thought he could return (October?), or where Alexandrine might go (Genoa?) to sit out his exile.

At the very end of August came the seemingly wonderful news that one of the leading anti-Dreyfusards had been arrested, confessed that he had forged key documents, and then committed suicide. The news arrived in suitably coded form as a telegram: 'Tell Beauchamp immediately victory'. Now, surely, Dreyfus would be brought back from the hell of Devil's Island where he was wasting away, have his case reviewed and be found innocent. Surprisingly, oddly, and tragically for Dreyfus and his supporters – and equally for Zola stuck in Addlestone – no such swift conclusion was in the offing. France did not rise up and demand justice. Again, Zola felt isolated and lost in this strange place with hardly anyone to talk to. In his notes, he returned yet again to cursing France's ruling regime. They were guilty of backward-looking royalism and militarism and suffering from the incurable cancer of defeat (referring all the way back to the Franco-

Prussian War of 1870–1). People were still fixed on the image of the French flag flying over all Europe, when shouldn't it be enough for them to be part of a generous and just nation? At exactly the same moment in France that the police were, in Zola's eyes, attacking the populace, he witnessed a scene on the road in front of 'Summerfield' where a man broke his leg and a policeman bandaged it by the light of a lantern. The heavy sliding door to the room where he worked made a terrible rumbling noise in its grooves as if, he wrote, he were shut away in the bottom of a dungeon, over which someone had pulled a slab, forever.

On 18 and 25 September the *Sunday Observer* printed several important stories: they had interviewed Esterhazy, who was in London at the time. He admitted that, yes, he had written the *bordereau*; he had done so in order to incriminate Dreyfus. Esterhazy's justification for having written a false document, though, was that Dreyfus was guilty anyway! Even so, these developments seemed to present the pro-Dreyfus camp with fresh possibilities.

But then disaster struck. Anyone who has loved and lost a pet will sympathise, even if it's a little excruciating to read in great detail spread out over many letters. Back in Médan, little Pinpin, or Monsieur Pin, the couple's favourite dog, sickened and died. No amount of Alexandrine's cuddling and soothing could save him. There is no doubting their depth of feeling about this matter. In the midst of the crisis, Denise recalled Zola struggling to open a heavy door on a day he felt ill, her mother anxiously rushing towards him to help. It seemed to Denise that he felt the loss of his little dog as if it were a very dear friend.

He had indeed lost a dear friend – several, in fact. He had lost France, lost money, lost the comforts of his own home, lost seeing his friends, colleagues and political companions and lost the daily routine of seeing both of the women in his life. The death of Pinpin, we might guess, must have represented the sacrifices that Zola had made in pursuit of what he had thought was a right and proper fight for truth and justice.

To divert him further, Vizetelly bought him a set of Nelson's 'Royal Readers' for children, which Zola himself followed up by buying an illustrated edition of *The Vicar of Wakefield*. This further acquaintance with English had him questioning Vizetelly about why the English 'I' merits a capital letter. He deemed it a triumph of egotism – 'tall, commanding, and so brief!' More seriously, amongst the many real conflicts or the shadow-boxing between the Great Powers, the imperialist squabbling known as the 'Fashoda Incident' loomed large for a brief moment, giving the impression that war was possible between Britain and France. Zola told Vizetelly that if matters between the two countries became too hostile, he would have to return to France. Briefly put, the 'incident' or 'crisis' was the outcome of long-standing imperial territorial disputes between Britain and France in eastern Africa. A French expedition went to Fashoda on the White Nile, with a view to controlling the area and excluding Britain from Sudan. After a war of words the French withdrew, leaving the area under Anglo-Egyptian control. Zola did not become an enemy alien and the foundations of the Entente Cordiale that has lasted since that time were laid.

In the last weeks of Jeanne's and the children's stay, Zola became bolder and more public in his ramblings. He removed his Légion d'Honneur from his jacket, swapped his white French hat for an English straw hat and on occasions even wore an English bowler. Vizetelly himself was regularly plied with requests for information about Zola in order to hear what Zola thought about the events unfolding in France. One reporter tried bribing Vizetelly's wife to see if she could give more information. Unmentioned by Zola, Vizetelly or Denise in any of their writings is the fact that the very newspapers that they were reading advertised the fact that a tourist in London could take a spin down to 'MADAME TUSSAUD'S EXHIBITION. Baker-street Station.' and see alongside a scene of 'GORDON'S LAST STAND AT KHARTOUM', 'All the most NOTORIOUS CRIMINALS of the CENTURY' and 'DR. W. G. GRACE', a 'PORTRAIT MODEL of ÉMILE ZOLA'.

Throughout this whole period, we have to remember that the person we tend to think of today as an inspired novelist and campaigner was at the same time an international celebrity.

Zola's place alongside Gordon of Khartoum also reminds us that at the very moment Zola was in England, on 2 September at the Battle of Omdurman (like Khartoum, in the Sudan), one of the worst massacres of British imperial rule took place: around 10,000 Sudanese soldiers were killed, 13,000 wounded, 5,000 taken prisoner; the British force, under Kitchener lost 47, with 382 wounded. To explain this mismatch in deaths and casualties, we have to bear in mind that this conflict marks one of the first uses of the machine gun in a major battle. The British army at Omdurman had forty Maxim machine guns, each capable of firing up to 600 rounds a minute. Zola, the great believer in the virtues of science and technology, straddled the precise moment when modernity was experimenting with new instruments of mass death.

Back in Paris, the crisis concerning Zola's property reached a head at the end of September, with the bailiffs ordering a sale of Zola's effects. Wealthy friends stepped in, bought key articles and thereby brought the sale to a close. Zola's editor Charpentier and his wife came over from Paris to see Zola and his family in early October just as Zola was describing it as one of the most beautiful autumns he had ever seen. They all went out in a landau to Windsor. For Denise, this was a day to remember, the woods, the squirrels, the deer, the park – it all seemed glorious. Baskets of flowers on the terrace of the castle reproduced an image of the crown, while in the chapel, everyone wanted to sit on the Queen's chair, she wrote. There's a nice irony in this scene, France's most celebrated anti-monarchist enjoying a little monarchy-worship on the other side of the Channel. In a restaurant, they ate an extraordinary turtle soup, while Zola and Charpentier made up crazy stories for the children as explanations of how the soup had been prepared. It's an image of gaiety, fun and enjoyable family social life.

One problem: on her return Madame Charpentier recounted the story of the day to Madame Zola. The Zolas appear to have had some kind of deal whereby Zola had agreed not to share his family life with people whom Alexandrine regarded as her and Zola's friends – like the Charpentiers. A letter full of dire anguish and despair followed. Alexandrine reminded Zola of what she had been through: how she had suffered and struggled at his side –

right from the start when things were hard; how she had found courage from looking forward to a contented old age; how she had enjoyed Zola's tough life and work; how they had clung to each other against the thorns that lay in their path. And now the reverse had happened: near in time to her and Zola's deaths, these thorns had cruelly cut into her skin.

The arrangement that Alexandrine, Zola and Jeanne had made may have enabled them all to carry on from one day to the next, but it also came at a price: they often caused each other real pain.

Zola revealed in his letters to Alexandrine that when the children would no longer be with him in England, he would be terrified of being all alone.

Zola was told that the anti-semitic newspaper *La Libre Parole* had made the group's domestic arrangements public – albeit in a garbled fashion. On 13 October, it announced that Zola was accompanied during his exile by (hint, hint) 'a friend' (*'une amie'*), one Madame Rozereau [*sic*]. Madame would be returning to France with two children. M. Zola would leave the train in the suburbs while Madame continued to Paris. A similar story ran in another paper of the same persuasion, *Le Petit Journal*. For reasons that are not entirely clear, this scandalous situation, so elegantly hinted at by Zola's enemies, was not then shouted from the rooftops by all and sundry. In spite of Desmoulin's and others' terrible warnings, the skies did not open, no great finger of accusation was pointed at him, Jeanne or Alexandrine. Zola's *ménage* did indeed turn out to be grist for the mill, but ended up in the bin. Perhaps it slipped out of sight in *fin de siècle* France for no other reason than that people from the professional classes laying blame

THE DISAPPEARANCE OF ÉMILE ZOLA

and opprobrium on the irregular domestic arrangements of others would lay themselves open to the same accusation.

On 10 October the little household made one more move: to Bailey's Hotel, Gloucester Road, South Kensington. At the time, its adverts described it as 'Under Royal patronage also American and Colonial families; renowned for many years for its home comforts and thorough completeness in every detail: 300 APARTMENTS, including self-contained suites facing gardens free from all noise; careful attention given to children's meals, which are served in special dining-room . . . elevator to all floors; electric lighted throughout . . .'

It was the best they could find, Vizetelly assured Zola, giving privacy in their room as they could dine there rather than with the other guests. Jeanne and the children left from Bailey's on 15 October and Zola moved, on his own, to the Queen's Hotel in Upper Norwood, under the name 'M. J. Richard'.

Adverts told newspaper readers of the time that the Queen's Hotel was 'close to Crystal Palace, in its own beautiful grounds of five acres. Renowned for healthy position. Highly recommended by physicians. Table d'hôte 7 o'clock. Good stabling. Lawn tennis.' *London Standard*, 27 July 1898.

Vizetelly and Wareham the lawyer chose it for Zola: they thought that he would be able to stay as secluded as he wanted to be in one of the suites and, as there was no 'vast hall' to cross, he would be able to come and go without a dozen servants standing around scrutinising guests. At first, Zola stayed in rooms overlooking the back garden but once the trees lost their leaves, he moved to a ground-floor suite facing the road. Apart from a short spell in another hotel,

[80]

the Queen's was where Zola would stay until his return to France in June 1899. In considering Zola as the Paris novelist or campaigner for the liberty of Dreyfus, it's almost farcical to think he spent nearly eight months of his life holed up in a suburban hotel in Norwood.

As ever, when the situation was desperate, Zola immersed himself in work. He broke off from his daily regime of working all morning, every morning, on *Fécondité* and took up Vizetelly's offer to write something inspired by 'The Castle', the derelict mansion near 'Penn'. He called the story 'Angeline ou la maison hantée' ('Angeline or the haunted house') and he transferred the setting to France. While Zola was absorbed by questions of truth in the Dreyfus Affair, he transformed the Vizetellys' researches into a tale about seeking the truth. The observer-narrator in the story passes through several accounts of what may or may not have happened until he witnesses 'the truth' for himself . . . or is it? Vizetelly translated it and it was published in *The Star* a few months later before Zola returned to France. Incidentally, when I visited 'Penn' in 2014, I looked for 'The Castle' but it has long since disappeared. At a short distance from 'Penn', though, I came across Castle Road, an unacknowledged presence of what was once a supposedly haunted house.

Reading the story not only allows us to picture the state of Zola's imaginative life at this time, we can also imagine it landing on breakfast tables and being read all over Britain as it was syndicated across many newspapers even while Zola was still living in England.

At first glance, the central motif of this odd little story appears to be Angeline herself, yet on reflection, my feeling is that the real theme is how the narrator is haunted. Haunting involves a 'return' – or several returns – over which the haunted one appears to have little or no control. Just as happens on the narrator's final visit to the house, the story hovers somewhere between dream and reality, between sleep and wakefulness. Again, at first glance, the reason for the haunting seems straightforward: the murder or suicide of Angeline. But behind the death are several transgressive motives: jealousy of Angeline by the stepmother, jealousy of the stepmother by Angeline, the stepmother's perceived disrespect towards the late wife/mother, a hint of over-intimate love in the 'passionate embrace' between father and daughter, and, of course, the desire to kill – to remove the rival from the scene. Some of this is a playing-out of the classic Electra trope. In this particular instance, though – as with Snow White – 'mother' is split between mother and stepmother, the first rendered perfect and idealised by being dead, and the second on to whom is displaced the sexual rivalry for the love of the father. The tale 'permits' the telling of unacceptable desires – including murder – precisely because they are channelled through the more socially acceptable rivalry between daughter and stepmother.

The narrator is a man, so his haunting is from a father's perspective. What returns as a haunting, seen purely from this perspective, is a father's role in the incestuous feelings. In this sense, it's not so much that the truth has to be found but that it has to be suppressed. This is done by the narrative of the story itself. The artist, 'V', banishes the haunting by telling the narrator that the girl simply died of natural causes, and that the calling-out for Angeline was real, and not a return. The narrator is relieved. Yet, there is no reason offered in the story itself as to why this account should be more believed than any other. Why should an old woman's version be any less reliable than a dreamy poet's, the narrator's own dream-vision, or a celebrated artist's version? In that sense, the hauntings are as 'real' as the 'real' explanation.

If we think of Zola at this point in his life, in the midst of various crises, creating these images of mental and emotional struggles, can we say that the story shines a light on any of his fears and anxieties? Or should we say that it stands alone as a playful game within the ghost-story format? In one respect, the triangle he had set up in real life with Alexandrine and Jeanne created an Electra-like situation. He was having a father–daughter-like relationship with Jeanne while staying in his relationship with the woman who had been a mother-figure of sorts to Jeanne and was even now, 'mothering' Zola, managing his affairs in Paris. This wasn't regarded at the time as being of itself beyond the pale, though: the mistress-figure was regarded by many as acceptable, so long as one was discreet about it. However, in Zola's case, as we've seen, Alexandrine's discovery of the affair resulted in a huge crisis and many small ones thereafter.

Later, once the daughter-like figure of Jeanne became a mother, perhaps we can say that the next phase in the classic psycho-drama was starting to play out. In her memoir, Denise wrote:

I was a little jealous of my mother, of the affection she bore my father; I always wanted to take his arm, I really lived in the atmosphere of glory that I sensed surrounded him. My mother never ever let go of him; she smiled at my authoritarian tenderness. In that way, she let me enjoy the infinite kindness of holding myself up against my father's arm, something I've never forgotten.

Through 17, 18 and 19 October, as Zola was writing the story, sitting alone in the Queen's Hotel in Norwood, he was painfully aware that, by returning to France, Jeanne and Denise had 'vanished' and that each of them in their own way was in constant danger of being harmed – or worse. Fear of absence is a kind of haunting too. Separated from his loved ones, Zola conjured up their images, imagined possible mishaps and misfortunes, wrestled with the complications and consequences of his divided life, and reflected on his role in altering the lives of everyone near to him. I suspect that this little, rather unghostly ghost story not only played with the difficulty of ascertaining truth, symbolically replaying some of Zola's concerns with the Dreyfus case, but also enabled him to safely explore some of the emotions swirling round in his mind: transgressive feelings in the story don't appear to happen directly to Zola, it's not a confession. They happen safely to an impersonal narrator, and are then banished. In the autumn of 1898, in the suburban surroundings of the Queen's Hotel, fiction-making was doing its work.

6

'A little corner of life'

Early on in Zola's stay at the Queen's Hotel, on 19 October, the *Daily Telegraph* ran a story under the heading 'Search for Zola'. Madame Zola had assured the journalist (or the journalist's informant) that Zola would not be returning to Paris until the Dreyfus case had been reviewed and the judgment of the court martial that had found Dreyfus guilty had been revoked. The paper reported that the person sent by the court that had found Zola guilty had roamed about looking for Zola, but it was said that Zola had a double, one M. Ignace Ephrussi of the 'famous Jewish financial family, which has a matrimonial connection with the house of Rothschilds'. Detectives had been duped by this double and as a result had given incorrect information to the court that was chasing Zola: the court official had trailed the wrong man. Zola told Alexandrine he had read all this and praised her for what she had told the journalist.

However, their final letters to each other before Alexandrine set out for England returned to the theme of their mutual pain. Zola explained that he hadn't fully told her about a crisis he had experienced at the end of September. He had felt so utterly lost that he had stayed in bed for two days, more through despair than an actual illness. He was physically and morally shattered (*'brisé'*).

Alexandrine told Zola that her life was also *'brisée'* forever, and every day it was crumbling away even more. This was something she could tell him only now, as she hadn't wanted to write before about how much she had suffered during the previous few months. She spoke of their 'torments' and questioned Zola's view that these would end. This was a hope she couldn't have herself; they would only end when she was deep in the ground, because after the torments of today there would be others. Yes, she read that Zola had cried over her letters to him, but 'let's not talk any more about the thing that's brought this sadness between us'.

Zola was also writing to Jeanne, keeping her up to date with how the food at the Queen's was even worse, the Sundays were just as terrible, and the hotel wasn't very clean. He didn't mention it, but the contrast with the luxury of his and Alexandrine's stay at the Savoy five years earlier must have been stark. He was extremely anxious that no one should know about Jeanne's stay in England, telling her to do what she could to prevent the children from talking about it. He urged her to defend them against even the most terrible threats to say where they had been and what they had been doing. One indiscreet word about the name of the country or town would set their enemies on his tracks and start off an investigation: this would be disastrous, he said, for his peace of mind. He asked her to remember the form of conduct he had told her to keep to: 'silent and indifferent'.

The fact that the *Libre Parole* had spilled the beans about Zola's domestic set-up anyway wasn't mentioned. He told Jeanne that he treasured the memory of the places they had lived together in England. In his mind's eye, he said, he could see the pair of them going for bike rides – on their own or with the children. He thought that the two months together in England had tied them even closer.

In the midst of this ardour, Zola was very concerned with the children's progress and reminded Jeanne that she had promised to keep him up to date with details of their studies. She had to be honest about it, too. He had some instructions for her: she had to remind the children that they had promised to be good when they were with her, and, if they were, they would get a present from Papa. And they must try very hard not to do anything to make their mother angry. He told Jeanne that he had put the little silver swan ornament on his desk and it was right by him, while he did his writing. He said it spoke to him of the three of them, a time in his life that he would never forget.

On 25 October, Alexandrine arrived at Victoria at 4.50 in the afternoon escorted by M. Fasquelle, Zola's publisher, and they made their way immediately to the Queen's Hotel. A cause for optimism cropped up at this point: the Criminal Chamber of the Supreme Court of Appeal agreed to investigate the Dreyfus case. Perhaps, Zola thought, he would be able to return to France sooner than expected.

Madame Zola would stay with her husband at the Queen's Hotel, Upper Norwood, until 5 December. We can capture a sense of this time and place from the photos that Zola took. He took a photo of the hotel itself, a neo-Georgian pile which had opened in 1854 and had attracted many famous visitors including Florence Nightingale, Kaiser Wilhelm II, the German Crown Prince Frederick (who became Kaiser Frederick III) and King Faisal I. Zola's camera shows us the road outside as if it were a wide continental boulevard.

A woman in a boater pushes her bike past the hotel. An elderly couple walk their dog. A man on a horse trots past.

From his room at the rear of the hotel, Zola snapped the ornamental garden. In another part of the grounds, chickens and a donkey graze peacefully. Opposite the hotel, across the road at the front, Zola took a picture of the detached houses that he wrote about:

I have never seen a soul in those houses during all the months I have been here. They are occupied certainly for the window blinds are pulled up every morning and lowered every evening, but I can never detect who does this and I've never seen anybody leave the houses or enter them . . .

Down the road there was a livelier house, one which had a balconied window, which Zola noticed was almost invariably open, and here he often spotted servants and children: 'That is the one little corner of life and gaiety, amidst all the other silence and lack of life. Whenever I feel dull or worried I look over there.'

We have to imagine many afternoons of Zola's stay in Norwood with him loading his camera into the front basket of a bike and cycling out of the Queen's Hotel to seek scenes to snap. His attention was drawn to the busy streets around Church Road, catching shoppers, horses-and-carts, shop displays, and workers laying electricity cables along the street. These are images of south London middle-class bustle. Modernity, movement and travel come even more to the fore in his many pictures of the local Southern Railway stations, trains, cyclists and, above all, the Crystal Palace itself, which he showed rising out of his pictures, too vast, too wide and too high for the frame, displaying its thousands of panes of shiny glass.

Sometimes, it's a solitary person who attracts his eye: a road sweeper in the middle of an empty street, a policeman, a lone horse or a woman striding across the road with her dog, with shops and houses stretching away from her, Alexandrine reading in the window of the hotel, or poignantly standing on her own by an oak tree in the middle distance. The coal-man delivers coal, cows walk by the hotel on their way to or from being milked, and many women cyclists cross Zola's viewfinder.

We can look at these photographs as pictures of a new kind of London, the modern suburban fringe to the old city. The railway system had been adapted to snake out of the centre into the surrounding stretches of countryside, hamlets and villages, which, in turn, gave the cue to builders to create hundreds of estates and terraces for a new way of living: menfolk would work five days a week in offices in central London, while their wives stayed at home and their children went to school. At the weekend, a round of suburban activities opened up to the new urban middle class: shopping, gardening, cycling, motoring and sports clubs – tennis and rugby. Though Médan, Zola's country house, was in a similar position in relation to Paris, and the railway out of Paris bisected the Zolas' garden, the settlements in France retained a much more 'villagey' feel. Clearly, the person taking these photographs was interested in the ordinariness of everyday life in Norwood as well as its modernity but we can guess that he was also interested in the ways in which these ordinary – yet fairly prosperous – Londoners were creating a settlement that was different from the Parisian one.

But, of course, this wasn't an anonymous photographer, it was the novelist who had put the bitter, difficult lives of the French poor in front of the world's reading public. He had explored their daily existence in minute material detail, along with their passions, sex lives and ways of dying.

Once Zola had brought the great *Rougon-Macquart* cycle of novels to an end, photography became something of an obsession for him. The roots of his interest went back to the 1860s when he met up with one of France's early professional photographers, Félix Tournachon (known as 'Nadar'). Nadar was part of the circle which included Manet and, thanks to Zola himself, Zola's school-friend Cézanne. From 1876 onwards, Nadar took portraits of Zola and from the letters between the two men it's clear that Zola received advice from Nadar about how to take photos. By 1888 he was hooked and, at the time of his death, Zola owned at least ten cameras and had installed a darkroom in the Zolas' house in Paris, another in the house in Médan and yet another in Verneuil, where Jeanne and the children lived when the Zolas were at Médan. Sometimes he would spend hours on end – whole days even – developing, fixing, printing and enlarging in the gloom of his darkrooms. It became a major part of his life. He broke new ground too: he perfected a little device that allowed him to take selfies, which he applied in particular to group shots of himself with Jeanne and the children. He discovered that a camera could be used to preserve and sanctify his family, with a place for him, as paterfamilias, right at the heart of it. He experimented with different kinds of paper, including the most modern platinum paper which was less likely to age and deteriorate.

He was interested in taking photographs from above the subject or of views across the cityscape, as if he wanted to capture the urban landscape in one glance. In Paris, he took pictures from the top of the Trocadéro and the brand-new Eiffel Tower. He tried out different cameras and, unlike most of his contemporaries, worked in rain, snow and even at night, using plate cameras as well as the most modern film cameras. In relation to his writing, Zola claimed that his visual memory was equipped with an 'extraordinary vividness' and that he could evoke objects he had seen in ways that meant he could see them again as they really were. Photography supplemented and enlarged this for him and is linked to what he thought of as the scientific approach to writing. Naturalist writers sought to inform themselves with the latest, most accurate, most scientifically reliable data and observations. In the theory, this is what made their work 'natural', the idea being that it was closer to the real (that is, 'nature') than what could be imagined. Photography, with its scientific modernity, was seen by some as related to this by appearing to document what was really there, representing it with verisimilitude.

In England, Zola worked with a camera described by Alain Pagès as a *'jumelle photographique'* so it would either have been his 'Jumelle Carpentier', a highly portable plate camera, shaped like an enclosed pair of binoculars (*jumelles* =

binoculars or, literally, 'twins') with one lens used for viewing the subject and other for taking the exposure; or it could have been his 'Joux Steno-Jumelle' which could take eighteen pictures on one plate. The ever-faithful Desmoulin put the *jumelle* in Zola's trunk which Desmoulin had brought with him to the Oatlands Park Hotel on 29 July, along with the scores of books he needed for writing *Fécondité* – camera and books side by side as part of the 'science' of Zola's work. On 10 August we find Zola writing to Vizetelly asking him to buy six boxes of plates and on 9 September Vizetelly was explaining to Zola that he'd tried to get his plates developed and had shopped around various dealers but the cheapest would charge 28 shillings (£1.40) to develop and fix seventy-two plates. Vizetelly explained that developing and printing the work of amateur photographers was 'very rare' in London and several shops refused to do it at any price. Zola was clearly unhappy with the price but said that he was 'obliged' (*'forcé'*) to accept local prices.

In amongst his pictures of the Norwood streets and ground-level views of the Crystal Palace, Zola caught an even more striking perspective of this spectacular building: it rises up above the terraced houses, with rows of chimney stacks leading the eye to the cathedral-like curves of the Palace's tower. The viewpoint of the photographer is clear: he is grabbing a vista – near and far, side to side, great height down to ground level. Both photographer and viewer are made small in proportion to it.

Little wonder that the Crystal Palace should have figured so strongly in his photos: only five years earlier, Zola and Alexandrine had visited the 'Palais de Crystal' in very

different circumstances. It's worth tracking back to this
earlier episode in London, as it would have still been very
alive in the Zolas' memory.

7

'The Republic of Letters'

On the evening of 23 September 1893, there was a banquet laid on in the great dining-hall of the Crystal Palace for the annual conference of the Institute of Journalists. A toast was drunk to 'Our Foreign and Colonial Guests' and Zola, with Alexandrine at his side, rose to speak. Full of optimism and hope, he said,

> Above the secular hatreds of races, the accidental mis-understandings of peoples, the interests and jealousies which trouble Empires and Republics, there is a kingdom serene and calm, vaster than any, immense, containing them all – the kingdom of human intelligence, of letters, and of universal humanity . . .
>
> [T]he initiative taken by the institute seems to me to promise happy and fraternal results. We can for an hour forget our different nationalities and our quarrels . . .
>
> And above all, ladies and gentlemen, I should like to see this brotherhood between the literatures of different peoples extended to the works of each literature taken by itself. Yes, I should wish that now, after the battle, there should no longer be realists or idealists, positivists or symbolists, and that only work which sows good seed and the genius that creates life should remain.

This was in essence an internationalist and pacifist vision. Its seriousness was acknowledged at the time, as much of the speech was reproduced in many European newspapers in the following days (the above is how it appeared in British newspapers of the time). Soon after Zola's speech and the votes of thanks, the guests made their way out into Crystal Palace Park where there was a huge fireworks display, which included a moment when the fireworks lit up a portrait of Zola in the night sky above London. He was being greeted and saluted as an international hero.

The Crystal Palace event was one of a series at which Zola was wined, dined and fêted over ten days as part of this visit to the annual congress of the Institute of Journalists. In some respects, Zola's experience of London in 1898–9 can be viewed through the prism of his first heroic stay in 1893.

It had all begun on Wednesday 20 September, when Zola and Alexandrine left Gare Saint-Lazare at 11.30 a.m. At Calais, they met twelve eminent French journalists, Ernest Vizetelly and Zola's biographer Robert Sherard. After a good crossing in spite of the wind, the party arrived at Victoria Station at 7 p.m. on the same day. The director of *Le Figaro* was waiting for them. Zola was flattered to be greeted personally and publicly by Sir Edward Lawson, the former president of the Institute of Journalists and chief editor of the *Daily Telegraph*, along with a sizeable crowd. Lawson spoke in French, leading Zola to suspect that no French newspaper director could have greeted a British writer in English. Lawson spoke of his respect and admiration for Zola's prolific output. Zola replied in French that he was touched by the welcome and thanked England in the name of the Society of Letters, and French literature as a whole. It's amusing to think that this formality took place at Victoria Station, which at the time would have been full of clouds of smoke and steam and the sound of whistles, porters' shouts and snorting engines.

In the build-up to the visit, Zola had expressed reservations about going to Britain, pointing out to Vizetelly that his work was 'still very much questioned there, and almost denied'. Yet he thought that, by coming, his presence and words might wipe out 'much of the misunderstanding'. What was Vizetelly's view on the matter? Vizetelly replied at great length, pointing out that things had improved – though he said he should also point out that the Institute of Journalists represented journalists from all over the country and he couldn't vouch for the response Zola might receive from provincial delegates. Even so, Vizetelly had strongly recommended accepting the invitation.

Following the meet-and-greet at Victoria Station, the Zolas headed to the Savoy where a basket of flowers, sent by Oscar Wilde, waited for Alexandrine. That evening, they visited the Alhambra Theatre, and chatted for a few moments with Wilde, described by Zola in his notes, as the 'charming and remarkable *poète*'. The show was called *Chicago*.

The following day, Thursday 21 September, Zola noted that the Thames in front of the Savoy Hotel disappeared under a thick fog. He was told it was the first of the season but he was delighted by it as he would have been greatly disappointed to have visited London without seeing one of its famous fogs. He took a ride in a landau under a 'smoky red sky' and, as the fog lifted, he was impressed by the size of everything – the enormous black buildings which appeared and disappeared, the many statues and columns throwing dark shadows. The only gaiety was provided by the red coats of the soldiers. The fog, he thought, turned the place into a 'pays de rêve' – a dream-land.

That afternoon, Zola attended the first session of the journalists' congress and heard the attorney-general, Sir Charles Russell, welcome everyone and Zola in particular. Zola began to realise that he was being cast as the star of the week and journalists clamoured to meet him. Russell reminded everyone that Zola had begun his writing career in journalism and led the delegates in three cheers for him.

That evening, the Zolas visited the Drury Lane Theatre with Lawson to see *A Life of Pleasure*, a five-act play by Henry Pettit and Augustus Harris. Following the show, he had to attend a reception at the Imperial Institute in South Kensington, which at the time was a colossal building celebrating the Victorian imperial vision. Zola wasn't so happy on this occasion as he felt that the organisation was very poor.

At some point in the day, Zola found time to write to his 'adorable wife', Jeanne, to tell her that he hadn't been ill on the crossing, he had been greeted with a very beautiful speech and that he was a great success 'here'. Invitations were coming in from all sides, and he was worried that it would all make him ill. Even so he was happy and convinced that the result of this trip would be excellent for him. He assured her that he was not forgetting his 'three dear children' (who apparently included Jeanne). He had thought of them only the night before, just as he was going to bed. In the middle of even the biggest of crowds, Jeanne was in his heart. He had been able to find a moment when he could be alone, and say to himself that, over there in a little corner of France, there were three dear little darlings who were thinking of him. He didn't dare ask Jeanne to write to him, he said, as he did not know who her letter should be addressed to.

The following day, Friday 22nd, was a double triumph for Zola: he read his first speech, 'Anonymity in the Press' to a full session of the Congress at Lincoln's Inn Hall. Following that, the Zolas retired to the Savoy and strolled for a while by the Thames, which Zola found 'adorable'. In the evening, he was received at the Guildhall, by the Lord Mayor at a sumptuous reception with over 4,000 guests, toasted and cheered again and again. While trumpets heralded him and Alexandrine, they descended the staircase into the vast hall. This red carpet moment was capped when Zola realised that he and Alexandrine, preceded by shouts of 'Monsieur and Madame Zola!' from the master of ceremonies, were to walk through a cordon of what he described as 'a double hedge of women', adding, 'there is no ensemble more delicious than all this milky flesh, and the hundreds of beautiful gleaming eyes staring at us'. This was of course immensely gratifying for Zola and the Vizetelly family, both in the moment and by way of a reversal of how Zola's work had been treated in the past. After all his novels had been banned in Britain; Henry Vizetelly, Ernest's father, had been imprisoned for publishing them, and was, even at this very moment, dying from the effects of his time in Pentonville Prison.

Following the triumph of the Guildhall reception, the Zolas repaired to the Café Royal where they ate oysters, before returning late to the Savoy.

The following day (Saturday 23rd) the Lincoln's Inn speech on anonymity was published in the London papers, alongside long commentaries and editorials. The newspaper-reading public could muse on how Zola admitted that the practice of signing political articles in France had undermined the authority of the French press, yet it had to be recognised that much of the passion in politics sprang from that. He understood and accepted that it was the practice of British journalists to write anonymously, but pleaded strongly for signed articles in literary and dramatic criticism, which, he noted was starting to happen in British periodicals. He claimed that one consequence of this was that British newspaper men were well paid (much laughter), and he likened some journalists to mere writing-machines at the beck and call of a superior (dissent). Not so, said some later; after all when the *Pall Mall Gazette* changed hands, most of the staff left.

Zola continued:

To my thinking, when a writer does not sign his work, and becomes a mere wheel in a great machine, he ought to share the income earned by that machine. Have you retiring pensions for your aged journalists? After they have devoted their anonymous labour to the common task, year after year, is the bread of their old age assured to them? If they signed their work, surely they would find their reward elsewhere; they would have laboured for themselves. But when they have given their all, even their fame, strict justice demands that they should be treated like those old servants whose whole life has been spent in the service of the same family.

Vizetelly drily noted in his biography of Zola, '... in journalism as in other matters, Zola was on the side of the worker and against the capitalist.'

Judged by the extent to which the speech was reported and commented on, it was clear that Zola seized the attention of the British press, with the commentaries and correspondence following every word he said.

On the day this all appeared, the 23rd, Zola and François Magnard, editor of *Le Figaro*, had lunch at the Athenaeum, with Baron d'Estournelles de Constant, the chargé d'affaires at the French embassy. Zola found the place 'cold and silent', with everyone keeping their voices quiet – 'comfortable and very melancholy'. Then he was taken off to the Travellers' Club ('less exclusive but very aristocratic') and then to the Liberal Club where he met up again with Alexandrine and had a cup of tea(!). Next stop was the National Society of Teachers of French in England at 20 Bedford Street where he was given champagne and made an honorary member. Yet again, Zola expressed his deep gratitude to the people honouring and fêting him. That evening the Zolas attended the great banquet at the Crystal Palace, already mentioned. In his notes, he expressed the fear that his speech had been too literary. Though it was the climax of the visit, there were still more outings and receptions to come.

Again, at some point in the day, he wrote to his 'adorable wife', telling Jeanne that he had been acclaimed everywhere. He told her of the 4,000 who burst into applause at the

Guildhall and he was telling her that, he said, because he had thought of her just then. He said to himself, at that very moment, she would be having a big snooze. (*'un gros dodo'*). He wished that Jeanne and the children could have been there to take part in it all. One day, his children, he said, should be known by the world as his; he wanted them to share the name of their father. He kissed them with all his strength, his big Jeanne, his little Denise and his little Jacques.

On Sunday 24 September, there was a garden party at Sir Edward Lawson's house in Taplow on the Thames, which Zola was enchanted by. In the evening, they went off to dinner at the house of Campbell Clarke, the Paris correspondent of the *Daily Telegraph*.

On the Monday evening (the 25th) there was yet another reception, this time at the home of Sir Augustus Harris, director of the Covent Garden Opera House and on the 26th, the party of French journalists including Zola visited Hatfield House. On the 27th Zola could devote himself to photography and then, with Alexandrine and Vizetelly, he had lunch with Andrew Chatto, who had published the final volumes of the *Rougon-Macquart* cycle. From this point on, Chatto became Zola's preferred English publishers, as the proceedings against Henry Vizetelly had broken the Vizetelly firm.

In the afternoon, Zola and Vizetelly visited the British Museum. Dr Richard Garnett, the poet, critic and curator of the Prints Department, met them and took them round the library where Zola was much impressed with the Reading Room, voicing that it was superior to the equivalent at the Bibliothèque Nationale in Paris. Following that, Zola visited the French Hospital and then the 'French Circle of London', a group of Francophiles who met to discuss French books and ideas. According to Vizetelly, Zola formed a very poor opinion of Hyde Park, while the royal barracks and Buckingham Palace were, he thought, a national disgrace.

On this day he wrote to his 'beloved wife' again. He hardly had a minute to himself, he wrote; the list of what he had to do was frightening. He wasn't used to this kind of life and it was tiring him out greatly. He said that he would be back in Paris by Sunday evening, so could Jeanne tell Denise to prepare a good cup of tea and some nice cakes for her Papa, and that he very much wanted to kiss Monsieur Jacques?

He had been received like a prince, he said, but of course *Le Figaro*, which didn't really like him, was hardly saying anything about it. The newspapers in Britain, though, had been full of it for some eight days now and he hoped that the echoes of it would reach the French ones. In any case, what had just happened would have enormous consequences for him, and this was making him very happy. He finished with a million kisses for his big Jeanne, his little Denise and his little Jacques, all three of whom he was carrying in his heart.

On Thursday the 28th, he was taken to the Greenwich Observatory and the Naval College in the company of the Irish novelist George Moore, who had been Zola's greatest champion and imitator in Britain up to that point. That evening, Zola was the guest of honour at a dinner hosted by the Authors' Club at the Whitehall Rooms of the Hotel Metropole. This was the most literary of the dos and bashes that Zola was taken to. Here, he was fêted again, this time specifically as the great French novelist and literary giant. The list of invitees included Walter Besant, George Moore, Thomas Hardy, Jerome K. Jerome, Arthur Conan Doyle, Oscar Wilde, Ernest Vizetelly and Andrew Chatto, though Doyle, Wilde, Hardy and Moore do not appear on the list of those who actually attended.

In his address, Oswald Crawfurd, director of the daily illustrated paper *Black and White*, made a clear reference to the upheavals of the past when he mentioned the 'great resistance' that Zola had met prior to this day, but now he was being received as the 'imperator litterarum'. He was more than a literary artist, Crawfurd said. By being the apostle of realism, writing under the banner of 'Reality is truth', Zola was also a philosopher.

Zola replied, modestly pointing out that the members were honouring French literature as a whole and he had only wanted to 'disappear', being no more than his colleagues' delegate. He added that in the midst of all this applause, he understood that the critics had not changed their opinion on his work, but now they had seen the man himself, they had found that he wasn't as 'black' as it had been claimed. 'You have said to yourselves, that I struggled a great deal, worked a great deal and, by honouring my work, you have honoured the great working people.' He said that he would never forget the royal welcome he, a simple French writer, had received in this enormous city of London. He then toasted the novelists of Britain and France, the good fraternity of writers in our 'universal republic of letters'.

It is interesting to note here that the 'kingdom of letters' of the Crystal Palace jolly had now turned into a republic. Once again, the papers wrote up the speech in the editions which appeared the next day, the 29th. Also on this day, Zola was taken to the National Gallery by Campbell Clarke, where he was excited by the Turners – oils and watercolours. Lunch was at the Nation Club with editor and publisher William Heinemann. Next stop was Westminster Abbey where he whispered to Vizetelly, 'I did not know that this was still a Catholic Church.' Vizetelly whispered back, 'It is Church of England – Protestant.' 'Protestant?' asked Zola, 'Well, all that is very much like Mass to me.' Then he shrugged his shoulders and led the way outside. A trip to see the Metropolitan Line followed, which by that time was thirty years old.

He wrote to his 'adorable wife' to remind her how, in two days, they would be together, after four months of separation (the Zolas had been away on holiday prior to this trip). What a joy it would be for him to kiss all three of them, his darlings, and to see them almost every day throughout the coming winter. He would see them on Monday. In the meantime, he would do all he could to make sure that he could spend two hours with them, and they would have a nice meal together, all four of them.

In England, he told her, it felt like a dream, what with all the honours that were being bestowed on him, where ten years previously they hardly liked him at all. He had conquered England; in this enormous city they were talking of little else but him. Happily, though, it was now over, as he was terribly tired. It was beautiful weather now, but changeable, sun, rain, fog. Yesterday, he had had a very interesting walk beside the Thames. It was an immense river, where boats passed all the time, like vehicles on an enormous street. He was sorry that he would not be bringing back any little presents as there was nothing more difficult than trying to make oneself understood in a shop. And, anyway, he was hardly free, but he would try to bring a little souvenir of London for her. He sent his three darlings a million kisses. He knew that they were waiting for him and he could do no more than put his heart into the letter. They were three darlings whom he adored . . .

On Saturday 30th, a long article about Zola appeared in the *Daily Graphic*, written by its editor, Lucien Wolf. Wolf had done the formal inviting of Zola, in part because he was bilingual, having been educated in Brussels and Paris, and he played a key part in organising Zola's itinerary.

The article in the *Daily Graphic* came headed by an illustration of Zola sitting at a bureau in his room at the Savoy, with Alexandrine standing over him with a book in her hand, looking attentive and dutiful. Out of the window, across the balustrade of a balcony, the towers of the Houses of Parliament were sketched in. Wolf wrote that the expression on Zola's face was

severe with a touch of pain about the wrinkles in his forehead but his mobile features respond easily to the quiet gaiety of his conversation, and, although the brow never smoothens, the grey eyes are frequently lit up with pleasant smiles. Madame Zola is in this respect very much like her husband. In repose her face is grave, almost melancholy, but it takes little to make her smile and even laugh outright.

Zola told Wolf that he was struck by the number of towns there were in London, each one stretching over a vast area, and each one possessing some definite and peculiar characteristics. He noticed that the parks were primarily recreation grounds rather than beautiful gardens, but the lawns in London were unequalled anywhere.

On his day at Greenwich, he discovered the secret of the importance of London as he passed east of London Bridge; the greatness of Britain, seemed to be laid bare to him. The immense waterway, with its endless life and traffic, its wonderful quays and wharfs, in direct touch with every part of the world, explained everything to those who marvelled at the power of the British Empire. Between London Bridge and the sea was 'the stomach, the heart of England'. Hatfield House, Zola thought, expressed something of the concessions that the aristocracy had made in Britain, thereby avoiding the political convulsions of a revolution. He hoped that one day he could return to England and live incognito, revealing his presence to just a few friends.

He was sorry that Thomas Hardy had not been at the dinner of the Authors' Club. He had heard so much about him. 'I am going to interest myself in getting some of his works translated into French,' he said, 'especially "Tess of the D'Urbervilles".' He had been very glad to meet George Moore whom he had known for fifteen years. They had met for the first time at a gigantic costume ball given for the hundredth performance of *L'Assommoir*. All the women were dressed as washerwomen and Moore, Zola thought, was dressed as a cook. Manet the painter had introduced Moore to Zola.

He likened the Académie Française to the House of Lords, a 'collection of old Tories'; it disliked all new departures, and the founders and leaders of new schools of thought. Hugo, Taine and Renan had each been refused admittance many times. 'In a few years I shall enter,' he said. 'They tell me I am a man of enormous talent. When they have habituated themselves to this way of thinking they will vote for me.'

Wolf closed the article by telling his readers that at this point in the conversation Madame Zola came into the room, gloved and bonneted ready to leave for another outing.

The day the article in the *Graphic* appeared, Zola headed to the East End of London in the company of two editors from the London evening paper *The Star*, where, according to Vizetelly, he visited the 'Rowton lodging-houses, Rothschild almshouses, various sweaters' dens, sundry Jewish homes of Whitechapel, and Italian ones at Saffron Hill'. Zola observed to Vizetelly that he thought that the poverty of Parisian rag-pickers was worse. (In passing, I can't help but note that at this very time several of my own great-grandparents were living in 'sundry Jewish homes of Whitechapel'!)

In the evening, Zola had a function to attend at the Press Club in Fleet Street with Herbert Cornish, the secretary of the Institute of Journalists. This time, Zola's speech reflected on his career, how he had surmounted great difficulties, how he had been very poor and that it was through irregular paid work as a journalist that he could earn a living while he began his literary career. Some, he said, suggest that journalism spoils the writing of a person wanting to be a literary writer: he disagreed. Later that evening, the Zolas played host to Lucien Wolf, Ernest Vizetelly, George Petilleau from the

Society of Teachers of French, and their wives at an intimate dinner at the Savoy.

The following day, Sunday 1 October, the Zolas returned to Paris. Straight away, he was interviewed and was delighted to report on what felt to him like a transformation of opinion: from the hostility that had greeted the publication in Britain of *La Terre* to the heroic welcome he had just received. He was full of awe and wonder at the size of London, the hypnotic presence of the Thames and even spoke of how, one day, he would like to write a novel set in London, with the city itself as a presence, and with the Thames as the soul of the work. The protagonists would be French, with just a few English people sketchily represented. Yes, he was tempted by such a project. He had dreamed of a series of novels based in the capital cities of Europe. For the time being, he was taken up with a much shorter series called *The Three Cities*: *Lourdes* (looking at religious faith), *Rome* (looking at the attempt by the Catholic Church to reconcile itself with science and modernity) and *Paris* (where he would look at the socialist movement, based on labour and justice). Perhaps, he would return to London for a longer visit when he would be freer to go where he wanted to without having to attend official functions.

Scholars have noted that the visit marked a moment when a great European writer made an impact on the British literary scene. It silenced those who had pilloried, persecuted and imprisoned Henry Vizetelly for publishing Zola. It was a moment when the idea that a novelist could write about contemporary life and politics and could try to grasp the essence of an epoch (as Zola had done with the great

Rougon-Macquart cycle especially) started to be appreciated. Personally, Zola could be seen by many at this point as a man of massive persistence and devotion, a risk-taker, someone independent-minded enough to put his literary efforts in support of reform, and against the social and sexual constraints imposed in particular by religion.

This welcome affirmation must have contributed to the choice of London that Zola and his friends made when they were picking somewhere for him to flee to five years later. By and large, the same newspapers who had acclaimed Zola in 1893 supported him in his stand against the anti-Dreyfus camp in 1897–8.

The 1893 visit was not universally welcomed, though. The Bishop of Worcester rose to speak at the Church Congress in Birmingham to declare: 'Zola has spent his life in corrupting the minds and souls not only of thousands of his fellow countrymen and especially of the young but also, by the translation of his works, thousands and hundreds of thousands of young souls elsewhere.' This view was publicly shared by the headmaster of Harrow School and the Bishop of Bombay, while the Bishop of Truro complained bitterly that Zola's horrible books were sold at railway-station bookstalls, which, he said, would never have been allowed in the lifetime of that 'good man, Mr. W. H. Smith'. This controversy then moved to the correspondence pages of the newspapers where Zola – or at least the Vizetellys for translating and publishing him – found a defender in one 'Mr A. T. Quiller-Couch', better known today as Arthur Quiller-Couch, or even just 'Q', novelist, anthologist, academic, and credited with being a key figure in the invention and development of the study of English literature as an academic subject in universities.

Zola came away from London in 1893 glowing with pride, sure that it would be a platform for achieving yet greater recognition and honour in France. He had juggled his personal life, appearing in public as one of a bourgeois couple, whilst reassuring Jeanne that his love was constant and his devotion to their children was total. He had delighted the writing milieu, though the aristocracy of the churches thundered their disapproval from their conferences, something that Zola would only know of as filtered by Vizetelly or Chatto.

Though he didn't note it in his diary, and Vizetelly doesn't mention it either, it seems as if he met up with Henry James in London. They chatted about travel and what Zola was working on. As in all his interviews, Zola was happy to tell James that he was embarking on the *Three Cities* trilogy and James was pleased to hear that Zola was at the height of his powers.

The visit had even given Zola a vision of how he could spend time in London, moving about unknown and unnoticed, absorbing a feel of the place as a possible backdrop for one of his novels. That pleasing cosmopolitan scenario didn't ever materialise, though a bizarre version of it was what unfolded five years later.

8

'Nothing is decided'

Vizetelly closely observed Zola's arrangements at the Queen's Hotel where most of his nigh-on eight-month stay was spent in the topmost rooms. At the outset, he and Wareham promised Zola that he would have a French-speaking waiter to attend on him but that turned out not to be possible. The one provided could speak one or two words of French, though, and was, Vizetelly says, 'very intelligent, very discreet, very willing to oblige – a waiter of the good old English school'.

Vizetelly sets the scene for us for the next episode in Zola's stay, as if he were describing a stage set. The sitting-room at the Queen's, he tells us, was where Zola wrote much of *Fécondité*. It was spacious and low-ceilinged with three windows overlooking the road and a very large gilt-framed mirror over the mantelpiece where there were two or three little blue vases. The walls were covered in a light-coloured paper with a large, flowing arabesque pattern and broad frieze; but there were no pictures at all.

Opposite the mirror there was a small sideboard; on the other side of the room there was a sofa and half a dozen chairs. The room was 'rich in tables'(!) – five in all. A folding card-table in one corner was where Zola kept his letter-paper, his weighing-scale for letters, his envelopes, pens and pencils. In front of the central window was where he sat at another table and worked every morning. Whenever he raised his eyes from the page, he could see the road below him, and the houses – which are still there – across the way. On a similar table, at another of the windows, he kept the books and reviews that were arriving from France. No chaotic, bohemian, disordered life for Zola, then. There was a small round dining table and, by the fire, next to Zola's favourite arm-chair, was a 'little gypsy table' where he kept the day's newspapers.

In the centre of the room there were brand-new electric lights – fitted for the first time at the Queen's even as Zola was staying there. Before that, it was paraffin lamps. Zola used the hotel's inkstand and alongside that he kept a few paper-weights which stood on his 'memoranda', written on the Post-its of the day, small pieces of paper, three inches square. He used a 'yellowish' newspaper as a blotter, a pen with a 'j' nib and a heavy ivory handle. Vizetelly's long experience of translating Zola seems to have had the effect of letting the Naturalists' method of writing seep into his own here but it serves to give us Zola's eye-view as he spent many gloomy hours in this living-space.

There was a bedroom leading straight off the sitting-room where there was a chest of drawers; on top of that stood a pair of life-size, maroon-coloured porcelain cats, with sparkling yellow glass eyes and yellow spots. Zola had bought these as a souvenir of England and English art, as he had found them particularly odd. He had been tempted by some white ones with coloured landscapes printed over their backs and sides but, in the end, he decided it just had to be the yellow-spotted, maroon ones. One of Vizetelly's daughters was startled by them and thought that Tenniel must have seen them before he drew the Cheshire Cat, while Vizetelly predicted that Zola's artistic friends back in Paris would greet the cats with laughter and derision.

Zola was amused by the way Vizetelly would lean out of the window and talk to guests arriving in their broughams and landaus on the gravel sweep of the drive, and surprised that some wedding guests arrived with yellow flowers. In France, Zola pointed out, yellow was associated with jealousy and conjugal infidelity. 'If those flowers are to be taken as an omen,' he said, 'that happy pair will soon be in the Divorce Court.' No surprise that such thoughts should be in Zola's mind: throughout Alexandrine's first stay at the Queen's Hotel, Zola kept up his correspondence with Jeanne.

Two days after Madame Zola arrived, Zola's letter to Jeanne shows that he had become very agitated about Jacques's health. These were the first signs of Jacques's osseous tuberculosis that would last several years. Zola also warned Jeanne that he might not be able to return to Paris for at least another two months as they were waiting on the appeal court to call for an inquiry into the Dreyfus case. The date of Zola's possible return was a bell-like refrain that was sounded in almost every letter he sent, but with each letter the date moved. Time and timing became agonisingly important for Zola in this period. For the first time in his adult life, he had no control over when things happened. This was a loss. He was dependent on political events far away, minders, hotel timetables and colleagues' instructions. The daily routine he had devised to live in two households had to be discarded. Jeanne's letters, he told her, arrived the day after she posted them, just as they were serving him his cup of tea, an event that happened, on the dot, every day at half past four.

Would Zola have been on his own at these moments, or should we think of Alexandrine sitting with him in the hotel lounge as the boy from Reception brought him the latest letter from Jeanne on a little silver tray? Either way, as we read Zola's letters to Jeanne, we can hold in our minds the sense that Alexandrine must have been aware of the letters passing between Zola and her one-time maid, mother of Zola's only children.

On 30 October, Zola told Jeanne that he was delighted to hear that there had been progress in the Dreyfus case and he was sure that this would end up with 'poor Dreyfus' being acquitted. Even so, he said (again) it would be two months before he could get back to Paris. This period of waiting would at least enable him to make progress with his novel. Apart from that, he didn't have anything interesting to tell her. Well, yes he did. 'Even so, one bit of news: I'm not alone. *Ce qui devait arriver, est arrivé!*' – 'What had to happen, has happened!' or, 'What had to arrive, has arrived!' This was the coded way in which Zola informed Jeanne that Alexandrine had joined him. The exclamation mark possibly marks the fact that in French *'arriver'* can be a pun, meaning both 'to happen' and 'to arrive'. While he was trying to reassure Alexandrine that he wanted to be with her, loved her, and that they could be happy together, was he simultaneously telling Jeanne that the relationship with Alexandrine was an obligation, in some way beyond his control? The anonymity here – no naming of names – was a consequence of the constant fear that the letters were being opened by the police: Zola was still on the run, and both Jeanne and Alexandrine were under surveillance. All the same, wasn't anonymity, in its own way, rather convenient, as this enabled Zola to position Alexandrine in his correspondence with Jeanne as an external and inevitable duty, as if he had played no part in enabling 'it' to have happened/arrived? If so, it could have been one way he thought he could reassure Jeanne that the marriage with Alexandrine didn't really have any loving emotion left in it, whether this was true, half-true or untrue.

At this point, the Dreyfusards had cause for optimism. The Supreme Court of Appeal agreed to conduct an investigation into the Affair. Labori, the lawyer for Dreyfus and Zola, warned Zola against coming back to France just yet, though. He wanted the procedure of the Supreme Court to take its course. Again and again in this period, those who wanted Zola to stay in Britain pointed out to him that to return to France would jeopardise the attempt to free Dreyfus. At moments like this, we are reminded that, though we say it was Zola's exile, in fact it was his friends who had exiled him. To soften this, Labori lavished praise on Zola's role in the case: thanks to Zola, the hour of justice was beginning to dawn.

I don't want to let this day go by without sending you an expression of my admiration and profound affection. Your exile must seem to you to be too sad and too long. But what a piece of work you have done! You will have not only saved an innocent man; you will have saved, I still hope, France herself, and in any case, you will have thrown an incomparable and glorious light on the years of decadence.

The players in this drama were seeing themselves as national heroes.

Letters to and from Denise and Jacques cheered him up, and the children each in turn always drew from Zola very different and contrasting concerns and tones of voice. He told Denise that he was very happy to see that his darling hadn't forgotten him. He would have liked to have come back to Paris with them but what a party they would have when he did get back and what a nice cup of tea she and Jacques would make him. He knew that she had got herself a silver medal for playing the piano. 'Next year, you must get the gold.' Violette, Vizetelly's daughter, was well and sent kisses to them. He closed with, 'My dear Denise, love me well, just as I love you with all my heart. Your Papa kisses you tenderly.' On the other hand, in his letter to Jacques, Zola told him that now that he was going to the *lycée*, he was a man, and that he (Zola) was going to keep Jacques's letter as a souvenir of his first step in the world. But now that he was a man, he had to be good, work at school and above all not play about at mealtimes.

Soon, when I get back, I'm sure that Mummy will have nothing but good things to say about you, telling me that you've done all you can, both you and Denise, to help her forget my absence . . . I kiss you tenderly in the certain knowledge that I am going to be very proud to have a little boy like you: hard-working and sensible.

In his letters to Jeanne, he was starting to get anxious about Jacques's failure to pass into a higher class. He should have worked harder in the holidays. 'Keep me up to date with him and with what they tell you at the *lycée*, in as much detail as possible.' Then, reflecting on the pair of them, and trying to make the most of the fact that Jacques wasn't advanced for his age:

If he stays with children who are more advanced than him, he'll be discouraged and he won't do very well. I really want my little Denise not to do very much at all and that later she will be happy to be a good little wife ['*bonne petite femme*']. But I would be very sad if our Jacques was just lazy and ignorant.

He told Jeanne that his work, writing *Fécondité*, was taking up the mornings and without it, his existence would be utterly abominable. He closed with: 'My beloved Jeanne, I kiss your beautiful eyes, from so far away, alas! that I am only kissing shadows. So, when will I be able to be with you again, you and the children, in a hug that can embrace you all together with all my heart?'

He attached two photos: a view of Summerfield, and the other of 'Penn' with all three of them in the picture.

Was Alexandrine in the room when Zola was writing these letters? It's hard to imagine that she could have been anywhere else. She couldn't speak English at all, there don't seem to have been any French people at the Queen's Hotel and, anyway, the Zolas would have thought it was still too risky to talk to anyone in case their situation became too public. Alexandrine was only in England to support Zola in what she and their friends thought was a time of crisis for him and for France. They thought he was making a great sacrifice for the sake of truth, justice and republican values, but we can speculate about what Alexandrine might have thought and felt at these particular moments far from home, separated from the support that she had built up to enable her to cope with what had happened to her life. Sitting cooped up in draughty rooms in south London while her husband wrote to his other partner could not have seemed like the best way to spend her time.

On Sunday 6 November he wrote to Jeanne, and his friends Paul Alexis and Eugène Fasquelle. He told his friends that he was finding exile very difficult, especially as winter was on the way. In a bout of recrimination towards Jeanne, he chided her for suggesting that he was getting along better because, according to her, he was back to his normal way of life. Her writing this, he said, made him extremely sad.

How can you talk of 'my normal way of life', when you're not here? I'm not getting along at all well; and I don't know how I'll summon up the courage to carry on with this to the end. My days are frightfully empty, since you and the children haven't been here with me. When I finish my work each morning, I don't know what else to do, I just hang about till the evening. Going out pleases me even less and I'm happy when it rains, so as to have an excuse to stay by the fire and despair. If this is going to last much longer, it will be awful. And you are not being fair to make it seem as if it's all a bed of roses, you

who, at least, are in your own country, in your house, with
your children. I will not be happy, I will not be able to go
back to 'my normal way of life' until I get back to Paris,
when I'll be able to see you all whenever I wish and to
love you all with all my heart.

He then restated why it wasn't possible for the three of
them to come and stay with him in England – the children
being at school, in particular – and he asked her to give him
courage rather than making him despair, as at this moment
what he really needed was to be supported and loved.

This recriminatory tone seems to have paid off, as he was
able to tell Jeanne four days later that her latest letter really
cheered him up. He had explained that he needed to be
supported and loved, he said, in order to get through the
misery; he had run out of nervous energy after all the shake-
ups he had had. The smallest of difficulties – ones that hadn't
bothered him in the past – could send him off-track.

Jeanne knew that Alexandrine was with Zola throughout
this time, but he told her that he went out as little as possible,
one-hour walks only. He was studying the newspapers in
order to see if there was the tiniest fact to suggest that he was
coming back later or sooner, one way or the other. Vizetelly's
English grammar book was coming in handy because he was
now reading the newspapers more and more easily.

Ah! if you knew how I dream of my return and all the
beautiful projects I have in mind for the day when we're
back together. I am getting to hate this country more
and more – which is not fair. But everything's becoming

unbearable, though the weather's good after a period of rain and storms. For several mornings, there's been heavy fog.

It's at moments like these that Vizetelly's details of the two hotel rooms – the wallpaper, the five tables and the porcelain cats, Zola's fastidious laying out of papers – give a claustrophobic flavour to what Zola was saying. Then matters turned to the children again. Zola needed to know if Jacques was working well at school. 'Our little boy must not be bottom of the class.'

What a state of nerves he was in! Each of her letters, he told her, made his heart miss a beat, as he was always afraid that it would be bad news.

Be patient, my adorable wife, our worst days are nearly over. Kiss my little Denise and my little Jacques tenderly for me. And you, my beloved Jeanne, I shut my eyes to see you, to remind me of you and to hold you in my arms as hard as I can and with all my heart.

Writing to Denise, he was able to tell her that she was a big girl now as she had written to him in German. But it wasn't just a matter of being first in German. She had to be first in French from time to time.

Did the monkeys from the Zoo tell you and Jacques that when you're lazy and lying, you become as ugly as them? Because you know that the monkeys are little boys and girls who haven't done any work and who have lied. So, they were put in cages . . .

Sunday came round again too fast. 'My beloved wife, now this terrible Sunday is here again and I would have spent the day in a sad state if I hadn't received your good and long letter yesterday.' He was worried that Jacques came home hungry from school and he was concerned that the boy was shy; it wasn't good that he was keeping himself apart from the other children. He hoped that Denise was becoming a little less scatterbrained.

In a few of the letters between the pair there was also a conversation going on about their photos, in particular the portraits that Zola had taken of her and the children, or the photos that Jeanne had taken of the children in Paris since they had been back. He planned to get these framed and placed opposite each other in the hotel room. With his usual caution over his marital arrangements, though, he asked Jeanne specifically not to send any pictures of her with the children: too painful for Alexandrine, we can assume: 'You know how happy I would be to get them, but what would be the point, if I can't put them on my table where anyone could see them?' He offered Jeanne New Year's Day as a possible return date since good news seemed to be coming from the court. On the children front, it was essential that Jacques did not terrorise her or Denise. It was very naughty of him to make a scene when he got in from school. Zola wasn't too worried about it, he said, but he pleaded with Jeanne not to let the boy have his own way, as that would do him no good at all. There were domestic concerns, too. 'The food continues to be revolting, their vegetables are always cooked without salt, and they wash their meat after they've cooked it. I am so sick of it, I would give you a hundred francs for a steak cooked by Mathilde.'

On Sunday 20 November he ticked off Denise for making too many mistakes in her letter – fourteen in all. He wasn't too upset about it, but she should try as hard as she could. 'If you work, you end up not making any more mistakes at all.' Violette, Vizetelly's daughter, was back at school. Her mother had bought her a beautiful bicycle with the present that Zola had given her in Denise and Jacques's names. 'Tell Jacques that he's a little lazybones for not writing to me. Be nice to him and play well together.'

The news coming out of France by 24 November made Zola suggest to Jeanne that he would probably have to stay in England for the whole of winter. The weather was awful. The thick fogs were making it necessary to put the lights on in the middle of the day and the wind was pulling trees up. The bad weather had also prevented the newspapers arriving from France. What's more, it was as cold as hell ('*un froid de chien*') and he was shivering in these foul rooms ('*chabraques de chambres*') where the big windows shut so badly.

There's no use having big fires; while I roast my feet, my back's frozen. In the mornings it's death to have a wash. As for the food, it's more and more revolting. See how furious I am! But what's the point? I always end up being resigned to it, still glad that I can work. On this front, at least, things are going well, my novel is coming along. It's my only consolation in the midst of the uncertainty that's torturing me.

Then it was the wisdom (or not) of asking the housemaid to take Jacques to school. Was this sensible? The roads that their darling had to cross were so packed with vehicles that Zola feared he would have an accident. And being in thirteenth place in a class of twenty-two wasn't good enough. He had to do better. He should be in the top five; that wouldn't be asking too much of him. He asked Jeanne to tell Jacques to work harder if he wanted to please his father.

How it must make you feel bad about this little world, to be forever running about for them! But, on the other hand, what would you do, if you didn't have this to occupy you, to distract and console yourself in my absence? You're right to persist in getting Jacques to play the piano a bit. Later on, he'll thank you for it.

Sadly, he thought of not being able to have a meal with Denise or being able to kiss them all, every day. What with that and the news from Paris, he wasn't happy. 'No matter, have faith in the truth!'

There was good news for the Dreyfusards on 25 November: Zola's friend Eugène Fasquelle wrote to Zola to tell him that the experts in the appeal court had found that the paper used for the *bordereau* was exactly the same as letters seized from Esterhazy, same year, and probably from the same batch. It was impossible to manufacture the same paper in two different processes. Surely now, there was no reason for keeping Dreyfus on Devil's Island? Wasn't the whole edifice of the state, army and justice system, which had found him guilty and then conspired to prop up the judgment against him, collapsing?

On 30 November the infuriating matter of the libel case reared its head again. This was over the attempt to smear and dishonour Zola with a concocted story about his father deserting the army and whether, in reply, Zola had libelled the man who had made the accusation. Zola had confidence in Labori but was concerned that some of the proceedings could take place before he got back. It was yet another burden for Zola to handle.

On 1 December Zola raised the hope with Jeanne that he could be back by the end of the year. He had, he said, resigned himself to living like a monk. The only thing that made him suffer was her absence. If she were with him, he would be able to wait patiently for years. 'Tell yourself that everything is for the best and that apart from our separation, we have nothing to complain about.'

On Sunday 4 December Zola told Jeanne that, as of the next day, he would be alone for two or three weeks. Again this was his discreet (or furtive) way of talking about Alexandrine. Specifically, his wife was heading back to Paris. 'The beautiful roads that we [Zola and Jeanne] noticed were so good for cycling, are nothing more than mud-lakes; even so, I meet women who cycle in all weathers in order to go shopping.' (Zola was still showing great interest in the female cyclists.)

> My adorable wife, I see you alone, in the evening, when you write to me, having put our darlings to bed; and I want to be next to you then, to kiss you and to say how much I love you! In the end, I think the greatest of our troubles are over and I'll be back in a matter of weeks.

We have certainly earned the right to be left to live our lives quietly and for ourselves.

He told her that everyone was doing what they could to bring him back. He urged Jacques not to sit alone, away from his fellow pupils, otherwise people would think he wasn't nice.

Alexandrine left for Paris on 5 December.

December 11th was a hugely special date for Zola and Jeanne. He must have made a note, in his mind or in a diary, some years earlier of what he thought of as the true starting point of their relationship. Sitting on his own in the Queen's Hotel, Upper Norwood, wasn't how he wanted to celebrate it.

Dear beloved wife, I'm going to be so sad next Sunday, 11 December, not to be with you, not to be kissing you with all my heart in memory of 11 December 1888! That anniversary is as sweet for us as it has been throughout the ten years of our happy set-up ['ménage'] since then. I would have wanted to celebrate the three of you, you and our two darlings, those two beautiful presents that you made for me, who have united us, the one to the other, for ever! Since last year, I have dreamed of finding a way of celebrating our ten years of happiness, of finding a way of perpetuating the memory of it for us. And here I am, far away, in exile, not able to bring about my wish, prevented even from bringing the three of you into my arms in one big embrace! I have never suffered more from being locked up here in this beautiful country which I am finding more and more abominable . . .

Then, in another of his impersonal sentences, he indicated to Jeanne that someone (*'on'* in French, meaning 'one') had been told to send Jacques a box of model soldiers for Christmas and a box of *'petits travaux de demoiselle'* (little girl's things) for Denise. In other words, Zola had asked Alexandrine to buy specific presents for the children when she was back in Paris. He asked Jeanne to buy them each four or five things to put by the chimney. She should take Zola's place and say to the children that little Jesus had brought them as ordered by Papa.

He was now not complaining about his solitary life, he said. In the evenings he was immersing himself in an orgy of newspapers and there was a good chance that he would be back home between Christmas and the New Year. 'Kiss our Denise and our Jacques tenderly, who were born out of what was the best in us, my passion and your goodness.'

But then, later the same day, 11 December, he had to write again to Jeanne to tell her that, in fact, he wouldn't be able to get back in January. He knew that this would upset her but he could see from her letters how reasonable she was being. The children had to take care over their homework. 'Tell them, that if they win prizes, I will give them as many books as they have prizes.'

There was a third missive sent by Zola on this special day, 11 December. He (or was it Vizetelly?) bought a coloured card, decorated with flowers and with 'Joyful Greetings' written on it. On the card Zola wrote:

To my beloved Jeanne,
a thousand good kisses from the depths of exile,

in memory of the eleventh of December 1888,
and in thanks for our ten years as a happy couple
['*ménage*'],
and for the bond between us that has been forever
strengthened,
by the arrival of our Denise and Jacques.
England, 11 December, 1898.

He also wrote to Alexandrine on the same day. He thought that her calculation that he wouldn't be back till after April was pessimistic.

Meanwhile a French newspaper, *L'Evènement*, worryingly leaked the news that Madame Zola had left London, returned to Paris, and that she was accompanied by M. Ernest Vizetelly. M. Zola was living, the paper said, near Crystal Palace. The significance of this was that anyone who really wanted or needed to could track him down. Vizetelly confessed to Zola that Alexandrine must have been recognised at Victoria Station when he went off to get the tickets. Their cases were in another room and had a sticker on them saying that they had come from Crystal Palace. In reply to Vizetelly, Zola seemed more concerned with getting Vizetelly to send him a recipe for reheating and serving Christmas puddings.

On 15 December, he warned Jeanne of yet further delays in coming back – two months perhaps. 'Ah! if only we could take up our life at Summerfield again ...'

At this point, Zola mooted the idea that they could meet up in Italy. He told her that everything was the same, he didn't see a living soul, he didn't even open his mouth. He had put in the order (to the unmentioned Alexandrine) for

Jacques's and Denise's toys. Jacques would get his 'Cuban War' game – a board game that had been rushed out for boys to re-enact the very recent war between the USA and Spain over supremacy in the Caribbean. Denise would get a toy . ('*joujou*'). She seemed to have come first in class, so why not Jacques? All Jacques needed to do was work.

In a letter to Labori on the same day he lamented the state of France: 'Ah our poor country! It's it I worry about every hour of the day. On the morrow of our great victory, what a heap of rubble it is! Will we ever be able to rebuild the house, with such rotten materials? That is the terrible tomorrow.'

On 18 December Zola was still much concerned about presents. He had done all he could to send them a pudding, made by the baker nearby. It wasn't very beautiful and it wasn't very good, he told her, but in the end she and the children could eat it and drink to his health. With the letter he would enclose a note so that Jeanne would know how to reheat and serve the pudding ... but they couldn't expect to be reunited before the end of February. By now there was also the matter of Jeanne's teeth. He urged her several times to take care of them as he was in despair over what she had told him about her health.

On 22 December he received the proofs of the first twelve chapters of *Fécondité*. Alexandrine had taken the manuscript with her to Zola's publisher, Fasquelle, and the 22nd was also the day she came back to the Queen's Hotel. It was Alexandrine he would be spending Christmas with. The 22nd was also a day to write to Jeanne, in particular to tell her that he had been told (by Alexandrine, but again not stated), that the children's presents would arrive straight after Christmas. He advised Jeanne to keep them hidden until New Year's Day.

Tell yourself that the beautiful days will return, that the future certainly holds for us other journeys, other holidays where we will find ourselves alone again, with our tenderness, freer and happier. Happy Christmas! Happy Christmas! be full of joy and hope, my three dear little darlings, and I send you all the kisses from the bottom of my heart.

Zola also bought an English card with the message:

My recompense is thanks
that's all
Yet my goodwill is great
although the gift is small!

(This is a quote from Shakespeare's *Pericles*.) Zola then wrote:

Happy Christmas
to my adorable Jeanne
who I kiss with all my heart.
England
December 1898
Émile Zola

Neither Zola nor Alexandrine decked the rooms in the Queen's Hotel with anything other than a large sprig of mistletoe hanging over the mantelpiece. Zola had bought it himself after Vizetelly told him about what the locals did under mistletoe at Christmas.

On Christmas Day Zola told Jeanne that he was distraught to hear that the Christmas pudding had arrived in bits. He was still worried about the children's marks. Jeanne had to speak kindly to their little chap and explain to him how getting bad marks in composition was upsetting for Zola and Jeanne. He wasn't worried about Denise's spelling mistakes but he admitted he was very anxious, even frightened, that his little Jacques was refusing to become an intelligent and wise man.

Assuming that Vizetelly was as assiduous as ever in bringing Zola his newspapers, 27 December must have been more interesting than usual. *The Times* ran three Zola stories that day. The first was part of its extensive, regular coverage of the Dreyfus and Zola cases – the usual mix of fact and opinion. *The Times*'s tone by this point was blending incredulity with contempt for how the French justice system appeared to be making a mess of both cases, underpinned by shock that anti-semitism was so vocal and public. The paper's journalists engaged in some detail with the wisdom (or not) of Zola's tactics in the matter, speculating as to whether he had been 'vulgar' in bringing the Dreyfus case into public view in the way that he had.

The second story in the paper that day was a snippet on Madame Tussaud's exhibition. Here Zola would have read that the waxwork of himself in a cameo with Dreyfus, along with a separate one of Lord Kitchener, was drawing the 'largest share of the visitors' attention'. What a contrast between the clusters of visitors crowding around a waxwork of Zola in Baker Street and Upper Norwood where the man himself was sitting in a cold room with five tables.

The third story was a supposed scoop: the 'Paris Correspondent' could now reveal exactly what had happened on the day of Zola's flight from France in June. Yet again the article was a bizarre pot-pourri of half-truth and pure invention. One or two moments in the tale have the smell of melodrama, as with the detail of someone supposedly having the time and wit to sew some bank-notes into Zola's jacket just prior to his heading off to the Gare du Nord.

According to the story, Zola had ended up at Charing Cross Station, and from there travelled to a village on the Birmingham line. Wareham or Vizetelly are transformed into a helpful 'clergyman', Vizetelly's daughter Violette becomes Kate, and since his arrival Zola has stayed at five different places including a house in Middlesex. All the inhabitants local to this clergyman's house know where Zola is but there hasn't been the 'slightest indiscretion'. Zola, the newspaper claimed,

speaks with admiration of this fidelity in preserving his secret, which he had not even requested, and of the delicate attentions everywhere paid him, and if on his return he writes, as is expected, his impressions of England, they will certainly show his gratitude for these good people who have thus softened for him the tedium and bitterness of exile.

Perhaps this last point arose from Vizetelly feeding the correspondent some pro-British material for *The Times* readers. Though coverage of the Dreyfus and Zola cases was often couched in liberal terms, what underlay the tone was Great Power rivalry and casual but virulent anti-French sentiment. 'He now reads English newspapers fluently, studies the laws and customs of the country, and certainly appreciates the liberty, legality, and toleration the benefit of which he has enjoyed.'

Following *The Times* coverage, the story was taken up by several other papers. Anyone interested in French politics, the Dreyfus case, curious about the life and times of a notorious novelist, or just following celebrity tit-bits would know that Zola was still in England.

On 29 December, he wrote to Jacques telling him that Mummy had said that he had written his nice little letter all by himself and Zola congratulated him on it because it didn't contain many mistakes.

If you make good progress, you know how much this will make us happy ... You have to work at school with all your heart in order to try to be amongst the first in your class; as it would be shameful if you stayed amongst those at the bottom. Mummy and I wouldn't dare go out in the streets, while if we had a clever boy, we would take him to the theatre and everywhere in order to show how proud we are of him.

To Jeanne, he said that he thought Jacques was indeed doing better and his spelling wasn't bad. If it was Denise's own fault that she was getting a cold, she would have a red nose and no one would marry her. He also sent Jeanne a card with 'A Christmas Greeting' on it, in order to wish her Happy New Year. He told her he owed her a New Year's present which he would give her as soon as he got back to Paris.

New Year's Day was a Sunday which, he told Jeanne, he would have loved to have celebrated with them together. It seemed to him that they were coming to the last days of the 'monstrous Affair' so perhaps he would be back soon. He hoped that the person charged with giving them flowers, sweets and the little blue bird (ceramic, presumably) had done as asked. He told her not to worry about the story that had appeared in *L'Evènement*. The only real worry was if people found out exactly where he was, because he would be overwhelmed by letters and visitors. 'As for you, don't breathe a word to anyone ...'

He told Denise that Mummy had explained to him that she was making progress with the piano; she should learn a lovely piece to play when he got back. 'We'll have a party and you can get us all dancing.' He said to Jacques that he hoped he would show him all his toys and they would play with them together. 'You'll also tell me how you're doing at school and I will give you good advice so that you can sometimes come first, which would make Mummy and me very pleased.' Now that the holidays were over, Jacques should get down to some serious work. Then, when he became clever, Mummy would be proud, Zola would be very happy and he would see how lovely this all was. 'And you, my beloved wife, will make me a nice cup of tea, every evening, so that we can stay together for the longest possible time, holding each other, looking after our children.'

By the 3rd – and subsequently – he was telling his friends that Alexandrine was suffering from a heavy cold, didn't dare go out and it was driving the pair of them mad. Vizetelly called it 'bronchitis and kindred ailments', and noted that Alexandrine was unwilling to see 'any medical man' and that she remained 'absolutely imprisoned' in their rooms for three or four weeks. In a letter to one of the leading Dreyfusards, Zola said that their unhappy country was sick and was showing all the signs of acute dementia. 'How will we ever restore it to health?'

On the same day, 3 January, he voiced worries about the articles about him that were appearing in the daily press. He tried to reassure Vizetelly that the claim by *The Times* journalist that he had interviewed him was purely and simply a lie. Meanwhile, it seems as if one Frederic Lees, an American journalist based in Paris, had fetched up at Wareham's house asking for information on Zola. This worried Vizetelly because he thought it would compromise the letters passing between them all. It would also enable the justice system in France to write to them. From now on, all letters should go via another intermediary. Meanwhile, the *Daily News* was ramping up the pressure by claiming that their correspondent had met a lady from Scotland Yard who had learned that the police had received an order from the French government to arrest Zola!

On 5 January, rather curiously, he told Jeanne that he thought the children had nothing to complain about as she had taken them to the Nouveau Cirque ('New Circus'). In all this, it was only her who had suffered from his being away. (Presumably, Zola had little sense that children cared about such things as an absent father.)

He had asked Fasquelle, the publisher, to send Jeanne four or five of the most recent interesting novels he had published. He was also sending her 5,000 francs. 'The last year has been disastrous but we're not going to do without bread.' He told her that Clemenceau (who had published 'J'Accuse' a year before) had been to see him at the hotel on the 3rd and that Clemenceau had been full of hope that it would all be over by the end of February.

The weather was superb, though, and he had been for a two-hour walk. Work wasn't going too well. Even so, he reckoned that he would have *Fécondité* finished before the end of April. He wanted to hear about the books that Denise was 'printing', the boats that Jacques was putting on the water and whether he was sticking to his big promise to work better. He was thinking of the happy day, when he would arrive home, carrying as usual a bouquet of violets for each of them. 'A million kisses, my three adorable darlings.'

For the children directly, he asked Denise to print a page of her writing so that Mummy could send it to him and later, 'I will give you one of my books to print.' He told Jacques that everything he told him about the Cuba War game was making him want to get back straight away to see such wonders.

When I get back, you must put it all in front of me on the table and show me your beautiful books, as well. If you're good, I'll give you some more even more beautiful ones. But now you must make good progress at school . . . It wouldn't be honest of you to have presents and not work hard.

THE DISAPPEARANCE OF ÉMILE ZOLA

By the 8th he had got news that the Truth–Justice–Liberty Committee was going to celebrate the one-year anniversary of the publication of 'J'Accuse'. They would have a banquet on 12 January. Zola was asked if he would send some words that could be read out before they toasted him. No, he wouldn't. He didn't want to perform any public act in France as long as justice wasn't victorious. He would come back, and resume when justice itself had resumed. If he were to send a couple of lines that could be read in public, he thought it would spoil his legal case. 'I am like Lazarus, dead, for as long as the sacred trumpet of justice which will eventually triumph has not awoken me.'

On Sunday 8th he told Jeanne not to worry about the stories about him that were coming out in the papers. It was all lies. No law could allow him to be extradited. He was 'lost in the crowd' in England, as unknown as when Jeanne and the children were here.

Nobody looks at me, or suspects anything, when I'm out for a walk. In the hotel, I don't think that either the managers or the waiters know who I am . . .

Six weeks more – and I'll be in your arms. I'm not on my own here any more, as you know. But I will spend a fortnight on my own before coming back. I would prefer to arrive on my own . . .

Jeanne should tell Jacques that it was very good (*'gentil'*) of him to finish fourth. One more little effort, and he'd be first. It's the place he must strive for. Did Denise dance at Madame Dieterlen's party? Jeanne hadn't told him. Then he begged Jeanne to write about what was going on around them. It gave him great pleasure when she talked to him of their little daily round ('*petit traintrain quotidien*'). 'Now, with each letter, we can say, that was one fewer. And when we kiss, it won't be coldly, on paper, but in each other's arms, on the mouth.'

On the 12th, knowing that back in Paris they would be calling out his name at the banquet, he expressed some doubts to Jeanne: perhaps this 'monstrous abomination' wasn't going to end well. But the only thing that made him suffer was being separated from her and the children.

> I am ready to come and live with you in the land of the sun ('*pays du soleil*'). It would do us all good. We could spend several years, very calmly and very happily . . . Our great strength is that the truth is with us, and the truth will always end up triumphant.

On Sunday 15th Zola had a major worry that Jeanne hadn't sent him a letter. But all was well, it turned up later in the day. 'You tell me that you are sad, without knowing why.' But Zola knew (he was trying to be positive for Jeanne's sake) that the Supreme Court could find Dreyfus innocent without having to send the whole case back to the Council of War. If the court did not find Dreyfus innocent, it would delay his return by two or three months. Yet it was his intention, he told her, to come back in spite of all this; he couldn't wait till Dreyfus returned to France. This time, if his friends thought he shouldn't, it was nearly certain that he wouldn't listen to them, at least so long as they couldn't produce unanswerable reasons. He also said that she was right to be worried about Jacques's piano lessons and dear little Denise was very good to do her work so carefully. It was three months, to the day, that Jeanne and the children had been gone and it was his firm hope that he would be with them in around one month.

Though he doesn't mention it, on 16 January Zola would have had the satisfaction of seeing 'Angeline', the ghost story he had written in the early days at the Queen's Hotel, translated by Vizetelly and illustrated by Sir James Linton, published in *The Star*.

On the 17th Alexandrine wrote to a friend to tell her that she was getting better and had gone out for half an hour. The violent coughing that had floored her wasn't so bad; rubbing herself with turps(!), and taking a malt and cod liver oil mixture must be doing her good. Outside, though, it was pouring with rain, with constant wind. Morale was low.

On the 18th Eugene Semenoff, a Russian journalist and friend of Zola, came and spent the afternoon with him. The bad news was, according to Semenoff, that it was unlikely the court would send the judgment to a new council of war (a new council would be more likely to quash the original judgment). On the 19th, in his letter to Jeanne, Zola questioned his idea of coming back to Paris because he would have to stay at home, or only risk going out in a car or carriage. So it would be better to carry on making this sacrifice all the way to the end. 'So I dare not fix a date for when we'll be back together.'

Zola could see from Jeanne's long letter that being alone was weighing her down and the afternoons were empty. 'I'm pleading with you, try to entertain yourself as much as possible. Think up something to occupy yourself with, go out a lot, arrange to go to the theatre in the evening sometimes.' In the three months since she had left England and been back in Paris, he had worked every morning, but he was getting tired and he might have to give up for a few days, if he wanted to avoid getting ill again, as he had in the last weeks of Jeanne's stay with him. When he got down to work, he was getting headaches and dizzy spells. She had to tell Denise, he said, that each time she finished first, he would pay her. And if Jacques worked well, he would give him something too.

On the 22nd – Sunday as usual – Zola's letter took on the quality of a prose poem:

> You can't have an idea of weather like this, the wind hasn't stopped blowing since the day before yesterday. There's a torrential downpour and it seems as if the house I'm living in is going to be carried off. The nights are especially shocking, the roaring of the wind in the chimneys sounds like thunder, while the windows, those windows you know are so practical, are shaken about as if someone wants to rip them off. And even though the sun has reappeared a little, today, Sunday, the wind hasn't stopped, it's still moaning.

On a long walk he had taken yesterday (Can we assume he did it with Alexandrine? And if we can, would Jeanne have assumed it too?) he had noticed little green shoots on the lilac trees and had the sad thought that he might yet see the leaves grow and even the flowers coming out.

He had had to give up studying English. He was too tired and working in the morning was giving him problems. He was struggling to read the papers. It was better to do nothing, rest for a bit – he needed that a lot – because in the end, what with all these shocks, he would end up not being so strong.

But the worst was the food. The perpetual badly cooked meat and boiled potatoes made him want to heave, even just looking at them. There were days when all he could eat was fruit and jam. He missed the cooks they had had at Summerfield and 'Penn' and eating at Bailey's Hotel. The only reason he was staying at the Queen's was because it was out of the way, in a quiet place, and the little apartment was convenient. Nobody saw him, and he didn't see anyone. Good old Vizetelly was coming to see him from time to time but Vizetelly was in a state. His wife had confided in Zola. She was unhappy. Mr and Mrs Vizetelly had sent Violette to another boarding school, but he feared that the poor little girl would have a hard life.

On the 26th he had to reassure Jeanne that he hadn't been deliberately deceiving her by saying that he would be back in a month or in six weeks. The truth was that he was saying these things in good faith but it wasn't actually possible to fix a date. Maybe they would be able to see each other in a foreign country somewhere . . . that's why he had mentioned Italy. His dearest hope was that they would be able to spend two good months together in August and September, in some little out of the way spot.

Then came a moment in the letter where it's possible to see that Jeanne very much had her own ideas about what

Zola had been saying about the children. 'As you say,' he wrote, 'maybe we will make something very good with our Denise and that we should let our Jacques just sort himself out at school before asking him to be top of the class.'

He had been for a long walk along magnificent avenues which would surely look superb in summer, with their big trees. 'How nice it would be for us to cycle along them!' Perhaps Zola knew that Jeanne would think that it was likely he had been out with Alexandrine and that was why he popped in the thought of how nice it would be if he and Jeanne were cycling there, just as they had done at 'Penn' and Summerfield?

By the 29th, he was saying to Jeanne that he couldn't go on much longer living without her and the children. They would have to come and set themselves up nearby. He was telling her this, he said, not to make her anxious, but to convince her that he wasn't deliberately separating himself from them. He wanted them to be with him wherever he was.

He was very pleased to hear that their good little Jacques had come first in reading and, if he had done it once, he could apply himself to do it again. There was more good news coming from Denise. She was a very good little girl, at heart very sensible. And even if she was a bit dizzy, without much of a memory for things and a not very good attention span, she would end up all right because of her regular getting down to work. He thought she was on the right track both for piano and for French. It would be really awful if these events would force all this to be messed up. It was good news that Jeanne had been out for a walk in Versailles and he thought that their friend, Madame Alexis, could come to dinner with her. 'Go to exhibitions, go shopping, run about a bit in Paris.'

He was feeling stronger and doing his five pages, every morning. This week, friends from Paris were coming. 'I miss you all so much, my three darlings, and there are days, like today, when I am so sad.'

He asked Jacques whether he had enjoyed the champagne at the party and told him that he had to work hard – 'it's the only way to be happy and to make Mummy and me very pleased'. It was also a good idea to play the piano well. 'You'll be able to get the girls dancing.' When he got back, Zola would pay him really well for all the times he came first.

Other than Jeanne's mild plea to lay off Jacques and just let him get on, we don't ever find out how the boy took this relentless stream of requests to work hard, constantly inter-twined with the rationale that it would make Mummy and Papa very happy if he came first. Here, though, is the heavy point that work was the only way to be happy. Clearly, Zola thought this of himself, and that working away at the novel every morning was saving him – just – from depression and a nervous breakdown.

On 2 February Zola returned to the idea of bringing them all out to England or going to Switzerland or Italy. They had to think about the possibility of defeat over the Dreyfus Affair. In which case he wanted her to consider the possibility that they could all end up in exile somewhere. They would know one way or another in six weeks. He told Jeanne that he was going out on his long walks in his cardigan and the cape she knew well and he was keeping very warm. 'Let's hope that this summer, in spite of everything, we will be free again to *courir en pleins champs'* – a phrase that means literally to run about in open fields. It was a phrase he also used in the book he was writing.

On the same day, he wrote to Alexis (the friend who had asked him to send a few lines for the anniversary banquet) thanking him for the news that it had gone so well. He was very touched. Zola wanted him to thank everyone who was in sympathy with what he had done.

On the 5th he told Jeanne that those of his friends who were in the know were certain that Dreyfus would be acquitted. The court had established clearly that he was innocent and, when this was made public, there wasn't a tribunal in the world that would be able to condemn him again. That's why the 'bandits' were doing all they could to suppress the court's investigation. Victory was certain. 'Alas! yes, the violets will be finished before I'm back with you, and I will perhaps see the lilacs bloom. Yet more weeks and weeks of kissing letters.'

On 9 February Zola was flip-flopping: he felt he had to explain again that he could not return to France if Dreyfus was not found innocent and that he would have to wait two, three or four months for it all to be settled. But now, he was going off the idea of Switzerland or Italy. That should only be an option if France was closed to them. And he had also gone off the idea of them coming out to England again. They wouldn't be happy. The Vizetellys wouldn't be able to help out. Yet, if they did come, he could work something out. But then, for the sake of the children's studies, it would be better if the separation continued. His friend Octave Mirbeau had written to say that the worst outcome was possible. The wind was blowing violently.

'Where are we going? I'm not hiding from you that I know nothing and that there are times when I would like to have the courage to take you all to Italy, without waiting any more, so that we could at least live there in peace.' He had just finished the twentieth chapter of *Fécondité* – twenty out of thirty. He needed three good months to finish it. He would write the last lines before the end of May. 'Where will I be?' 'All I ask is for a little corner where we can live together.' Did he mean 'live together' or live together in the way that they had lived before, nights with Alexandrine, afternoons with Jeanne and the children? It's not clear. But then perhaps it wasn't clear to Zola either.

On the 12th Zola had to reply to Jeanne's news that she was getting angry. 'Alas! that won't help anything apart from make me feel bad. You have an air of triumph, as you claim that you had foreseen that this separation would last six months.' Today, he said, she was telling him that she didn't want to come back to England. 'Believe me, that makes me even sadder. In the end, if I have to stay, you have to come and join me here again.' For the last two days, he told her, he had been in a state of great sadness. He was in the midst of a crisis that was as bad as the one that she had witnessed at Summerfield. That's why they had to hold on to each other.

Can we say then that during Zola's exile in England he broke down twice?

On the same day, he tried to reassure his friend Mirbeau. Mirbeau had been threatened on the street by a gang of anti-semites. Zola told him this shouldn't make him dream of isolating himself as Zola was doing. Mirbeau told him that he didn't feel as if he were at home; in France, he was in some

'J'accuse': Zola's open letter published on 13 January 1898, which led to him facing imprisonment for libel and ultimately to his flight to England later the same year.

Captain Alfred Dreyfus (left), before his arrest and imprisonment in 1895 for the alleged crime of treason. Major Ferdinand Esterhazy (right), the actual perpetrator, was acquitted.

M. Labori, Zola's lawyer who advised him to flee the country.

Le Petit Journal, an anti-semitic newspaper, reports Zola's departure from the trial at Versailles, 18 July 1898.

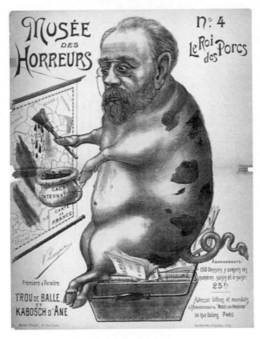

'Le Roi des Porcs': anti-semitic cartoon relating to the Dreyfus Affair which depicts Émile Zola painting 'caca international' (international excrement) on the map of France.

In the garden of Jeanne's house at Verneuil: Zola with Jeanne Rozerot and their children, Denise and Jacques, in 1899.

Zola's wife, Alexandrine, with Zola in the 1880s. Both Jeanne and Mme Zola would visit him during his exile in England.

The front of 'Penn' in Weybridge, Surrey, with Denise, Jacques and Violette Vizetelly, August 1898.

Zola writing *Fécondité*, at 'Penn', 1898 (photograph by V. R. Vizetelly).

Ernest Vizetelly, Zola's translator and friend, who wrote an account of Zola's exile in England which was published in 1899.

Jeanne with Denise and Jacques at 'Summerfield' in Addlestone, autumn 1898.

The Queen's Hotel in Upper Norwood, where Zola moved on 15 October 1898.

Alexandrine in the window of the Queen's Hotel.

Jasper Road off Westow Hill in Crystal Palace: one of many photographs Zola took of everyday life in south-east London.

Mme Zola near the bottom of Hermitage Road, Upper Norwood, November 1898.

Zola 'in his English garden': photographed by V. R. Vizetelly, September 1898; and with his children, Denise and Jacques, not long before his death.

kind of foreign and hostile country. He couldn't even walk about freely.

The letter to Jeanne of 16 February marks what was perhaps Zola's lowest moment of the exile. The most recent events had given him a crisis, which he was coming out of little by little. The worst was that his work had suffered. He had also feared that he and Jeanne were breaking up:

> The truth is that over the last few days, I have been convinced that everything's over for us, and I admit, I still think it . . . Even if the injustice and lies win out, we have to have the strength to go on living amongst the debris . . . For my part, I don't know what I'll do. I have to be on the side of a brave and honest man.

He said he was spending his days banging his head against the wall, trying to find a solution in the face of invincible obstacles. There wasn't any point in the family coming to England if it was just before he went back . . .

Other news: it seemed as if Vizetelly was feeling worse and worse. His wife was suffering. Violette hadn't gone off to school and was wasting time at home. Unhappy people, but it was their fault. The children were naughty to fight. 'Tell them that if they carry on, I won't love them at all, when I get back . . . It seems to me certain that I will be with you in six weeks.'

That day, the 16th, he wrote to Vizetelly on the matter of keeping visitors away. Yes, he would really like to have seen Chatto and Spalding but both Alexandrine and he were ill. They would be poor hosts. Vizetelly also put off an Irish academic, William Graham, and the novelist George Moore. He told Zola that he wouldn't let any Englishman he knew come and see him. Graham had come to see Vizetelly on behalf of the owner of the *Observer*, Rachel Beer. She wanted to meet Zola, and she had told Graham that she had many Jewish friends in France who would vouch for her.

On the 16th a sensational piece of news broke. The anti-Dreyfusard President of France, Félix Faure, had died in the arms of his mistress, Madame Steinheil. Faure had always opposed any 'revision' of the Dreyfus trial. His death, and the appointment two days later of Émile Loubet, who was more sympathetic to Dreyfus, offered immediate hope to the Dreyfus camp as Zola was quick to tell Jeanne. Even so, he added, throwing in a touch of fatalistic determinism, 'the days drag, nothing comes along, nothing is decided. It even seems as if events themselves were taking pleasure in prolonging things.' He could see that being on her own for this length of time was disastrous for a woman of her age. At times of his greatest concern, this thought gripped his heart. (Or did he mean, but not say, it was disastrous for a man of his age in a relationship with a woman of her age?) 'Today, a thick fog, no one on the road in front of my windows. You know the terrible Sundays here.'

In France on the 23rd, following the funeral of President Faure, there was an abortive attempt at a nationalist uprising. That it failed was good news for the Dreyfus camp. Zola wrote to Jeanne bemoaning the fact that he thought he would end up celebrating his birthday, 2 April, on his own in England:

You can imagine how, from time to time, I'm seized by anger and sadness because there are moments when I am at the end of my patience. But what's the point? The more I wait, the more it makes sense to me to wait some more. A year has been stolen from my life. At my age, that counts.

Then, in one of his extremely rare pieces of news about Alexandrine, he told Jeanne that the weather had been really good these last three days: 'I go out on my own all the time,' followed by a sentence that is not easy to express in English *'on est très malade près de moi'* (literally: 'the one who is near me is very ill'). This is Alexandrine, who is hidden behind the word *'on'* when Zola speaks to Jeanne about her in his letters. But in any case he had been for a long walk, thinking of Jeanne:

How troubled our poor life is! Where are the days when I was so happy to come and have tea with the three of you, bringing you violets? I see your lovely apartment in a dream, when, even if I didn't find you, I would be happy just to rest for a bit and wait for you. I got so much pleasure sorting out this apartment! It pleased me so much that it was on the lively rue du Havre! and we haven't enjoyed it again. I've often been afraid, and I still am, that I won't be able to come back and see you there. Here, the little leaves are sprouting, I thought of Verneuil [Jeanne's house near Médan] on my long walk this afternoon. Ah! all that seems far away; will our peaceful life ever come again? – Yet, happily, I'm well,

I've started working again, let's hope everything's going
to be all right.

News of Denise's and Jacques's studies was good – that
was one care less for the future. Ten times, he had thought of
bringing Jeanne out again, but it was the children's schooling
that prevented it happening. 'When one has children, their
needs must be put before the parents' pleasure. In the end,
the sacrifice is made and I hope that we will be compensated
for it.' ('Compensated'?!)

He also wrote to Denise that day, telling her that Mummy
must be spoiling her by taking her to see the big wheel,
buying confetti for Mardi Gras and doing whatever Denise
wanted. So they mustn't fight, that made Mummy and him
feel bad.

We don't often get a glimpse of what Alexandrine was
thinking at this time but she wrote to one of her friends on
the 23rd, saying that she would much rather have been ill at
home, where at least she wouldn't die without help, which is
what would happen in London. She said she would be back
on the 27th, making it the fourth time since she had first
come to this country that she would have been on that route
– a country that had been so deadly ('*funeste*') for her.

On the 26th, Zola told Jeanne that he would be alone
again as of the following morning. Yet again, that was his
way of reminding her that Alexandrine would be leaving and
going back to Paris. This meant that it would be possible he
would also be on his own till he came back to France. 'You
know that being alone doesn't scare me,' he said. He would
go for long walks every day and think of Jeanne. The exile

had been good for one thing: he had been able to write a novel.

He was surprised that Denise was becoming so serious with her work, as she was so scatterbrained. Maybe she was going to stun them with her progress. As for Jacques, he was still very young and they shouldn't ask too much of him – both things being precisely what Jeanne had written to him a few weeks earlier, though he didn't acknowledge it.

He wrote to Jacques that he was counting on him ending up on the honours board and it was making him feel bad that he wasn't there yet.

If you don't devote yourself to study, there's no reward and you end up being sad about it and making your parents sad too. If you are not careful about your homework and if you are not very good it would be utterly shameful. Mummy is very nice to have given you a book from the 'Pink Library' series, all the same. I hope that you've thanked her for it and that you love her with all your heart.

On 27 February Alexandrine left for Paris.

Zola told Jeanne that Vizetelly visited him regularly. He knew to do this only in the afternoons and they would talk business and chat about the news or Zola's work. As Zola was deep into writing *Fécondité*, he was glad to take from Vizetelly a summary of the views of one Rev. R. Ussher on 'Neo-Malthusianism' (the view that poverty was caused by over-population), the very idea that Zola was fighting against in the novel he was writing every morning. Vizetelly filled Zola in on details of ongoing legal cases in the English courts against 'medical men' and midwives. Zola was much interested in the case against the Dickensianly named brothers Chrimes who had been up in court for selling bogus medicines – we can presume for abortion purposes – and were also in trouble for blackmailing the women who had bought the medicines. This, in Zola's eyes, not only made the Chrimes brothers culpable but also the hundreds of women applying to them for supposedly abortion-inducing treatments.

Zola was amazed to find that the British newspapers hardly spoke of these matters. He suspected that some kind of 'mythical innocence' was being protected by non-publication when, in his view, the welfare of the whole nation was being sacrificed. 'Let all be exposed and discussed in order that all may be cured,' said Zola to Vizetelly, which was precisely what he thought he was doing by writing *Fécondité*.

He was very interested in the statistics of the British birthrate, with its year-on-year decline, a direct result, as he saw it, of the 'Bradlaugh–Besant' campaign. Charles Bradlaugh had been Britain's best-known atheist and republican, and Annie Besant Britain's best-known champion of working women, having greatly assisted the notable Bryant and May matchworkers' strike. Scandalously, Bradlaugh and Besant lived together. Zola's interest in the pair stemmed from the fact that in 1877 they had published a book by the American birth-control campaigner Charles Knowlton. Knowlton's position was the exact opposite of Zola's, with Knowlton claiming that working-class families would never find happiness unless they had the means to control the number of children they had. Besant and Bradlaugh were arrested, charged with obscenity and found guilty. The case attracted a great deal of attention, with the Church opposing the pair and 'liberal' opinion supporting them. Eventually, the case was thrown out on a technicality. In the midst of proceedings, Besant founded the Malthusian League, which would go on to campaign for the decriminalisation of people promoting contraception. One immediate and personal consequence of the trial was that Besant lost the custody of her own children.

This conversation between Vizetelly and Zola reveals that the turn-of-the-century fault-lines on either side of the Channel around questions of childbirth, contraception, eugenics, birth control and class don't fit easily into modern left/right, liberal/conservative categories. Various well-known people in Britain who are often seen as 'progressive' were advocates of eugenic control of working-class birth-rates, while Zola, the progressive, scientific, liberal socialist, was deeply hostile to this view.

As they chatted on, Vizetelly and Zola were in agreement that the 'English race' was 'physically deteriorating' and one cause, they thought, was that English women were becoming less inclined to breast-feed their babies. Even worse, the nannies employed by well-off women could be seen around the streets of Norwood, neglecting their charges, standing about flirting, gossiping or looking in shop-windows. The mothers, Vizetelly and Zola presumed, were out visiting or 'receiving', reading novels, bicycling or playing lawn tennis. 'Ah well,' said Zola, 'that is hardly my conception of a mother's duty towards her infant, whatever be her situation in life.'

These man-to-man chats on the state and role of woman-kind sometimes took place on their afternoon walks, heading down the hill from Upper Norwood, past Beulah Spa, round by the fields and the recreation ground, punctuated by some photography. Life for Zola at these times seems much less claustrophobic and oppressive from these accounts than it appears in his letters to Jeanne.

Zola told Vizetelly that sometimes he amused himself by counting the number of hairpins he spotted lying on the pavement. This was, he thought, symptomatic of the 'careless-ness' of English women. At other times, he thought about writing an essay on the effect of the capital 'I' on English character and another on the English 'guillotine' window. Vizetelly was glad to put Zola right about the hairpins. They were lying about in the street as a result of 'penny-wise and pound-foolish' spending: the cheap ones never 'caught' properly in women's coiled-up hair. These cheap hairpins, Vizetelly pointed out, were made in Germany.

Another aspect of life in Norwood that caught Zola's attention at this time were the grandiose names of the suburban houses, especially the French-sounding ones, Bellevue, Beaumont and the like, but Vizetelly was happy to translate Oakdene, Thornbrake, Beechcroft, Hillbrow, Woodcote, Fernside, Fairholme and Inglenook. One colonial one puzzled them – Ly-ee-Moon – derived, they eventually figured out, from the name given to ships sailing in the China Seas. The householder, they discovered, had been a ship-owner and sea captain.

The way back to the hotel from these strolls included a visit to the post office, where Vizetelly bought Zola his stash of postage stamps. The sheer scale and steady regularity of Vizetelly's stamp-buying, they noticed, caused a bit of eyebrow-raising by the 'lady clerks' in the Norwood post office.

On 2 March, now on his own, Zola put Jeanne off from coming with the children at Easter. He might be back before then. If he came back straight after Easter, then it wouldn't be sensible for them to make the journey for the sake of a few days. In the end, 'if everything is ruined and I can't come back for several months, it's certain that "one" won't leave me on my own and "one" would come here'. Again, Zola seems to want to show Jeanne that he is helpless in this matter and that it is Alexandrine who makes the decisions and controls the situation. On his walks he had again encountered groups of women on bikes. The tea in the hotel was making him sick. It felt like he was swallowing medicine.

On 5 March, he told Jeanne that, since the death of Faure, everything was getting better and better. Jeanne had written again about coming at Easter, but he said he didn't know if he would be 'alone'. His great joy wouldn't be to see her again here, in this damn country, but in Paris, in their home. She should tell the children that this would be the year they would get their bicycles. That was a promise. In July, before going to the country, he and Jeanne would take them to a velodrome so that they could learn to ride their bikes.

Watching the bicycles go by outside, beneath my window, makes me think of ours. If yours is asleep in your toilet at Verneuil, mine's asleep as well, at Médan, in my study. Let's hope that we're going to wake them up next. And it's true, we're going to be a little more free, the two of us, now that our children are taken up with their school work. We can benefit from that by the two of us arranging for a little part of our lives to be closer together.

The next two weeks were going to be decisive, he said.

What had been revealed in France that week, and had been repeated in the press in London, was the testimony of Esterhazy, the man whom Zola had accused of writing the *bordereau*. This testimony had been with the Supreme Court since November but had now been released. According to the Dreyfusards, this testimony showed the whole public how the General Staff had colluded with Esterhazy and how he had been in cahoots with one of the key anti-Dreyfus figures, Colonel Henry. (As it happened, Esterhazy was himself lying low in England too.) Surely now the stage was set for the release of Dreyfus and the glorious return of Zola to France, with 'J'Accuse' and all its allegations vindicated.

On 9 March Zola asked Jeanne why she had given up on the idea of coming at Easter. (A curious thing for him to write since he had offered her three reasons why she shouldn't.) It was now possible that not only would Dreyfus be acquitted but he would be too. The end was in sight.

On the 12th he shifted his view yet again. There would have to be anything up to twenty sessions at the court and it was his great fear that it would end up with a judgment summoning Dreyfus to appear again rather than finding him innocent. That would push matters on till 10 May. He had agreed with his friends that he wouldn't come back while these proceedings were under way in case it might jeopardise the outcome, or even be the cue for attacks and persecutions. (This reminds us of how often the Dreyfusards, including Zola, were on the end of abuse and mob violence. Many thought that if Zola had been found innocent he would have been murdered on the street outside the court.)

He repeated the expression of not knowing whether he would be 'alone' or not. 'You won't be buying me a cake at Madame Louise's before June.'

There was good news about Jacques but he hoped that like all mothers she wasn't falling into doting on her son. He was good and intelligent but he was also capricious and had little bouts of rebellion. It was very bad of a little boy to say to his teacher that he didn't want to do his homework. With Denise, you couldn't ask her to do more than she could. She would end up being good at spelling. With that and a bit of piano, they would find her a prince.

He could also tell her that he had finished his twenty-third chapter of *Fécondité*.

Finally, this letter had a note about a meeting he had had a day or so earlier with a key figure in the leadership of the pro-Dreyfus campaign, one of the leading voices amongst the French socialists, Jean Jaurès.

9

'Here we have, alas!, no Zolas'

At the time that Jean Jaurès came to England in March 1899, he was engrossed in writing a book about the French Revolution and editing the newspaper *La Petite République* ('The Little Republic'). The year before, he had lost his seat in the National Assembly but was looking towards the end of 1899 to a conference which was aiming to unite all the different socialist organisations, groups and parties of France.

It may seem unsurprising now that someone calling himself a socialist should go out of his way to meet Émile Zola but this was to fraternise with a fugitive from the law, who had sided with a convicted traitor and spy, had defended the corrupt, conspiratorial 'syndicate' aiming for world domination ('the Jews'), and who was the kind of novelist who, according to some, was just a pornographer of the gutter. What's more, only a short time before this meeting, Jaurès was still convinced that Dreyfus was guilty. In December 1894 he had contrasted the usual fate of simple soldiers guilty of a moment of aberration with that of Dreyfus, who had not been sentenced to death. Why hadn't he received the death sentence? Because, according to Jaurès, he had benefited from the 'prodigious deployment of Jewish power' (*'prodigieux déploiement de la puissance juive'*).

There is some debate whether it was 'J'Accuse' that convinced Jaurès of Dreyfus's innocence. Later, he would approvingly cite his fellow socialist, Jules Guesde, for calling 'J'Accuse' 'the greatest revolutionary act of the century'.

A few days after the sensational appearance of 'J'Accuse' he signed a manifesto which refused to take sides in the Affair, accusing 'free thinkers and Jewish capitalists who, discredited by numerous scandals, were trying to rehabilitate themselves', through siding with Dreyfus ('*les libres penseurs, et les "capitalistes juifs" qui, discrédités par des nombreux "scandales", cherchent à se réhabiliter*').

The matter isn't clear cut, though. On 22 January 1898, nine days after the appearance of 'J'Accuse', Jaurès defended Zola in the Chamber, saying that the charges against Zola were based on nothing but lies and cowardice – a speech which won him the instant accusation that he was a mouthpiece of the 'syndicate'. On 12 February Jaurès appeared for Zola at his trial. In prosecuting Zola, he said, the ministry, the army, and the Church were wreaking vengeance on a man who had too long defended the downtrodden and exposed their oppressors.

They prosecute in him the man who defended the rational and scientific interpretation of miracles: they prosecute in him the man who, in *Germinal*, predicted the springing up of an impoverished proletariat, rising from the depths of suffering and ascending towards the sun . . . They can prosecute him, they can hunt him down, but I think I speak for all free citizens in saying that we bow down before him in deference.

As a sign of how Jaurès's views were evolving in the crucible of the Dreyfus Affair, on 19 February he spoke in the Chamber following an outbreak of anti-semitic violence in Algeria:

Our duty as socialists is not to preach reactionary and deadly hatred against the Jews; no, it is to call attention to the suffering and exploited among the Jews, who, standing at the side of oppressed Arabs, should form, with the European proletariat, a party of all those who toil and suffer.

The final trigger that brought Jaurès and many, but by no means all, socialists into the pro-Dreyfus camp was the 'Henry Affair': Colonel Joseph Henry was unmasked as the forger of a secret 'dossier' that supposedly further proved Dreyfus was guilty. This happened in August 1898, while Zola was in England.

At this point, Jaurès made his position clear: if Dreyfus had been condemned illegally, this made him innocent, and so, if he was innocent, then in Jaurès's worldview he was no longer an officer or a bourgeois – in the language of socialists, no longer the 'class enemy'. Jaurès expanded on this: Dreyfus was 'no longer anything but humanity itself' (in other words someone who socialists could and should support). This line of thinking went on: Dreyfus's fate at the hands of the courts had become a protest against the social order and this drew him to the side of the working class. (This formulation was how Jaurès pulled many in the socialist wing of the labour movement into the Dreyfus campaign.)

Then to back up these arguments, in September 1898 he published *The Proof: The Dreyfus Affair*, a lengthy book, which put the case for the innocence of Dreyfus in great detail.

By the time of his visit, then, Jaurès was an unequivocal supporter of Dreyfus and Zola.

His visit was not solely for the purposes of meeting Zola, though. He had come to attend a conference called by the Social Democratic Federation (SDF) in the St James Hall, Piccadilly, to promote 'universal peace and international fraternity'. The SDF was the forerunner of the British Labour Party, the Independent Labour Party and the Communist Party of Great Britain and this conference was chaired by its founder, H. M. Hyndman; speakers included Jaurès, Wilhelm Liebknecht from Germany, Britain's first socialist MP, R. B. Cunninghame Graham, Harry Quelch, the Marxist editor of the SDP's newspaper, and Dadabhai Naoroji, who had for three years been Britain's first Asian MP. Someone else who was asked to speak, declined, but attended all the same was the novelist Joseph Conrad; though, according to Cunninghame Graham, it wasn't a happy experience for him.

The Times of 9 March, reporting on the conference, quoted Jaurès saying, 'It was absurd to believe that there could be universal peace under the present capitalist system, which was itself based upon letting loose war throughout the world and encouraging strife among the working classes. Socialism was their only hope in the direction of true peace. (Cheers.)'

This was the Jaurès of the moment of the visit to see Zola. The organisation that had invited him had an official periodical, the *Social-Democrat*. Its December 1898 edition included an article called 'L'Affaire Dreyfus'. It was a summary of the Dreyfus Affair, from a totally pro-Dreyfus stance, saying clearly that the government and the anti-semites were to blame. Zola was named and praised for having 'done much to awaken the French people to a sense of the injustice which had been done'.

The article went on to explain to any doubting readers (and if you track back through socialist and anarchist journals of the mid-1890s, in France and Britain, you can find plenty such people) exactly why socialists should support someone who was a wealthy Jewish army officer: in brief, the writer says, it is because 'socialists stand for the justice of all', citing Jaurès as an authority to back him up. In conclusion, the article took a different twist: it warned readers against 'throwing stones' at 'our French neighbours'. Justice being enacted by the British at that very moment in the Transvaal (that is, in the Boer War) was no better, but

here we have, alas!, no Zolas, no Clemenceaus, no Guyots. All our public men, the whole of the Press, outside the Socialist ranks – which are, unfortunately not nearly so powerful as in France – were on the side of our Esterhazys, our Paty du Clams, our Henrys, and our Cavaignacs.

This volley of villains had been identified earlier in the article as being the key anti-Dreyfusards – especially Esterhazy, the man who had forged the document which had incriminated Dreyfus in the first place.

Had Zola read the article, or had anyone from the SDF made their way to the Queen's Hotel to tell him about it, we might guess that Zola would have been pretty pleased with what the *Social-Democrat* had to say. This imaginary person might also have shown Zola an article which had appeared in the same magazine only three months before Zola began his stay in England. Credited to A. S. Headingley, it was headed 'The Dreyfus and Zola Case'. As with the December article, the writer summarised where both cases had reached, echoed Zola's and Jean Jaurès's words in highlighting the nature of the injustice, the government's and high command's role, ending with a tribute to the 'honour and integrity of M. Zola'. With these two articles, we can say that, by the time the year turned at the end of 1898, the *Social-Democrat* had signalled to left-wing readers in Britain that Zola's politics were to be respected and admired.

About the same time as Headingley's article had appeared, an Austrian-born London-based socialist, Max Beer, had visited Paris to interview Zola. The article he wrote wasn't actually published until 15 October 1902 (also in the *Social-Democrat*) three years after Zola's stay.

In March 1898, M. George Clemenceau gave me a letter of introduction to Émile Zola, who at once consented to receive me 'at any time after nine o'clock in the evening'. It was but a few weeks after his condemnation to a year's imprisonment, consequent upon his letter, 'J'accuse' published in *L'Aurore* of 13th January 1898 . . .

Zola bade me take a seat on a sofa, while he moved a chair opposite to me, and scrutinising me very attentively, sat down. He bent forward, so that his head was close to mine, and asked me to begin with my questions.

'The subjects that always interested me most,' asks Max Beer, 'were Socialism and the Jewish question. It is, therefore, natural that I should look upon the author of *Germinal* and the defender of Dreyfus with deep admiration. But *cher maître*, I cannot conceal the fact that your *Rougon-Macquart* series and *Trois Villes* do not contain a single Jewish character worthy of our sympathy.'

Zola: 'Yes that's true. All my Jewish characters have so far been quite despicable. They are, however, such as I saw them.'

'Exactly. I do not impugn your power of observation. It is, as all the world knows, very comprehensive; and your studies are painstaking, sincere and scientifically correct. You will, however, permit me to say that your observation of Jewish life did not go far enough. You had no opportunity of seeing the whole of it.'

Zola: 'During these last few months of anguish I thought a good deal of the Jewish question. And I had good reason for it, too. As you know, I was for a long time under the influence of the historical theories of Hippolyte Taine, who laid so much stress on the racial factor in human development. My novels might surely give the impression that I regarded the Jew chiefly as a money-mongering and luxury-loving human being. My recent struggle, however, taught me that there are many Jews who belong to quite another category. There are in human history some factors more potent than race or religion.'

'Economic ones!'

Zola: 'Precisely. You see, the rich Jews and Jewesses hate me as much as the Nationalists and the Catholic bigots do. A few days ago a Jewish lady positively insulted M. Anatole France, our greatest critic and essayist, for having signed the petition for revision of the Dreyfus trial. But I am glad to say that the Jewish intellectuals are on our side.'

'And the Jewish proletariat too. One object of my coming to you is to express to you the respectful thanks of many thousands of Jewish workmen in New York for your defence of social justice.'

Zola: 'I am deeply touched by this sign of recognition on the part of Jewish labour. I have seen their poverty, their wretchedness, and their toil when I was in London in 1893. I went round Whitechapel to convince myself of the evils of the sweating system.'

'The anti-semites see only the few Jewish millionaires, and shut their eyes to the misery of the toiling Jewish masses in Russia, in Austria, in England and in America. There is no Jewish question at all, but there is a struggle between the owners of the means of production and the owners of labour-power. This struggle knows neither race nor religion. It is a struggle going on, consciously or unconsciously, in the whole civilised world. Abolish this antagonism and Dreyfus trials will be no more.'

Zola: 'You are, of course, pointing to socialism.'

'Yes, *cher maître*. The final chapter of *Germinal* expresses the advent of socialism in words so powerful that it would be exceedingly presumptuous on my part

to deal in your presence with this subject. Although you
do not belong to any socialist organisation, all socialists
look upon you as one of their great leaders.'

Zola: 'I am not a leader in socialist thought, yet I
sincerely wish to have all socialists as my friends. You
see, only Jaurès and his friends are supporting me.
Some Guesdists are standing aloof; some of them are
behaving badly. They do not see that I am not fighting for
a certain individual, but for the liberty of our great and
noble France and against a conspiracy of mighty foes,
militarism and the Catholic Church. I need all sympathy,
all assistance I can get.

'It is, therefore, painful to see socialists taking no
interest in the stormy events which are convulsing the
French nation. They think I entered into a deadly struggle
for a rich Jewish captain. He is for me only a symbol, a
victim of terrible forgeries, a witness of the degradation
of our Republic, which inscribed on its portals the
democratic trinity: Liberty, Fraternity, and Equality . . .
But, after all, truth is almighty. It will prevail.'

Zola was speaking passionately and with great fluency.
He was easily accessible, eager to impart knowledge and
imbued with a modesty as sincere and deep as his love of
truth. He actually thanked me for the trouble I had taken
in calling upon him. At the conclusion of the interview
he enquired again about the position of the millions of
Jewish workingmen, about their aspirations and ideas.
He also asked a good deal about England, and regretted
that he was no linguist. 'Je suis du Midi,' he remarked
smilingly; 'mon cerveau n'est pas organisé pour des

langues.' ('I am from the South: my brain is not organised for languages.')

After a hearty handshake, I left the little house in the Rue de Bruxelles, having spent one of the happiest hours of my life. It is, perhaps, an echo of that interview, when Zola in his last novel, *Truth*, now in course of publication, says:

'And at the sight of that paradise acquired by Jew wealth, at the thought of the splendid fortune amassed by Nathan the Jew money monger, Marc instinctively recalled the Rue du Trou and the dismal hovel without air or sunshine, where Lehmann, that other Jew, had been plying his needle for thirty years and earning only enough to provide himself with bread, And ah! how many other Jews there were, yet more wretched than he – Jews who starve in filthy dens.

'They were the immense majority and their existence demonstrated the idiotic falsity of anti-semitism, that proscription en masse of a race which was charged with the monopolisation of all wealth, when it numbered so many poor working folk, so many victims, crushed down by the almightiness of money, whether it were Jew, or Catholic, or Protestant. There were really no Jew questions – at all; there was only a Capitalist question – a question of money heaped up in the hands of a certain number of gluttons and thereby poisoning and rotting the world.'

This passage is probably the most socialistic in all Zola's writings.

Max Beer's testimony is amongst other things a reminder that Zola had a readership that saw and relished the links between his fiction – especially *Germinal* and *Vérité* (*Truth*), the third of his *Gospels* – and his public political stance. He also suggests here that thousands of 'Jewish workmen' had discovered Zola and Zola suggests that he had discovered them. Is there any evidence in the press in Britain that reflected this? Jewish working-class papers in Britain and elsewhere were written in Yiddish, using Hebrew letters. They were read mostly in London's East End, and in Manchester, Liverpool, Newcastle and Glasgow. The newspapers tended to appear, disappear and re-appear and there are no complete runs of them in libraries. Through these, it's possible even so to build up a picture of how Zola was being viewed by this group at the time of his stay in England. In July 1898, the *Yiddisher Express* reported how Zola had lost his second trial and then, a fortnight later, how there was a 'new sensation' in the Dreyfus case: Under the heading, 'Where is Zola now?' the paper said that this was a question that 'everyone' was asking. 'It remains a mystery. No one knows where he is . . .' The article suggested that the Dreyfus campaign had lost its leader: 'The army has been left without its general.' In that sense then, the paper saw Zola's role as pivotal. But, it goes on:

the government thought that with Zola's departure, the campaign would fall apart, but in this case they were mistaken as the campaign pushes forward with or without Zola. It seems that a new general will be elected to lead the fight against the government.

So – pivotal but not indispensable.

We catch another glimpse of how this turmoil was being viewed from a leaflet sent by the East London Jewish branch of the Social Democratic Federation in support of the Republican James Connolly who stood for election in Dublin in 1902. (On a personal note, my great-grandfather was a member of this branch of the SDF.) Written in Yiddish, the leaflet called on Jews in Dublin to support Connolly, who was standing for the Irish Socialist Republican Party. It warned readers not to vote for the Home Rule candidate because Home Rulers 'speak out against the English capitalists and the English landlords because they want to seize their places so that they themselves can oppress and exploit the people'. Home Rulers were part of the same class of people who 'provoke hatred of the Jew and seek to throw the blame for everything upon the Jew in order to deceive the people and conceal its sins against its own people'.

The writer of the leaflet, the Secretary of the East London branch, Boris Kahan went on:

The Socialists are the only ones who stand always and everywhere against every national oppression. It is the Socialists who went out onto the streets of Paris against the wild band of anti-semites at the time of the Dreyfus case. In Austria and Germany they conduct a steady struggle against anti-semitism. And in England, too, the Socialists fight against the reactionary elements who want to shut the doors of England against the poorer Jews who were driven to seek refuge in a strange land by the Russian government's brutality and despotism.

The point here is that the campaign against the imprisonment of Dreyfus, and Zola's part in it, were helping to create a new kind of politics. This new politics was combining ideas that were internationalist, against poverty, against injustice and against what we now call racial discrimination – four ideas that hadn't always sat together in one worldview. Zola had been approached by the Dreyfusards to support their campaign because, much to the surprise of many in his milieu, he had written several impassioned articles against the rise of anti-semitism. At that precise moment, he was a lone non-Jewish public figure saying these things. The anti-semites in France forced the battleground to include the question of race. For them, an army officer who was a Jew was a contradiction in terms because a Jew could not be loyal or honourable. This then encouraged socialists like Jaurès to find a response to racism, drawing on what Zola had written and the stand he had taken.

Zola mentioned to Alexandrine that Jaurès had come to see him and Jaurès himself wrote up his meeting with Zola too. He talked of Zola's 'glorious' exile near Crystal Palace: on a table were the sheets from *Fécondité* that he hadn't quite finished yet; Zola spoke to him with an 'admirable serenity' about the comfort and joy he found in work. He reported Zola as saying to him:

Ah! how this crisis has done me good! How it's made me forget the self-glorifying vanity to which I – like many others – become attached! And how it's opened up my life, along with problems and profundities that I didn't ever suspect! I want to devote all my efforts to the liberation of man. I wish that we could all put ourselves up for the test that our group of humanity might come out of this being braver and more fraternal . . .

As for me, I read, I do research, not in order to imagine a new system . . . but in order to extract from socialist works those ideas that chime most with my sense of life, with my love of activity, good health, abundance and joy.

A friend lent me Fourier; I'm reading this at the moment and I'm stunned by it. I don't know yet what's going to come of this research, but I want to celebrate work, and through that, get people who curse it, are slaves to it, or who disfigure it with ugliness and misery, to end up respecting it.

As Zola was finishing off *Fécondité* he was thinking ahead to the second of his four *Évangiles – Travail (Work)*. As Jaurès notes, one of the inspirations for this novel was the work of Charles Fourier (1772–1837). As Zola sat during his last days in the Queen's Hotel he was conjuring up a new kind of hero, an enthusiast for Fourier's work. This young engineer, Luc Froment, would take from Fourier the idea of the phalanstery, a harmonious utopian community of 1,600 or so people, cultivating some 5,000 acres of land, where capital, talent and labour would join forces for the collective good. The book, begun in England but finished in France, brought this utopian vision to life: next to modern industrial plants, a new kind of city grows up: a community of single-family houses, each with gardens watered by fresh streams. At the centre of the city, there are communal buildings: an assembly hall, a library, public baths. Religion fades away, co-educational schools transmit knowledge, boys and girls learn partnership. Over time, even the social hierarchy (the class system) fades away too.

When *Work* appeared, Jaurès reviewed it and this review appeared in the *Social-Democrat*. He pointed out that Zola's utopia could not be reached in the way that Zola had showed it being achieved; it had to be reached through organisation and the struggle of the working class. Even so, Jaurès writes,

> Read and re-read the last pages. Luke and Jordan have finished their work, they are talking for the last time at sunset. They see the old familiar landscape. Luke looks for the last time at the Communist city, joyful and fraternal, which has risen from the co-operative seed which he sowed long ago; Jordan rejoices at having captured the sun's heat for the science of man.
>
> This appears to me finer than anything I know of in fiction or verse. In the old days the poets exalted gods, but now it is man who, older than any god, is the poet's hero.
>
> In Zola social revolution has at last found its poet.

H. M. Hyndman replied in the same issue. He enjoyed the powerful descriptions of the coal and iron men on strike, and the hunger and misery experienced by the families; similarly, the scene when the old foreman of the smelting furnace commits suicide on seeing the new electric smelters, or the 'terrible death struggle' when the head of the great iron works burns down his house so that his selfish wife should die in the fire.

(A thought in passing on this aspect of Zola's interests during his time in Britain: if he had been more fluent in English, he might have been interested in the news coming out of South Wales while he was in London. After a bitter six-month dispute between the coal-miners and the owners had ended in defeat and poverty for the miners, they formed the South Wales Miners' Federation in October 1898. The following year they affiliated to the Miners' Federation of Great Britain. Over the next ninety years, some of the most powerful advocates of the kind of political ideas that interested Zola would come from this source.)

Overall, Hyndman thought that Zola had lost his capacity for that 'close and continuous analysis of the situation which compels the reader to follow him . . .' When it came to the utopian passages, Hyndman read against the spirit and mood of the novel, sympathising with the anarchist who complained of the monotony of the utopia! Hyndman said that the founder of the enterprise would 'never have had a ghost of a chance of success against the organised forces of progressive capitalism'. He went on to describe how the 'powerful Trustifiers' would have ripped into the co-operators of the novel and destroyed the enterprise. The 'pretty little bubble' that Zola had created would be 'pricked into nothingness'. But why should a great writer like Zola, Hyndman asked, 'condescend to such unthought-out and crude imaginings'? He doesn't answer the question but suggested that the book was dangerous because it would 'divert the minds of the mass of the people' from understanding the 'stupendous developments' in capitalism going on around them. He closed by warning socialists against thinking that they could compete on a large scale with these newer developments. The results of 'such misplaced energy will be nothing better than disappointment and regret'.

On this plane of highly politicised left-wing literary criticism: the Fabian group, credited with being the nursery (or university) for moderate socialist intellectuals, also had Zola on their agenda around this time. The June 1898 edition of *Fabian News* announced that their next meeting at Clifford's Inn, Fleet Street, 8 p.m. Friday 10 June, would feature a talk 'Émile Zola as Artist and as Doctrinaire' by Sydney Olivier, CMG. The magazine laid out the 'Syllabus' for the evening, which would include: 'The Zola Bogey. Zola's Doctrine. Limitations of both: throwing back the tremendous force of the man into practical revolt against institutions.' Coincidentally, the Fabians were on Zola's patch in another way too: the following talk, a fortnight later, was from a neo-Malthusian – in other words diametrically opposed to the views that Zola was expressing in *Fécondité* at that very moment. The 'Syllabus' here included: 'Poverty and Population. Socialism and the Birth Rate. The Real Population Problem'.

In the following month's issue, there was the write-up of Sydney Olivier's talk. He had opened by discussing the common accusation against Zola's writing that it was full of 'nastiness, indecency, and dreariness'. He dismissed this as superficial and irrelevant. He was interested in what he called 'connecting intentions' across Zola's twenty-novel *Rougon-Macquart* cycle. He thought these were: the scientific study of heredity and determinism in human life and society, and an anatomy of the characteristics of middle-

and working-class life in France under the Second Empire. This second intention was, he said, closely bound up with Zola's own ruling passion, 'his real democratic feeling and his hatred and contempt of all that he typified in the Second Empire'. He was now becoming more and more an accuser of the established order from the point of view of utopian socialism, and in his greater works, such as *Germinal*, his accusation spoke through powerful artistic methods.

Olivier was much less keen on the turn Zola had taken in his last book in the cycle, *Doctor Pascal*, and the *Three Cities* series that followed. He thought Zola was working under the illusion that 'his works represent a body of scientific truth', and that the scenes in these books represented 'the promise of a re-created society and a wholesome future for France'. He thought that Zola's ideas of the essentials of such a society were ones that most Socialists would applaud, but his 'denunciatory method', albeit with a moral purpose, marred the literary effect. Now, though, Zola's passion and power and fearlessness and enormous industry had forced him into action in revolt against injustice (in other words, the Dreyfus case). This experience could not fail to affect his writing, Olivier thought. He hoped that this would have a better outcome in his fiction.

Fabians reading about Zola in their magazine at that time would have found him alongside a review, 'Plays: Pleasant and Unpleasant', of Bernard Shaw's works, including *Mrs Warren's Profession*, a play about prostitution which some have thought owed something to the literary, social and political opportunities that Zola's writing had opened up. And in the June issue there was a write-up of a talk on 'The Social

Teaching of Thomas Hardy', whose last two novels, *Tess of the D'Urbervilles* and *Jude the Obscure*, owed a good deal to Zola. While Zola was turning up in places like Weybridge and Upper Norwood, his works were also arriving on the bookshelves of Britain's liberal left.

'Grossest bad taste'

Two events at the Queen's Hotel give us a glimpse of how Zola's books were seen in Britain at the time of his exile: a major dispute with Vizetelly over his translation of *Fécondité* and the visit to the hotel of the Irish novelist George Moore.

The dispute with Vizetelly had its roots in the scandals surrounding Zola's work in the years prior to Zola's visit to England in 1893. Between April 1884 and May 1888, Vizetelly and Co. had published eighteen Zola translations, seventeen novels and one collection of short stories, some of them in cheap, illustrated editions.

The editor of the *Pall Mall Gazette*, W. T. Stead, founded an organisation called the National Vigilance Association (NVA), which set up a Literary Sub-Committee to keep an eye on immoral writing. The NVA brought prosecutions against Henry Vizetelly for publishing Zola's novels, some of which had prefaces written by George Moore.

The anxieties expressed by the NVA were partly alerted by the rise of new readerships created by the 1870 Education Act. Worrying for guardians of decency was that working women were reading books which were thought to 'pander' to them. Others, from the Social Purity Alliance, said that 'there never was a time when greater efforts were made to poison the minds of the young'.

A battle was on. 1879 saw the publication of *Pioneer*, a 'Magazine Written to counteract the Effect of Pernicious Literature Amongst Youths'. The Pure Literature Society supplied 'sound and healthy reading'; the National Home Reading Union was founded in order to 'check the spread of pernicious literature among the young'. In 1885, the Criminal Law Amendment Act raised the female age of consent to sixteen, and the NVA vowed to enforce the 'social purity' of this law, along with a promise to suppress the publication and sale of indecent or obscene books, papers, prints and pictures. The Literary Sub-Committee of the NVA promised to target indecencies that were 'obviously subversive of the best interests of the growing generation and opposed to the ideals of a true citizenship'. In 1886, it successfully brought prosecutions against an individual who sold 'art photographs' of nudes and a newspaper for printing details of a divorce case. In 1888, it brought a case against a street-seller of photographs from Paris. Significantly and ominously, they wrote, 'Every clerk and shopboy knows enough French to pick out obscenity, and it is sometimes difficult in these days to distinguish between high class French fiction and mere pornography.'

And that was the core of the problem. Was Zola high art or smut? Though consumers of high art – presumably readers of a high enough class – were safe from corruption, low-class readers were not. If unexpurgated Zola was available through cheap publications coming out of the Vizetelly house, then this line could not be held. The *Contemporary Review* of 1884 placed Zola as part of the 'photographic school' of literature and said he was notable for his 'odious indecency', adding with a sneer, 'this is how we are told clever writers think it worthwhile to write'.

Via a planted letter on its letters pages, the NVA warned readers of the *Pall Mall Gazette* in December 1887 that *La Terre*, 'too vile to be published in either France or Austria, is being brought out here with impunity in English'. They lured Henry Vizetelly into boasting how his 'unabridged translation' of *Nana* had sold over 100,000 copies. He wasn't afraid of talking up his publications: his advert for Alphonse Daudet's *Sapho* said that it was 'A glowing picture of Parisian life, with all its special immorality . . . with numerous French engravings . . .'

On 8 May 1888 matters reached the House of Commons when the MP for Flintshire, Samuel Smith, proposed a motion that deplored the 'rapid spread of demoralising literature' and that the law against obscene publications should be vigorously enforced. His concern was that 'low bookstalls' were carrying an endless supply of English translations of French novels. He named Vizetelly as the chief culprit, particularly as he claimed 'artistic grounds' for books that were 'only fit for swine'. This all constituted a 'gigantic national danger', it 'corroded the human character' and 'sapped the vitality of the nation'. He asked the government whether it was content 'to wait till the deadly poison spread itself over English soil and killed the life of this great and noble people'.

The NVA rushed out 120,000 copies of Smith's speech as a pamphlet and, by October 1888, Vizetelly was on trial for issuing translations of the 'three most immoral books ever published', Zola's *La Terre*, *Nana* and *Pot-Bouille*. The trial began with the prosecution reading an extract from *La Terre* in which the young farm-girl Françoise assists – with her hand – a bull to mate with a cow. Vizetelly pleaded guilty and was fined £100 and bound over not to publish the novels in their present form.

In May 1889 he was back in court, for his editions of Maupassant and Flaubert's *Madame Bovary* and on the issue of whether he had sufficiently expurgated *La Terre*. He hadn't. He pleaded guilty again, was fined £200 and sentenced to three months' jail with hard labour, despite his defence's pleas that at seventy he was too frail and had been punished enough. Simultaneously, the NVA was bringing charges against a publisher of an English translation of Boccaccio's *Decameron*. Again, the case was that, though the Italian text couldn't be objected to, the English versions could be found on sale in the 'filth-market of our large towns'.

Literary critics struggled with this wave of prudish hostility. In the *Contemporary Review*, one Percy Bunting argued that the *Decameron* and Zola were 'literature', and could 'plead the privilege of art' albeit 'feebly'. The NVA was now in a strong enough position to warn 'writers of what is called the realistic school' that they would not allow Britain to be 'flooded with foreign filth, and our youth polluted by having the most revolting and hideous descriptions of French vice thrust upon their attention.'

George Moore organised a petition on behalf of Vizetelly and managed to hook in atheist and campaigner Charles Bradlaugh, drama critic William Archer, the sexologist Havelock Ellis, writers Thomas Hardy, H. Rider Haggard, A. W. Pinero, Edmund Gosse, Frank Harris, Olive Schreiner,

John Addington Symonds, Max O'Rell, the actor Sir Henry Irving, and the chief librarian for W. H. Smith, William Faux, but the petition failed in securing Vizetelly's release. The liberal counter-attack wasn't strong enough yet.

Around this time novelists who dared write about sex started to be accused of 'Zolaism'. Zola was the yardstick by which the level of filth could be measured. George Gissing's novel *The Nether World* was reviewed by the *Glasgow Herald*, which found 'the horrible brutality, the crime, the filth and squalor, the very language are reproduced with a fidelity which Zola himself might commend'. The *Contemporary Review* noted that it lacked the 'leprous naturalism that disgusts every honourable reader in the works of Zola and his school'.

George Moore's *Esther Waters* of 1894 (previously serialised in the *Pall Mall Gazette*) was banned from the circulating libraries of W. H. Smith by the same William Faux who had signed the petition, complaining that readers were 'not used to detailed descriptions of a lying-in hospital'. The act of birth seems to have outraged critics of this school easily as much as the act of sex. The *Gazette* criticised *Esther Waters*, the book it had itself published, for being 'hampered by the trammels of Zolaism'. Writers need approval to survive and Gissing, amongst others, was made nervous by the outcry against smut and switched his focus from the society of the street to the safer environs of the middle class. The one true victim of the battle, though, remained Henry Vizetelly, who served his time in Pentonville jail, was forced to close down the publishing house, and died some three years later in January 1894, with son Ernest always blaming his time in prison for having finished him off.

On 27 March 1899 Ernest Vizetelly wrote to Zola agreeing with him that *Fécondité* was a moral work which stigmatised the vices and processes that it described. On the other hand, if he (Vizetelly) had to think about publishing the book in English in Britain, it was in his opinion impossible. To do so would lead to six months' imprisonment for whoever dared to publish it. Vizetelly deeply regretted having to tell Zola this. What's more, making cuts in the work was impossible too. Looking at the ten chapters he had in front of him, there wasn't one of them that he wouldn't have to cut by a third or perhaps a half, the reason being that in a cheap book, distributed to the general public, the descriptions just wouldn't be tolerated. There would be some who would say that the book would corrupt people, the clergy would rise up en masse, and the whole thing would be a repetition of what had happened to Vizetelly's father after he published *La Terre*.

Vizetelly proposed telling Chatto the situation: if they wanted to publish, he would do the translation. He insisted that this had nothing to do with his own personal feelings about the book. The problem was the prejudice of the British and Americans and the laws being so severe in the two countries.

Vizetelly would go on to make these misgivings public in *The Athenaeum* in October 1899, adding that he felt he could not 'fight, or help to fight, the battle which the publication of a faithful rendering of *Fécondité* would, in my estimation, entail'. Yet, Chatto & Windus convinced him that a much cut version could be published and it did appear in May 1900, after Zola had returned to France, with a preface from Vizetelly himself. Even though he had indeed heavily reduced the novel, this preface shows signs of him still being nervous that the book would be condemned. The novel, he writes, is a 'tract' in relation to 'certain grievous evils'. By writing the book, Zola was 'discharging a patriotic duty ... absolute freedom of speech exists in France which is not the case in this country'. He, Vizetelly, had been of the opinion that publication in England would be impossible but that view became 'modified', because the book's 'high moral purpose' was recognised by several of its 'most bitter detractors'. (He meant recognised by those who had read the original French version.) Vizetelly then mustered forces in his defence: among the reviewers were two well-known lady writers(!), Madame Darmesteter (formerly Miss Mary Robinson), and Miss Hannah Lynch. The first had said how 'honest', 'moral', 'human' and 'comely' the book was, and the second, how 'eminently, pugnaciously virtuous' it was. Vizetelly added, 'nothing in any degree offensive to delicate susceptibilities will be found in this present version ...' and reassured readers that in the book, 'the punishment of the guilty is awful'.

He could have added in here *The Times* reviewer who had said that it wasn't

easy to explain completely to an Anglo-Saxon audience the full signification of M. Zola's remarkable work. Naturally such a theme carries him amidst scandalous habits and customs. But side by side with these terrible scenes he describes for us almost romantically, and in pages which are among the most eloquent he has ever penned . . . the book itself is a series of contrasts, at one time full of beauty, and another reeking with monstrous suggestion.

The point is, Vizetelly was a worried man. In a letter to the publisher Macmillan he filled in the details behind his concerns:

> . . . scene follows scene of women at midwives' establishments, of operations of all sorts performed on them, of some of them dying from the effects thereof in <u>lakes of blood</u>, of others being unsexed by surgical operations, of others taking every precaution to prevent childbirth <u>so boldly, so vividly, at such length, in such detail</u> that neither British nor American hypocrisy could for one moment tolerate such a recital. [All underlinings his.]

In fact, large parts of *Fécondité* have never been translated into English. And it is disturbing. This passage describes what can only be termed as infanticide. Madame Rouche, a backstreet abortionist, relates what she has seen:

> 'And what do I find in one of the two beds? The wretched girl, legs splayed, in a pool of blood, hands twisted, still tight around the neck of the infant they had strangled, when it had barely made the journey out; and she dead herself, Monsieur, dead from a ghastly haemorrhage, the flood bursting through the mattress and bedstead, to seep onto the floor. But the extraordinary thing was that the

other woman, the cook, who had been asleep no more than two metres away, had heard absolutely nothing, not a cry, not a whisper. She only became aware of all this upon waking ... Can you picture the poor child, compounding her pain, swallowing back her cries, expecting the infant only to suffocate it with her own feverish hands? And then can you picture her, with no strength left after that final exertion, letting all the blood drain from her veins, and drifting off into death with that tiny being, but never releasing her grip?'

Remembering the consequence of his father's publication of Zola, Vizetelly reminded Macmillan that his father was 'imprisoned, ruined & hounded to death for his pains'.

This was true but it doesn't tell the whole picture. The situation had not been uniform. Whilst Vizetelly senior was indeed being hounded, a group of editors, critics and writers in Britain slowly emerged to fight back against the onslaught. They had either taken Zola seriously from the start, evolved into admirers, or let 'Zolaism' into their writing, so that, by the time of his exile, Zola's influence was felt across a good part of the literary world. The list of names on George Moore's petition tell part of the story: but we can add (with significant caveats) the names of Arthur Symons, Henry James, Thomas Hardy, George Bernard Shaw, Arthur Quiller-Couch and the institutions of the Independent Theatre Society, the Lutetian Society and journals like the *Westminster Review*.

Chronology may not do full justice to how this sphere of influence grew and spread but it gives an indication all the same. Back in 1880, Henry James reviewed *Nana* and, though he complained about its 'monstrous uncleanness', he conceded that the English novel was constricted by its need to be wholesome for 'virgins and boys'. 'Half of a life is a sealed book to young unmarried ladies,' he wrote, 'and how can a novel be worth anything that deals only with half of life?'

In 1884 James wrote an essay on 'The Art of Fiction' and seemed to hold back from condemning Zola. By 1903, though he was still struggling with Zola's 'indecency', he produced one of the first full-length, serious reviews of Zola. In private, through the '80s and '90s, and presumably in conversation with friends, he had been taking Zola's writing seriously.

Much more in the open, George Moore was a conscious and public champion of Zola, though never unafraid of being highly critical of his work. According to his own account, *Confessions of a Young Man*, his conversion to Zola happened in 1879 when he read Zola's manifesto for Naturalism in *Le Roman Experimental* (*The Experimental Novel*). Moore was astonished 'at the vastness of the conception, and the towering height of the ambition'. Moore was one of the few English-language writers who consciously and publicly made an effort to imitate Zola's Naturalism. As mentioned, his *Esther Waters* appeared in 1894.

The work and critical reception of the era's greatest novelist, Thomas Hardy, was intertwined with the Zola effect. In 1890, Hardy produced the essay 'Candour in Fiction' and in 1891 another, 'The Science of Fiction'. Beneath the surface in these essays and over several decades, Hardy's attitude to Zola flip-flopped between uneasiness, contempt, envy, pretended ignorance and admiration. In France, Hardy knew well that Zola had precisely the freedom to write about love and sex in ways that he, Hardy, yearned for. In a letter to a woman friend, he wrote, 'I think him no artist & too material.' He conceded in 'The Science of Fiction' that Zola was a 'romancer' but later condemned him for not being an 'artist, but at bottom a man of affairs, who would just as soon have written twenty volumes of, say, the statistics of crime, or commerce, as of fiction – a passionate reformer, who has latterly found his vocation'.

This last comment can be taken as a sneer at Zola's involvement in the Dreyfus case. Hardy had refused to comment on the Affair, having stated his position on writers and politics a few years earlier with 'The pursuit of what people are pleased to call Art so as to win unbiassed attention to it as such, *absolutely forbids political action* [my italics].'

Though Hardy told Edmund Gosse that he barely knew Zola's work, claiming to be 'read in Zola very little', behind closed doors he collected Zola's books in both French and English. He penned notes on some of these (including *Germinal*) and hand-copied extracts from the books into his notebooks.

In his dealings with editors and the press, Hardy worked in the shadow of the NVA's campaign, and its successful use of Zola as its test case. *Tess of the D'Urbervilles* (1891) and *Jude the Obscure* (1895) both had a rocky road in their production and reception. They were seen to be touched by the presence of Zola, if only for such scenes as Jude's encounter with the pig's 'pizzle', which some think is reminiscent of the cattle-mating scene in *La Terre*. The review of *Tess* in the *Manchester*

Guardian said that it was 'coloured throughout with Zolaism'. Zola himself (as mentioned in an earlier chapter) hoped in 1893 that *Tess* would be published soon in France. A close reading of Zola's *La Faute de l'Abbé Mouret* in relation to Hardy's novels shows Hardy working through some of Zola's ways of writing. While Zola had had a free ride in France, Hardy spent years wrestling with publishers: literary magazines turned down versions of *Tess* in serial form, so for them, he self-censored – resentfully – the rape of Tess, along with the birth and death of the illegitimate child and he spent a good deal of effort in negotiation with his publishers over what could or could not be allowed. With *Jude*, Hardy had to negotiate with *Harper's New Monthly Magazine* so that it could fit in with their demand that he avoid material that 'could not be read aloud in any family circle'. The two novels can be read in part for their sub-textual commentaries on the NVA and its effect on people's sexual behaviour. When *Jude* appeared, the *Pall Mall Gazette*, dubbed it 'Jude the Obscene' and Hardy retreated from writing fiction from then on.

Meanwhile, in 1891, the poet and critic John Addington Symonds praised Zola as an 'idealist of the purest water' and celebrated *La Bête Humaine* as 'the poem of the railway'. These flourishes may seem like hyperbole now but in the context of the struggle over Zola, they were weapons.

We can get a sense of the stream that Zola's works were swimming in at this point from the fact that, in the same year, a dramatised version of *Thérèse Raquin* played at the Royalty Theatre for the Independent Theatre Society. This was a private theatre club, more responsible than any other institution at the time for bringing the works of Ibsen to

Britain, along with premières of Shaw's *Widowers' Houses* and plays by Maeterlinck. A Zola adaptation had been seen before on the London stage: in 1879, a version of *L'Assommoir* had played at the Princess's Theatre, with the *Gentleman's Magazine* regretting that it was a toned-down version of the novel! A 'melodramatic-burlesque' adaptation of the play followed soon after and in 1885 a suitably watered-down version of *Nana* had played at the Theatre Royal, Wigan, with a brief showing in London. In the 1880s, British drama critics in Paris went to see Zola adaptations, filling their reviews in the Britain newspapers with the usual health warnings: 'tiresome, loathsome and repulsive in the extreme'. The Independent Theatre Society production was a different matter. The society had to be private in order to avoid the censorship of the Lord Chamberlain; its members included Henry James, Thomas Hardy, George Bernard Shaw, George Moore and Arthur Conan Doyle, with Oscar Wilde, Shaw and James coming to see the Zola play. The *Daily Telegraph* critic, Clement Scott, thought the incidents of the play needed to be in the 'hands of Euripides, or Sophocles, or Shakespeare' as they 'required to be lifted ... out of their squalid atmosphere'. Not much rehabilitation of Zola there.

The *Morning Post* review, though, showed the kind of ambivalence that was starting to creep into mainstream attitudes to Zola. 'Happily for visitors of refined tastes, Ibsen's "Ghosts" no longer exhibited their hideous shadows upon the stage, but the morbid revelations of "Thérèse Raquin", by M. Émile Zola, were quite strong enough for ordinary nerves.' Having laid out the usual warnings to readers who, after all, would not even be able to see the show, lower down in his article the reviewer sneaked in a smidgeon of admiration for the play: 'powerful situations ... the fate that eventually overtakes the guilty couple is in harmony with poetic justice ... the sombre drama affords scope for vigorous acting'. And a comment you could take either way – though Zola would have thought of it as a compliment – the play was 'rather a story such as the police court reveals'.

The *Standard* of the same day offered the same mixed fare: first the reviewer pointed out that the Lord Chamberlain had licensed this production. Then it acknowledged that Zola had his 'devotees' and 'credit must be given ... to M. Zola's imagination', though of course this came with the usual proviso about Zola trespassing 'far beyond' the 'legitimate bounds of art'. A major bother for the reviewer was the 'grossest bad taste' of showing a young girl helping Thérèse dress and wash – if the Lord Chamberlain had licensed this then he had been 'unduly lenient'. After outlining these drawbacks, the review approved of the last scene which 'in its own horrible and exceedingly painful way' was 'certainly effective'. 'There is something terrible in this silent witness [the speechless mother] of the hell which the guilty pair have made for themselves.'

Frederick Wedmore in the *Academy* found it 'original and fearless' and an old champion of Zola, William Archer, was 'enthusiastic'. When the French version of the story ran in Paris in 1892, *The Times* reviewer reported back to British readers that Zola had 'undoubtedly made out his case ...'

In his essay, 'The Tyranny of the Novel' (1892), the literary critic Edmund Gosse offered real and serious praise of Zola as the 'one novelist' who had written 'a large, competent, profound review of the movement of life'. In the same year, Zola's *The Attack on the Mill and other sketches of war* (*L'Attaque du Moulin*) became the first Zola fiction to be published by a traditional publishing house – Heinemann – and it was the first to appear without the customary flamboyant and alluring cover image. Gosse wrote the preface saying, 'Whenever M. Zola writes of war, he writes seriously and well.' This same year, *La Débâcle* was reviewed in *Harper's Monthly* and described as 'a work of genius and immense power'.

1893 was a really good year for Zola in England. A literary biography appeared, written by the journalist Robert Sherard, which brought to English-speaking readers a solid survey of Zola's life and work that trod carefully around the pitfalls of whether Zola was smut or not. On *La Terre* for example, Sherard writes:

> It is . . . the book about which Zola has been most blamed for deliberate pornography, and it is certainly a matter of fact that there are many passages in it which never can be approved by Anglo-Saxon readers. But it happens that Zola does not write for Anglo-Saxon readers . . . And it must be remembered that the delight in a certain kind of coarseness is a trait of French character, just as in England under Elizabeth.

Criticism like this, I suspect, was just as likely to attract the curiosity of some Anglo-Saxon readers, as repel others.

In 1892 and 1893, the *Westminster Review* took up a good deal of space with discussions on Zola's influence on Thomas

Hardy. 'The coarseness of Zola's "L'Assommoir" cannot blind us to its wonderful vividness of description, its harrowing presentation of the miseries and vices of the scum of the Parisian population, its pitiless but faithful, portraiture of life's bitter realities. So with "Tess of the D'Urbervilles".' The influential critic V. Lee gave Zola that Victorian seal of approval by dubbing him 'moral'. (One sidenote here is that V. Lee was in fact Violet Paget, who used the pen-name because she had herself run into similar trouble to Zola because of her frank discussions of sexuality.) Zola-like she wrote in her diary, 'I will show, fight, argue, prove that I am in the right, that the restrictions placed upon the novel in England are absurd, that my novel [*Miss Brown*] is legitimate and praiseworthy.' In her essay 'Moral Teaching of Zola', Lee said that she 'aim[ed] to suggest the moral lessons Zola may bring to his worthier readers'; 'Zola exposes the sort of misery and wickedness the world contains'. Then September of that year saw Zola's hugely successful visit to England, though some at the time spotted the contradictions between the acclaim he received coming so soon after his books were banned.

In 1894, Zola's *L'Attaque du Moulin* (music by Bruneau) played at Covent Garden and the Independent Theatre Society had a second stab at Zola with a production of *Les Héritiers Rabourdin* at the Opera Comique. This was a complete flop, not for the usual reason of disgusting its critics, but because the comedy wasn't funny. In the history of Zola's reputation in Britain, the attempt to put it on is more significant than the outcome. Prompted by the death of Henry Vizetelly, the *Daily Chronicle* hosted a passionate debate on 'Literary Freedom', including strong defences of Zola and Hardy.

In 1894–5, a private male literary circle took up Zola's cause: the Lutetian Society published uncensored editions of *Germinal* (translated by Havelock Ellis), *L'Assommoir* (Arthur Symons), *Nana* (Victor Plarr), *La Curée* (Texeira de Mattos), *La Terre* (Ernest Dowson) and *Pot-Bouille* (Percy Pinkerton), each edition circulating 300 copies in two volumes, all printed 'for Private Distribution' amongst Lutetian Society members, on handmade paper at a cost of £25 per book. Though these editions were for the private consumption of wealthy men, the translations made serious attempts to do justice to all aspects of Zola's work that the NVA and others found so objectionable: primarily the many sex and childbirth scenes – both human and animal – along with the slang, curses and so-called obscenities. One small example of hundreds, this one from *La Terre*: Zola wrote: 'Tu peux te la foutre au cul, ta soupe! Je vas dormir.'* The Lutetian edition translated that as: 'Shove your soup up your bloody arse! I'm going to sleep', while Vizetelly translated it as: '"Stick your soup behind!" shouted the old man, turning round to her. "I'm going to bed."'

In 1895 the *Westminster Review* published 'Towards the Appreciation of Émile Zola' by E. C. Townshend. Townshend tried to save Zola from the accusation that he was a socialist; if his books preached socialism it was because he turned the unconventional insight of the true artist on modern life, on the hollowness of its shams, the cruelty of its contrasts. As with much of the Zola criticism of the time,

---

* Standard French is 'Je vais' but Zola represented local dialect with 'Je vas'.

this had a double-edged quality: the dangers or drawbacks in Zola's work drift into being its delights and insights.

The next year, Havelock Ellis followed up his translation of *Germinal* with an essay on Zola in the *Savoy* magazine, which some see as the first truly modern English-language critique. Ellis was perhaps the first critic to explain and justify Zola's exploration of working-class life and language: 'The main thing was to give literary place and prestige to words and phrases which had fallen so low in general esteem, in spite of their admirable expressiveness, that only a writer of the first rank and of unequalled audacity could venture to lift them from the mire.' He put Zola in the company of Rabelais, Chaucer and Shakespeare in his expression of the 'sexual and digestive functions'.

All the forces of Nature, it seems to him [Zola], are raging in the fury of generative desire or reposing in the fullness of swelling maturity. The very earth itself, in the impressive pages with which 'Germinal' closes, is impregnated with men, germinating beneath the soil, one day to burst through the furrows and renew the old world's failing life. In this conception of the natural energies of the world – as manifested in men and animals, in machines in every form of matter – perpetually conceiving and generating, Zola reaches his most impressive effects, though these effects are woven together of elements that are separately of no very exquisite beauty, or subtle insight, or radical novelty.

Ellis grasped here that Naturalism was not realist; it used the details of natural phenomena, culled from modern scientific sources, as the basis for metaphors and symbols. Ellis also pointed out how Zola had rendered a 'service' to his fellow artists by giving proof that they too could write about the 'rough, neglected details of life':

It has henceforth become possible for other novelists to find inspiration where before they could never have turned, to touch life with a vigour and audacity of phrase which, without Zola's example, they would have trembled to use, while they still remain free to bring to their work the simplicity, precision, and inner experience which he has never possessed. Zola has enlarged the field of the novel.

With that phrase, 'enlarged the field of the novel', Ellis signposted the full significance of Zola in the literary world.

Further defences and celebrations of Zola appeared in the *Fortnightly Review* (R. E. S. Hart) and from the poet Arthur Symons.

Several questions raised by all this are about the movement of opinion. Between, say, 1880 and 1900 were these members of literary groupings changing their attitude to the depiction of love, sex and class in literature? Did enthusiasts of Zola convince those who disapproved? Was Zola's work the catalyst for change – a process that runs through, perhaps, D. H. Lawrence and James Joyce, all the way to the *Lady Chatterley* trial of 1960?

I suspect that it was all these, with many nuanced variations in between. Apart from anything else, there was no one single 'Zola', there were censored and uncensored works, and there were novels that people could say to themselves were more 'moral' than others. And reading is social. Readers are people who talk to each other about what they read and this often leads them to range across several authors who they see as belonging together. It wasn't only the NVA who lumped Zola into a Paris or French school; the Lutetians named themselves after the Latin name for Paris; Zola's British publisher upped his sales by hinting at forbidden delights from across the Channel while literary critics spotted the tide flowing from Flaubert, Maupassant and Zola to Hardy, Shaw and James. Things were moving.

None of these issues stand on their own; they are linked to the question of the social order. Those who were opposed to Zola's fiction felt that he undermined that order, the implication being that fiction has or should have a role in sustaining the status quo and he was betraying that role. They had a problem: the status quo wasn't very 'status' – society was changing. The old certainties of church, state and power – 'the rich man in his castle, the poor man at his gate' – were under pressure from new political organisations, new organisations for working people and for women (many of whom, I hasten to add, were now part of what we mean by that phrase 'working people'), new technologies, new ways of moving over the earth's surface, new ideas about the structure of matter, the nature of time and what a human being is. People on both sides of the Zolaism wars recognised that Zola pictured the change.

What is odd is to think of Zola virtually alone in Norwood at the very point that a new 'republic of letters' (his words from 1893) was taking shape. I can't help thinking that it's a great shame that Zola wasn't able on occasions to gather up his papers, stroll out of the Queen's Hotel, turn left, walk up the road to Crystal Palace Station, take the train up to town to give a talk at the Authors' Society to follow up his speech from 1893, give a reading and have a discussion with the Lutetians, the Fabians, the members of the Independent Theatre Society, the readers of the *Westminster Review* or the *Social-Democrat*.

After all, waxworks don't talk.

'Cheque delayed. Invoice received.'

By 16 March Zola and Jeanne were figuring out how she and the children could come to England again, and how she should keep it secret from the authorities. The children had to stay patient, their bicycles would be bought when he got back. Any other place to meet was impossible: 'It'll be difficult to find a country where I won't be recognised and where we'll be able to live in peace, without the whole world on my back.'

On 20 March Zola and Alexandrine were back to struggling with their situation: Zola received this:

This day, the 17th, the holiday, is, in spite of your kind thoughts, a real day of mourning; I can put it amongst the days which, in these last years have been the most sad, because, through these thirty-five years together, I have to subtract a frightful ordeal ['*calvaire*'] of ten, which will only come to an end when my life ends. Today, living alone as I am, this flood of past sadness rose up inside me and a suffering so bitter that I've spent this day in the midst of flowers that I haven't arranged yet. When we reached thirty-four years together, on 28 December, I was by your side and neither of us spoke of it; I returned home, once more crying desperately. I was looking forward to the days when we'll be old and once again

I couldn't understand how the happiness I used to dream of could have escaped me like a flash of lightning.

ps You again wish me happiness in your letter but where do you want me to find it? Isn't my life finished for ever?

Zola responded, 'I thought sending you the flowers would make you happy for a moment, and I see that all I've done is give you grief...'

On the other hand, on 23 March, with a tone of delight, Zola wrote to Jeanne: 'Dear beloved wife, it's been decided, pack your bags and come ... This happiness isn't given to us very often, so I mustn't let it escape. This is going to make for a delicious Easter holiday...'

Plans were made for Jeanne and the children to come out on 29 March and go back on 11 April. He told Jeanne that Vizetelly would be at Victoria Station to meet them. He wasn't so cheerful about Jacques: he wasn't working hard enough. 'It's disastrous that we have a little Jacques who can't do well and, because of his casualness and inattention, can hardly get on.'

On the same day he wrote to Denise conjuring up a picture of the four of them riding bikes in Verneuil and going off to buy cakes. They would look so lovely that everyone would stop to look at them.

As planned, the family arrived on 29 March and spent the Easter holidays under the name of 'Roger', at the Crystal Palace Royal Hotel, listed as being 'near to Beulah Spa, with six acres of Pleasure Ground attached', where the manager was W. C. E. Francatelli.

Denise remembered that there was:

a valet at the hotel who stole my brother's watch, then pretended to find it again when my mother threatened him by telling him that the watch had never left our room. This caused inconsolable unhappiness for several days in our intimate circumstances . . .

On Sunday, to our great astonishment, the Salvation Army, stopped in the middle of the street, very solemnly sang hymns, handed out their leaflets and preached to passers-by . . .

At Crystal Palace, there were two poor people, 'Daddy's poor people' Jacques called them. One was an old beggar who swept the pavement and road and cleared a way through the mud and snow 'for the ladies'. The other drew pictures on the pavement, and my brother and I were full of admiration for his pastel pictures with their garish colours that he sold. Every day, Zola gave a little money to the artist and the sweeper.

We can get a picture of Alexandrine's role in the relationship when she warned Zola on 30 March to rely more on his own intuition and not just listen to political friends. 'For all your life long you have always done things your own way. Why don't you carry on now? . . . Don't take political friendship for any more than it is . . .'

Then, by way of reversal of the situation in which Alexandrine sat in a hotel while letters arrived from Jeanne, now – and on his birthday – a basket of roses arrived from Alexandrine. He told her on 2 April that he was delighted to receive them but it was hard, after nearly nine months of exile, torn from his country, on the end of all the relentless hatred. 'All I wanted was justice, not all these insults they've showered me with. All this comes back and smothers me on a day like this.'

Alexandrine replied, 'Listen, Monsieur Wolf-Cat-Dog, Dog-Cat-Wolf, or Cat-Wolf-Dog, I am going to give you a good telling-off for being so sad. I am sorry to see that even your dear little ones being there doesn't get you out of this frame of mind.' Perhaps this implies Alexandrine was acknowledging that Jeanne had a role of lifting him out of his depression too.

Jeanne and the children travelled back to Paris on 11 April, so from then on, it was back to living in the shadow of the Dreyfus Affair. Mathieu Dreyfus advised Zola not to come back yet and Alexandrine pointed out that the enemy were feeble and disorientated, so it was vital not to give them a distraction.

On 12 April Zola wrote to Jeanne to tell her that the days when they were with him made him feel yet again how alone he was, torn from everything he cared about, though the presence of Denise and Jacques had cheered him up: 'Tell Denise and Jacques how nice they were when they came to stay with me, and their Papa loves them even more.'

In a similar vein, three days later, he told Jeanne that he would carry the memory of them all on his walks and wherever they had been together. 'And I say to myself, I'll see you all again soon, whenever it turns out to be the end of the Affair. If it's a victory, we'll enjoy it. If it's a defeat, even so, we won't be separated any more.' But he had to warn her that there were still five or six weeks to go before he could come back.

The following day, he was starting to fantasise about being reunited with French food . . . if the new cook could make a good *ragout* and a good *sole au gratin* . . .

On 18 April, Alexandrine wrote: 'Thank you dear Loulou,* for the beautiful violets that brought me your dear kisses, and I have waited by them thinking that our dear comrades are there on this little table next to you.' This was also the day that Zola went back to the Queen's Hotel. Presumably, he had stayed at the Crystal Palace Royal to spare Alexandrine's feelings. Or was it to spare Jeanne's? Or was it just to avoid being turned away by the hotel management at the Queen's? No one would be allowed two wives, even if cohabiting on different occasions. Meanwhile the *Sunday Mail* and the *Daily Telegraph* were bombarding Vizetelly with requests for articles from Zola but he wouldn't play ball. By the 20th his food fantasies were turning to *poulet roti* and *pommes de terre frites*. Jacques had to work harder and Denise only had one spelling mistake in her letter to him.

On 27 April he had to handle the tricky matter of a request from the anarchists to publish *Germinal* in their newspaper for little or no fee. Zola thought not but would see if there was a way they could arrange things for when he got back to Paris. Meanwhile, in a letter to Jeanne, he was back to talking about the women on their bicycles who, amazingly, went out on them in the rain. He was dreaming of Verneuil . . . he had spent the last eight days seeing no one at all, not even a word

---

* This seems to be a nickname they called each other. It was also a nick-name for the Pomeranian dog they owned, 'M. Pinpin'. It can mean 'darling' or 'rogue'.

to the staff at the hotel. But then Vizetelly came for a chat, before he lapsed back into silence again. Now, there was only one chapter left of *Fécondité* to write. 'Our life will remain complicated but we will eventually be reunited and we won't have the weight of the horrible Affair weighing on us . . .'

On 30 April he had some domestic news for Jeanne:

Yes, I've had to buy some shoes and socks, because they were in tatters. But best of all, I've bought some needles and some black and white thread because all my clothes were coming apart. So, I've started sewing, and that's quite a spectacle, I can tell you. I'm not very neat but my buttons are sewn on really well.

He noticed that Jeanne had hired a cook who was against the retrial of Dreyfus. He wondered if the Affair was landing in the washing-up water. Soon, before hiring a servant, would they have to ask their opinion on whether Dreyfus was innocent or guilty? He explained he was joking but it did bother him a bit and that they had to be very wary about who Jeanne brought into the house.

On 4 May he told Jeanne that he made a fire every day to keep him company. 'I feel less alone when there are flames going up the chimney.' A few days later, his mind turned to *ragout de mouton* and *sole au gratin* again. He could see the pair of them having tea together once more like young lovers. Jeanne should tell Jacques that if he worked harder they would love him more; and that Denise wasn't to be jealous of her mother, because she was as beautiful as her mother, with a beautiful dress, a beautiful hat and beautiful hair. 'Tell her that she would be even more beautiful if she made fewer spelling mistakes.' He had gone out that day to take some photos and took one of the hotel that they had stayed in. 'I'm sewing without a thimble, and I'm sewing very well.'

A short while later he apologised to her for being depressed when she was there; it was because he thought that there was going to be a bad outcome to the Dreyfus case. If she could see him now, they would be having a much nicer time. But no need for recriminations, they would get all that back when they went for their next holiday. 'You'll see me on 10 June, or earlier.'

On 14 May he asked Jeanne to tell Jacques that he had taken a photo of where he saw 'Papa's artist'. The light was bright and it was just where the poor man was doing his drawings. He had other photos of the old poor people they had seen – he gave them a penny or two. He had many photos to show them. Taking photos kept him amused and they would see what a beautiful album of his days of exile he would give them.

In his letter to Jeanne on 18 May he told her he was noticing the lilac and chestnut blossom, the greenness every-where, the magnificent avenues. On 21 May he wrote to Denise saying, 'I hope I'll be back in three weeks' time. We will go out for beautiful walks, we'll go to the woods in a *fiacre automobile* [an electric landau], it will be a *fête* every day.' Not so cheerfully, he told Jeanne that stuck in his hole, he thought he was losing his memory. On 25 May he could tell her that he had a date: he would leave England on 6 June. Finally he would be able to kiss them all.

On 27 May Zola finished writing *Fécondité* and on the next day wrote to both Jeanne and Alexandrine with the news. Denise remembered him telling Jeanne: 'I am counting on all honest women, all wives and all mothers being on my side,' while he told Alexandrine, 'I started this novel alone on 4 August 1898 and I have just finished it alone on 27 May 1899, 1,006 pages in my handwriting.'

Finally with a great sense of relief, he wrote to Jeanne:

When you get this letter, you won't have to write to me any more. And how nice it is, isn't it, to stop getting these cold letters, and to find ourselves together again? . . .

Get out the teapot, order a cake from Mademoiselle Louise. This will be a day of celebration for all of us which we will enjoy to make up for the ones we missed because of us being apart.

Ten days more, then it will be the big, beautiful day.

On 31 May Alexandrine told Zola that she was delighted at how pleased he was that he had finished *Fécondité*. It wasn't unalloyed pleasure, though:

I think it's sad for us that at the moment you wrote the word *fin* [end], we're not sitting beside each other, with me reading your last page and you chatting loudly and excitedly about your new work, thanks to the relentless effort you put in.

She also had some words of warning. Their misery might be coming to an end but in Paris there was nothing but bother:

The frontiers are under surveillance, people here will want to cheer you, our door is guarded again. You don't have the right to be your own person any more; the public take you as their thing; your wishes, your desires will have to count for nothing in the face of this public, who don't understand and don't think that after your exile of eleven months, you must want above all to come back home in peace.

On 1 June he met up with George Moore and he had time to write to Jeanne: he told her that he was amazed to write that they were going to be victorious. 'I think, in the end, we will, all four of us, ride our bikes in the woods of Verneuil. We must order the beautiful bicycles.'

And to Denise:

If your dollies get indigestion when they're having tea, you'll have to take them for electric treatment with Doctor Delineau, or you could get electric treatment for yourself, in their place. *Maman* told me that you would really like that. See you soon, my good little Denise. Be very good, and you will see how we are going to have a feast together, all four of us, *Maman*, you two and me.

On 2 June, in Paris, there was a conference at the office of *Le Radical*: Clemenceau, Jaurès and several other leading Dreyfusards put their heads together and decided that it was all clear for Zola to return.

Zola wrote to Alexandrine:

Ah my Loulou, my poor Loulou, it all seems like a dream.
I can see the jostling crowd ['*bouscoulade*']. But we will
be together and we will struggle on together, if needs be.
A million kisses, dear wife, with all my heart which is
beating really hard.

On 3 June the Supreme Court of Appeal in Paris overturned the verdict of 1894 and ruled that Dreyfus should
appear before another court martial. This meant that the
now starving, sick, not-far-from-death Dreyfus would have
to take the journey back from Devil's Island and face trial
again. Alexandrine sent a telegram: 'Cheque delayed. Invoice
received. All goes well.' This was code for saying that the
three chambers had jointly quashed the 1894 guilty verdict
but that Dreyfus was to appear before another court martial.
This wasn't a total victory: Dreyfus hadn't been found
innocent. That's why the supposed 'cheque' was only 'delayed'
not 'arrived'.

There was also Zola's own case to think about: he wrote
to Labori, his lawyer: 'I'm being threatened with arrest at the
frontier but I'll come back all the same.'

On his last evening in England, Zola had dinner at the
Queen's Hotel with Vizetelly and the Fasquelles, then at
9 p.m. on 4 June, Zola left London through Victoria Station,
accompanied by the Fasquelles.

It was over.

'A frightful catastrophe'

Zola arrived back in France at 5.38 a.m. on 5 June. As he didn't reach home till the evening, he may well have gone first to Jeanne's apartment at 3 rue du Havre. While he was in England, he had prepared an article which would explain his position. This was 'Justice' which appeared in *L'Aurore*, 5 June 1899. 'All I've done is be a good citizen, devoting myself to being this, even so far as going into exile, a total disappearance. I agreed to be no longer active for the sake of the peace of the country, so as to not take part purposelessly in the arguments around this monstrous Affair.' He added that he had only one wish: to resume his place again 'in his national home' – peacefully, so that no one could take up his time any more.

Denise recollected this, but more important for her at the time: 'The bicycles that he promised us in England, my brother and me, he immediately gave us as presents.'

Zola also had to sort out his own case. On 9 June, he challenged the Versailles verdict that had found him guilty of libelling the military court. The Versailles sentence of 18 July 1898 was served upon him at his home in the rue de Bruxelles. On 31 August he was summoned to appear in Versailles on 23 November. On that day, however, his trial was postponed to some unspecified date.

Meanwhile, back in London, between 7 and 29 June the

Evening Standard ran Vizetelly's memoir 'Zola in London', published later in a short book as *With Zola in England: A Story of Exile.*

On 20 July Zola wrote to Vizetelly, enclosing some photos:

> You can't imagine the bother I'm being assailed by. I have often missed the peace of the Queen's Hotel. Even so, everything's for the best, the happy dénoucment is approaching, and I will get set up on Tuesday at Médan so I can rest . . .
>
> I read your articles on my stay in England in *Le Matin*. They are very good and sensibly stay within the limits that I asked you to stick to.

This referred to Vizetelly keeping quiet about the Dreyfus Affair.

In late July, in an interview with Philippe Dubois, Zola gave notice that he wasn't going to put the Dreyfus Affair into one of his novels: 'It would be base and ugly on my part to exploit the Dreyfus Affair.' (That's what he said. What he did was another matter.) Dubois asked him about the photos he was developing. Zola told him that they were photos of England, photos of pubs, houses and streets in London, as well as 'poor ragged cripples, hideous, pitiful devils. One sees many like that over there, alas.'

> I took some 300 with a little 'jumelle', 6.5 x 9, which I attached to the handlebars of my bike when I was going out and about. This 'jumelle' gave me photos that were marvellously sharp and clear. I'm going to bring

all the photos together. I will make an album of exile. This album will be full of documents and interesting memories. Sadly, during the trip, four of the photos, already developed, were broken. They were of the flower shop where I went every morning, during the two months that my wife was ill, for the flowers that I took to her.

Dubois finished with: 'Zola added, with the melancholy that one always notices in cases like this, with all photographers, "The photos that are broken were of course the best in the collection." When I took my leave, Zola went back to his laboratory.'

On 13 October, in *Le Temps*, Zola talked about *Fécondité* and his life in England. This was his chance to give France the picture of what he had been doing. He explained that all his research for the novel was finished just as the second trial at Versailles took place and he had to leave. 'I took the Calais train,' he said,

with my nightshirt, a flannel, and a piece of paper with four English words on it from Clemenceau. On the train that was carrying me far from rumours of death and also, alas! far from my home, I repeated the words, forcing myself to remember them in order to guide me through my first steps in London.

He said that he didn't stop in that huge, humming city, seeking out instead solitude and silence. He wrote to his wife asking her to find his papers in a corner of his study.

Zola clearly wanted everyone to know that it wasn't his choice to flee to Britain. 'I had accepted my sentence and I was prepared to serve my year of imprisonment.' Only guilty people were frightened of prison; he had nothing to fear, no remorse. The action he had taken came from his conscience. 'I would have been able to say to myself, "Honour is secure" and I would have been able to fill my cell with sweet thoughts like that.' Instead, he had accepted the tactical arguments that his Dreyfusard friends had put to him. So he gave in to the interests of the cause that he had already sacrificed so much for. 'I obeyed as a soldier would.'

In spite of the urbane way in which British people behave, he said that he felt surrounded with sympathetic but annoying curiosity. As a result, he chose an inaccessible place to stay in the middle of green fields and shade. He took on British servants who didn't know him and couldn't speak a word of 'our language'. Reading British newspapers made him familiar with a few expressions that he could use in order to make himself understood.

The final paragraph of the article is an extraordinary secular prayer to the future of France and how he saw his role in it, interweaving the Dreyfus case, his utopian novel, and his own life and beliefs.

While my enemies relentlessly try to ruin me, I have given my very best to my country, the wisest of advice. I induced her to touch her wounds so that she could salve them. And with *Fécondité*, which confirms the existence and greatness of my country, I have exalted beauty. The budding flower is pretty, the open flower is beautiful. The virgin is not as beautiful as the mother. A woman gives off a perfume, shows off her whole soul, takes on her complete beauty when she achieves her natural end. This was a useful truth to put forward, just as Jean-Jacques Rousseau became an ardent apostle for his views. I hope that my book will have the same good fortune – not for me, but for my country – as that which celebrated the ideas of the philosopher [Rousseau].

The Dreyfus case still had a long way to go. (According to some, it's still running!) On 9 June one of the key figures who had done so much to prove Dreyfus's innocence, Colonel Picquart, was released from prison after 324 days in detention. Most important of all, though, this was the day that Dreyfus left Devil's Island on board the cruiser *Sfax*. He arrived in France on 1 July and was taken to a military prison in Rennes.

On 18 July, in an article in *Le Matin*, Esterhazy admitted that he wrote the *bordereau* but stated that he wrote it 'under dictation' from his superiors. On 7 August the climax of the whole campaign arrived: Dreyfus's re-trial by court martial at Rennes. Zola kept out of the way, he didn't testify. On 9 September the Rennes trial ended: Dreyfus was found guilty but with 'extenuating circumstances'. After everything that had been revealed over the previous year and a half, to the Dreyfusards it was beyond belief. It was a disaster.

As a consequence, on 12 September, Zola wrote: 'The Fifth Act', which appeared in *L'Aurore*. 'I am terrified,' he wrote:

What I feel is no longer anger, no longer indignation and the craving to avenge it, no longer the need to denounce a crime and demand its punishment, in the name of truth and justice. I am terrified, filled with the sacred awe of a man who witnesses the supernatural: rivers flowing backwards towards their sources and the earth toppling over under the sun. I cry out with consternation, for our noble and generous France has fallen to the bottom of the abyss.

. . . for the past two years, suffering has been no stranger to me. I have heard mobs hound me with their death cries; I have seen a filthy flood of threats and insults flow by my feet; I have known the despairs of exile for eleven months. And there have also been two trials, two deplorable displays of baseness and iniquity. But, compared with the trial of Rennes, my trials have been refreshing and idyllic scenes, with hope in full blossom!

Back in Britain, by Sunday 17 September there were over 120,000 names on a giant petition on behalf of Dreyfus and between 50,000 and 80,000 people demonstrated in Hyde Park against the Rennes decision. Historians have asked why and how did the Dreyfus case arouse such feeling in Britain, and was Zola any part of that? This matter is complicated by a good deal of anti-French sentiment swirling around Britain at the time. The Fashoda Incident had only just ended, while others leaped on the story as the treatment of both Dreyfus and Zola 'proved' that something – or even a lot – was supposedly wrong with the 'French character'.

This raises the question of how exactly had Zola's 'J'Accuse' and his trials gone down with the British public?

We've already seen how the Left swung behind Dreyfus and Zola following Jaurès's move, but what of the rest of public opinion? To understand this, we need to go back to 17 January 1898, straight after Zola had published 'J'Accuse'. Vizetelly had instantly stepped forward to support Zola for writing 'J'Accuse'. He pointed out that 'literary men' had occasionally failed in promoting the cause of justice but he wanted his readers to remember someone who had succeeded: Voltaire.

> . . . there lives in France at the present day a writer of books, novels, stories, and essays on art, literature, and social problems, who is regarded by many as an individual of scurrilous proclivities, a picker-up of filth and garbage, a reviler of religion, who is personally excommunicated, and several of whose books figure on the 'Index Expurgatorius' of Rome. His name is Émile Edouard Charles Antoine Zola. Truth has been the one passion of his life.
>
> I . . . venture to say that if he has come forward so prominently in this Dreyfus case, it is not because he feels that wrong has been done, but he is absolutely convinced of it.

Vizetelly made an analogy between Zola's writing method – meticulous research – and the kind of knowledge and proof he would have brought to the Dreyfus Affair. But in doing this, Zola was running a greater risk than Voltaire had faced.

Fanatical Jew-baiters march through the streets anxious
for an opportunity to wreck his house and murder not
only himself but his wife also in the sacred name of
Patriotism . . .

At the end, possibly, lie imprisonment, fine, disgrace,
ruin. How jubilantly some are already rubbing their
hands in the bishops' palaces, the parsonages, the
sacristies of France! Ah! no stone will be left unturned
to secure a conviction! But Émile Zola does not waver.
It may be that the truth, the whole truth, will only be
known to the world in some distant century; but he,
anxious to hasten its advent and prevent the irreparable,
couragcously stakes all that he has – person, position,
fame, affections and friendships, possibly even the best
of his declining years. And this he does for no personal
object whatsoever, but in the sole cause of truth and
justice, ever repeating the cry common to both Goethe
and himself, 'Light, more Light!'

Punch printed a cartoon of Zola, entitled 'The Dreyfus
"Scape-goat"', a parody of the famous painting by Holman
Hunt, and in February, when Zola himself was sentenced,
the *Manchester Guardian* wrote:

The condemnation of M. Zola yesterday to a year's
imprisonment will come as a shock to every generous
mind. At a time when France is torn by doubts as to
the integrity of the chiefs of her army, which have been
confirmed by the efforts of the Cabinet, the War Office,
and the Chambers to stifle discussion, M. Zola alone of

all Frenchmen has had the courage to accuse the War
Office of double-dealing, with the express purpose of
compelling inquiry into the facts of the case.

It was a heroic act. M. Zola had everything to lose
– the popularity which he has earned by years of toil
and upon which as a novelist he has to depend for a
livelihood, and even his personal liberty. On the other
hand, he had nothing to gain but the satisfaction of
having repaired a judicial error and rescued an innocent
man from a horrible captivity. Yet, in the teeth of the
Government and of public opinion, M. Zola took up the
cause of Dreyfus, and by his outspoken denunciations
of the War Office authorities drove the Government to
prosecute him.

Then the article turned to how Zola's own trial proceeded,
where he was forced into defending one tiny part of
'J'Accuse' – the part where he claimed that Esterhazy was
found innocent by those who knew he was guilty. It was a
'shameful burlesque', the paper said.

At the pleasure of the judge, witnesses might be cross-
examined for the defendant or they might be told to keep
silence; military witnesses might discuss the Dreyfus
affair if they wished to pledge their honour that Dreyfus
was guilty, but other witnesses must respect the chose
jugée; generals in uniform might address the jury in
impassioned terms, and then hold their peace when
asked to substantiate their assertions; if a witness gave
evidence reflecting on the War Office, the head of the Bar

must apologise to the generals present and assure them of his sympathy.

Such scenes as have occurred during the past fifteen days in the Paris Court of Assizes would be thought incredible on the stage or in a novel, and yet, after this mockery of justice, M. Zola is condemned. It speaks volumes for the dogged bravery of the man that he should have fought this cause to the last, and his glory is the disgrace of those who have deliberately trampled on the law to bring about his fall.

The *Daily Chronicle* of 24 February 1898 singled out Zola for personifying the honour of France, while all others betrayed it. The *Daily Telegraph* of the same day appeared to praise Zola's 'courage' for 'confronting' a tribunal in what he 'asserted to be a just cause' – the word 'asserted' being the classic journalese get-out of not appearing to agree with the cause too closely. More positively, the article said that, on hearing his sentence, Zola 'looked defiant and still full of fight'. *The Times* of that particular day presented Zola as having failed to do what he wanted, which was to use his own trial as an opportunity for practical revision of the Dreyfus case, but, 'It has been a rare intellectual treat for educated men everywhere to watch the *splendid fight* made by M. Zola's counsel against the heaviest odds.' Zola's 'offence' was to make himself:

the mouthpiece of the intelligent and thoughtful portion of the French public whose conscience has been profoundly disturbed and whose apprehensions of the safety of social rights have been aroused by the proceedings carried on in the name of French justice. His real offence is that he has dared to stand up for truth and civil liberty at a moment when many saw the peril but no other was ready to brave the extremity of personal danger in order to aid in averting it. For that courageous vindication of elementary civil rights he will be honoured wherever men have free souls.

At the same time, it was noted that Zola had taken a stand on anti-semitism. In *The Humanitarian* of February 1898, Robert Sherard, author of the biography of Zola in 1893, wrote: 'The cry of "À bas les Juifs" ('Down with the Jews') is to be heard all over Paris. To this the cry of "À bas Zola" ('Down with Zola') is now added ...'

Zola told Sherard that he was greatly surprised to find how widespread the anti-semitic movement was, and how great its force:

'It seems incredible to me,' Zola said, 'that one hundred years after the French Revolution, by which the equality of men was proclaimed and an end put to all enmities between races and creeds, it should be possible to raise up so many Frenchmen, grandsons of the Revolution, against other Frenchmen, because the latter are men of a different ethnical derivation, professing a different creed.'

Anti-semitism had been accepted by the mass of the people, Zola claimed, as the 'newest form of Socialism':

'The Jews have been made to represent in the eyes of the ignorant, the Have-Alls, the Capitalists, against whom the demagogues have always directed the furies of the proletariat. Instead of crying as they used to cry ten years ago, "Down with the Capitalists", the people are now taught to cry, "Down with the Jews", the leaders of the Anti-Semitic Campaign acting largely in the interests of the Catholic party, having induced them into the belief that all the capitalists are Jews, that it is the Jewish money which employs the labour of France, that the whole nation is a vassal to the purse of the Rothschilds, and such-like absurdities.'

The people were saying these things, Zola argued, knowing full well that it was an 'imbecility'. The words 'Capitalist' and 'Jew' were not synonymous: 'there are some very rich Jews in France, there are also thousands of poor Jews – of very poor Jews'. Zola saw in the campaign a return to the Middle Ages, an undoing of all that civilisation and enlightenment had done towards the realisation of what is the ideal of us all: 'the federation of man, the commonwealth of nations'.

'I have no words to express my abhorrence of it.

'. . . the Anti-Semites are shouting into the ears of the people that the destruction of Jews would mean the dawn of a new era which the demagogues of social reform have always been promising to their followers . . .

'We are trying to wipe out the frontiers of the nations, we are dreaming of the community of the peoples, we draw together into congresses the priests of all religions so that they may fall into each other's arms, we feel ourselves the brothers in the common sufferings of humanity, and we wish to work for the relief of all from the pains of existence by raising up a single altar to Human Pity. And a handful of madmen, cunning or idiotic, come and shout in our ears every morning: "Let us kill the Jews. Let us devour the Jews. Let us massacre them. Let us exterminate them. Let us get back to the days of the gibbet and stake." Is it not inconceivable? Could anything be more foolish? Could anything be more abominable? . . .

'Anti-Semitism as it exists to-day in France is a hypocritical form of Socialism.'

As for the accusation that Jews have 'no love for anything but the acquisition of wealth by the labour of others', Zola pointed out that if Jews had 'superiority' in the matter of money-getting it was because 'we trained them to this in an apprenticeship of eighteen hundred years'.

During those eighteen hundred years of cruel persecution, when we herded them like lepers in the ghetto, when we insulted them and outraged them and beat them, living like a conquered people amongst their conquerors . . . [i]t was then and there that they learned the science of finance, for the trade of money was the only occupation which contemptuously was abandoned to them.

Then Sherard turned his attention to the 'syndicate' – the supposed conspiracy of Jews which was supporting Dreyfus. Zola replied,

'The famous syndicate of which I am supposed to be a member. That is all sheer nonsense. There are as many Jews against Dreyfus as there are for him, more indeed . . . There is no syndicate of Jews to free Dreyfus. There is no syndicate of Jews, the world over, for any purpose. That they are helpful to each other, that amongst members of no other religious faith is there such great solidarity, that a Jew can always count on the assistance of his fellows is a fact, and the primary cause of this . . . is that they were bound together by centuries of common suffering . . .'

In truth, though this was presented as an interview, much of it was taken from Zola's articles on anti-semitism written before he joined the campaign to free Dreyfus. However, this was one of the first occasions when these articles would have been seen in English and shows how Zola's profile in Britain was changing just prior to his exile. No matter how odd or imperfect Zola's arguments against racism towards Jews were, they remain one of the few examples at this time of a non-Jew taking a stance against anti-semitism. Even rarer was to find a socialist of any complexion taking up this position, and it was through Zola's attachment first to the Dreyfus case, then through convincing Jaurès to join in, that the socialist movement started to argue against anti-semitism.

The official voice for the British Jewish community at this time was the *Jewish Chronicle*. On 21 January 1898 it described 'J'Accuse' as a 'bold step'. It reported on the anti-semitic riots and attacks on Jews, with 'Anarchists' fighting the 'anti-Semites' in the fog in a Paris street. 'Professors' were almost the only people supporting Zola, it said. The paper criticised *The Times* for not giving Zola 'sufficient credit for the public spirit of his action ... but it fails, we think, to recognise the keynote of M. Zola's literary temper, namely devotion to truth for its own sake.' This will 'justify him in history even if he has to suffer very severely in the present ...'

A week later, Zola was described as 'incisive' and the paper published 'J'Accuse' in its entirety as a supplement. Again, in great detail it reported on the anti-semitic outbreaks and attacks. Just as Zola was leaving England in June 1899, one 'J. M. L.' wrote to the paper. The letter was given the heading, 'Testimonial to Zola':

It seems to me that the time has arrived when every Jew and Jewess in every part of the world ought to desire to shew their full recognition of the valuable service rendered to the cause of Judaism by the one man and he (an alien to the Jewish faith) the great man Zola, whose courage and energy in the cause of right and justice, has been the means of bringing to light the unjust sentence passed on the unfortunate Dreyfus. I therefore propose that a subscription be raised to present him with a suitable testimonial to shew that his great work has found an echo in the heart of every lover of Judaism and justice. Should this suggestion take root, I shall be pleased to send my 'widow's mite'.

How representative of mainstream Jewish opinion this was is not clear, other than to say that the paper wouldn't have published it unless it had some currency.

In the *Contemporary Review* of April 1898, David Christie
Murray reviewed the Zola trial and said of Zola, 'I still think
his methods mistaken. I still think his work baneful. But I
shall never again do him the injustice to doubt the loftiness
and essential purity of his desire.' He also brought an image
of Zola in court to English speakers: 'In his anxiety to be
heard throughout the hall he pitched his voice too high, and
the effect was painfully harsh and dissonant. He cracked into
a shrill falsetto, and the crowd at the back of the court broke
into a roar of insulting laughter.' Murray also made clear that
he was prepared to overcome his dislike of Zola's 'rhetoric' to
approve of his actions.

More positive was the *National Review*. Between March
1898 and October 1899 the editor, Leo Maxse, devoted many
pages to campaigning for the revision of the Dreyfus case and
analysed 'J'Accuse' in positive tones. As evidence of the way in
which Zola passed into mythic or proverbial consciousness at
this time, the historian Martyn Cornick cites the example of
Conan Doyle, who 'assumed Zola's mantle' when defending
a 'foreign' solicitor's wrongful imprisonment a few years later.

Three books appeared on the Dreyfus case in 1899, each
with thoughts on Zola's intervention. In order of how far on
in the progress of the Affair they were written, they were: *The
Dreyfus Case* by Fred. C. Conybeare; *A History of the Dreyfus
Case* by George Barlow; and *The Tragedy of Dreyfus* by G. W.
Steevens.

Conybeare devoted a chapter to Zola. As was customary,
he distanced himself from what he called Zola's 'indecencies'
but he didn't join with others in condemning 'the excessive
vigour of his denunciations' in 'J'Accuse'. It was only

Zola's 'fierce denunciation' that had brought the matter to the attention of the nation. 'The time was past for gentler methods, and he penned that most terrible of all philippics, his letter beginning "J'accuse".' Conybeare also bore witness to the vehemence of the language used in court against Zola:

> The Procureur-Général said, 'M. Zola has defamed others, because he is gifted with immeasurable pride, because he fancies himself as being the Messiah of the ideal, and representing the genius of France, to have the power of driving deep into the rebellious conscience of the nation a distrust of the court-martial's verdict . . .'

Barlow was more expansive in his admiration of Zola's actions: a man of 'perfect good faith ... he was fighting against France for the sake of France'. Readers of Zola's prose essays would know that 'he loves truth and hates humbug with a thoroughly English love and hate ...' What's more, anyone who had read his novel *La Débâcle* would know that he was someone who could write a 'complete and unflinching exposure of the causes which led to the disastrous break-down of the French army in 1870 ...' In fact, according to Barlow, the French generals had never forgiven Zola for telling the world the whole truth about their predecessors of 1870. And now, in similar fashion, what Zola had done was break down the 'conspiracy of silence' around the Dreyfus case.

In summing up the contribution Zola had made through 'J'Accuse' and his defence of it in court, Barlow claimed that Zola 'had acted from the most generous and humane motives, from love of France and true regard for his country's honour, and with the most absolute good faith' – all presumably extremely positive aspects of his character to lay before a British readership. What's more, Zola had 'saved the honour of French literary men'.

In contrast, everything thrown at Zola was, according to Barlow, 'illegal' because it was all based on what had originally been an illegality; Zola spoke 'the absolute truth' against someone like one M. Tessonnière, a candidate for the ninth arrondissement of Paris, who in his election address thought he could disprove the statement 'I don't know if Dreyfus is guilty or not,' with 'All Jews are traitors.' In other words, argues Barlow, Tessionnière was saying that Dreyfus was guilty because he was a Jew.

Barlow also reminded his British readers that Zola's opponents in the *Libre Parole* called him the 'Italian pig' and revelled in the moment at the end of Zola's trial when 'thousands of throats wild with fury' shouted 'Down with the traitors! Down with Zola! Death to the Jews!' Barlow quoted *Libre Parole* saying:

Zola's face is the colour of buttered eggs. He, so full of swagger when he left the Court, has now suddenly hidden himself at the bottom of the carriage. He is crouching quite down, and nothing but his head is visible, emerging from between the knees of the two Clemenceaus . . . The truth is marching along, and Zola is in flight, although, there are in the neighbouring woods such lovely branches . . . natural gibbets.

An incitement to lynching if ever there was one.

In supporting Zola against the 'argument' that his father was a deserter, Barlow countered that Zola had inherited from his father the 'capacity for ceaseless toil in the face of giant obstacles, and an invincible tenacity of purpose', a reference to his father's struggle to build a harbour in Marseilles (unsuccessful) and to build a canal in Aix (successful). Barlow also wanted to show that Zola did not flee justice in July 1898: 'It was not Zola's object *not to* be tried. It was his object to be tried, but *to be* tried fairly, and in the course of a fair and public trial to bring facts to light which would make the revision of the Dreyfus case a necessity.' Barlow quipped, 'Therefore ... M. Zola ... retired for a season to the North Pole.'

In Steevens, Zola is very much in the shadow of the main players, though seen as virtuous more by dint of backing a victim of injustice than anything said directly about him.

So, though Zola's reputation in Britain was in some ways inextricable from the Dreyfus case, it's clear that by the time of the demonstration against the judgment of Rennes, Zola's stand was widely admired and celebrated.

The Hyde Park demonstration took place on Sunday 17 September 1899. Two days later, Dreyfus was pardoned by the President of France, Émile Loubet. Though this was a momentous decision giving Dreyfus freedom, it was in a narrow legalistic sense meaningless: a military court had found him guilty, so it was only a military court that could find him innocent. To date, this has never happened, neither in Dreyfus's own life or posthumously.

On 22 September Zola published another article in *L'Aurore*, in the form of a highly emotional and rhetorical letter to Madame Alfred Dreyfus. For him the pardon wasn't

enough. He wanted the judgment overturned in the Supreme
Court of Appeal:

> The innocent, having been condemned twice, did more
> for the fraternity of peoples, for the idea of solidarity
> and justice, than a hundred years of philosophical dis-
> cussions, and humanitarian theories ... It is us, the
> poets, who have nailed the guilty parties to the pillory.
> Those whom we condemn will be scorned and booed by
> generations to come. The names of criminals, once we
> have heaped infamy upon them, will be no more than
> vile, human wrecks ['*épaves immondes*'] for years to come.

Fifteen months later, on 22 December 1900, another
double-edged decision was made: the National Assembly
passed an Amnesty Law that officially pardoned everyone
who had been part of the Dreyfus case.
Denise observed:

> When, in May 1900, the proposal concerning an amnesty
> law was put before the Senate, Zola made his opposition
> known against this measure, which would absolve the
> innocent and the guilty, the criminal and the just, without
> establishing any distinction between the two. He said,
> 'The law to remove the case from the courts ['*dessaisisse-
> ment*'] has been a legal crime, the amnesty law will be
> a piece of civic treachery.' Eventually, seven months
> later, on 22 December 1900, Zola wrote a last article,
> addressed to Émile Loubet, President of the Republic:
> 'That's more than eighteen months that I have been

waiting for justice, having been given notice every three months, and knocked back every three months to the next session.' Labori said of the amnesty law that it was a 'law of weakness and powerlessness'; Zola couldn't accept it without rebelling against it; he would have wanted the case to be heard again, as someone who 'had accused others on the facts, which a Supreme Court enquiry had shown to be absolutely true'.

The Dreyfus Affair was over but not over.

Denise wrote: 'From that time on, Émile Zola only wanted to live away from all this, having made up his mind to safeguard his peaceful working life as an intellectual.'

On the domestic front, while all this was going on, between 7 October and 2 December 1899, Alexandrine stayed in Italy. In remembering this time, Denise's memoir becomes emotional:

My father, my dear father! The image of the garden in Verneuil, the big white house, the apartment in Paris, rises up before me, along with that of my parents! There at Verneuil, what beautiful outings I had next to them, on our bicycles through the woods in the summer of 1899. The bicycles that he promised my brother and me in England, he didn't wait a moment to give those presents to us . . . My father took photographs with the passion he gave to everything. They remain as living testimony of our intimacy. Ah! the happiness of those years, between my father and my mother, in the tenderness of their relationship, so trusting and so faithful!

My brother loved science and with great pleasure Zola watched his son's interest in this grow; he found books on botany for him. Chantôme, our gardener, who loved his job, was almost a scientist; Jacques spent many hours asking him questions about the plants. My father did botany with us, and they ended up training me. We also knew an old sand quarry where fossils could be found. Zola talked endlessly about work, he never moaned about us, but he wanted to save us from laziness; he was very involved with our education, oversaw our holiday homework so that we didn't neglect it.

I was a very positive little girl, who wanted to get to the bottom of mysteries ['*fond des mystères*'*]. Yes, I was very pious, the poetry of legends attracted me no end . . .

My father enjoyed taking me through my learning of the catechism . . .

And also, throughout this time, Zola was writing novels.

On 24 October, in 'A Visit to M. Émile Zola at Home' in *Le XIXe Siècle*, he talked about his time in England, writing *Fécondité* and preparing to write *Travail*. He was looking forward to sketching out the ideal socialist city. The following novel, *Vérité*, would be based on science. 'I never stop believing in science,' Zola told the journalist. 'Science gives us the morality and the aesthetics of the future society.' While the Catholic doctrine said that work should be about punishment and suffering, he would show that work was a good thing, with a sacred function. It was only through work

---

* This has religious connotations as the phrase appears in particular in Christian commentaries.

that we felt good and we found happiness. That was one of his most dearly felt beliefs, he said.

Then, in his last book, *Justice*, he would throw himself into a total utopia. 'It'll be a dream, a lyrical apotheosis of humanity on the march towards beauty and goodness. All in all, a great poem.'

What after that? the journalist asked. Perhaps he would go to live on the Balearic Islands. There he would be far from his struggles, his defeats and his victories. He would spend his last years contemplating nature with great peace of mind.

In her memoir of her father, Denise described Zola writing *Travail*:

Hardly had he returned from exile, when he got down to bringing together the materials he needed for *Travail* in June 1899. He had accumulated more notes than ever, lingering for a long time over works which dealt with the social question or with industrial technique, anarchism, metallurgy, large furnaces and electricity. He was drawn to the works of Charles Fourier and his followers; he dreamt of creating a city in the image of the socialist phalanstery.

Having started on the book, Zola wanted to spend some time at the house of M. Ménard-Dorian, and at the factories of Unieux, in the Loire. He had thought of a glassworks for the setting of his novel, but he chose a steelworks instead. And that explained his attraction to the Gallery of Machines in the Champ de Mars at the Exhibition of 1900, Denise wrote:

We spent hours there. My father watched, listened, clearly fascinated; as for myself, I admit that this mass of fire, of wheels, turning in an indescribable racket wasn't at all enjoyable for me, while Jacques followed our father every step of the way, showering him with questions.

Denise noted that Zola's theory that work could be made attractive excited a number of young intellectuals. They jumped on the idea that science could be linked to co-operative action, a marriage of science and communism that seemed revolutionary. A sense of what he was thinking about in terms of literary intention and theory emerges in a letter. On 1 December 1900 he wrote to Maurice Le Blond, saying that novelists can't lock themselves up in an ivory tower, they can't isolate themselves in a pure dream world, and remain indifferent to the dramas of everyday life.

Everyone must take action, everyone understands that it's a social crime not to act in times as grave as these, when evil forces of the past battle against the energies of tomorrow. It's necessary to decide if humanity is not going to take one step backwards, not going to fall once again into error, into slavery, perhaps for another century.

Zola saw in Le Blond's work that he and his colleagues were giving affirmation to 'the necessity of life, of human truth and social usefulness'.

In an interview with Amédée Boyer he said that he thought that the literature of the twentieth century would be 'social'. The great movement for democracy that he had contributed to would influence literary taste, tendencies and the feelings of writers. More and more, books would paint an exact picture of the habits and aspirations of the people. Workers with their unions and committees would enjoy novels as much as the theatre. He thought that literature would tend more and more in the future towards being a great philosophical and social inquiry. 'In politics and literature, we can see a great movement amongst young people that gives me hope that the powers of reaction won't win in any long-lasting way.'

Far from *not* writing about Dreyfus, as Zola had promised, in actual fact the third novel in the *Quatre Évangiles* series, *Vérité* (*Truth*) was very much a reflection on the Dreyfus case. It tells the story of a Jew who is wrongly accused and unjustly found guilty of a crime. He is taken away from his family and sent to a prison camp for many years while his supporters fight for justice for him! After their campaigning, he is finally recalled for a re-trial where his supporters are able to produce new facts proving that the original verdict was wrong. The novel also follows the shape of the Dreyfus case in that it tells of the accused man being freed but then found guilty again in a new trial (as happened to Dreyfus at Rennes). He is finally pardoned. When Vizetelly put it in front of English-speaking readers he made it quite clear – in great detail, actually! – that *Vérité* was a reworking of the Dreyfus case. I suspect that by doing so, he thought it would help make the book more popular.

As always with Zola, even as he was finishing off *Truth*, he started to make plans for the fourth *Évangile, Justice*. The hero was going to be a soldier who was a pacifist, convinced of the need for world disarmament. Peace and happiness for all would come from the setting-up of a universal republic, which would defeat militarism and the nationalisms of separate countries. He envisaged France at the head of this project 'but for science, not armaments', he scribbled on one of his papers. One bête-noire of the book would have been Rudyard Kipling, whom he described in his notes as religious, egotistical, militaristic, colonialist and monarchist, with Kipling seen as an embodiment of Britishness at the time. The anti-colonialist stance that Zola seems to have been adopting here was in direct contrast to the pro-colonialist viewpoint he celebrated at the end of *Fécondité* where the fruitful Mathieu Froment fertilises and civilises a 'savage' Africa.

It could be said that one of the contradictions that Zola struggled with throughout the period of the Dreyfus case, his exile and the last months of his life was that the France he wanted (republican, humanist, secular, democratic and evolving towards socialism) was not the France he had written about in 'J'Accuse', faced in his own trials, or fulminated against in his most miserable moments in exile. So when, in his literary mind, he placed France at the head of a movement to humanise the world, this was a France that he knew didn't exist yet. What's more, by identifying imperialism as an evil that other powers were guilty of, he had either to efface the imperialism of France itself or claim that whatever France did, could do or should do outside of its own borders was as a humane, civilising force.

Returning to personal affairs: between 1901 and 1902, Denise says that Zola went out more often with them. Every autumn, Alexandrine went for the 'cure' in Salsomaggiore in

Italy so Denise and her brother looked forward to October when Zola would be with them more than usual. Zola wanted them to get to know Paris. He took them to the theatre. Sometimes he took them out to a top restaurant and once, after dining out in the one on the Eiffel Tower (very 'top'), they were there when the lights came on and they watched illuminated fountains of the 'Château d'Eau'. They went to hear Sarah Bernhardt in *L'Aiglon* – Zola thought she wouldn't be acting for much longer; they sat in the box at the Opéra Comique. But all this peace and pleasure came to an end on 29 September 1902.

At this point, Denise's account makes painful reading. In September, she says, he always had nightmares. He didn't like going back to the city from Médan. On 22 September he went out on the Seine in his new boat, *L'Enfant-roi*. They had all been out on their bikes and waited from him by the bridge at Triel. Then they all went out on the boat till it reached the islands at Médan.

> I thought it was easy to jump on to the bank and tie the chain to a tree, but my foot slipped and I sank into the soft mud. I called out for help from my father. He quickly came and helped me and didn't have too much trouble pulling me out of the water with all his strength. However, my mother hadn't realised the danger as I was running and laughing about it. The outing was spoiled thanks to me, as I had to stay in the sun in order to get dry. This was one of our last outings with my father.
>
> On 27 September, he came to give us a hug at Verneuil and we all had to go back the following day to Paris

... We stood at the door watching him going into the distance, turning his head towards us for a last time, before disappearing round the corner of the road. We wouldn't see him again till we saw him on his deathbed a few days later.

It was, says Denise, a 'frightful catastrophe' for Jeanne and her two children.

What happened was that Zola and Alexandrine made a fire in their bedroom. They noticed that the coal briquettes (*'boulets'*) weren't 'taking', the *'valet'* came and opened the flue. Later he came back again, saw that the fire was going well and closed the flue. In the night, Alexandrine got up to go to the toilet. No doubt she saved her life by breathing in some fresh air there. Zola was feeling ill but wouldn't call a servant at this time of night because it would have disturbed the servant's sleep. According to Denise, he wanted to get up, open the window to get rid of the awful sickness he had; Alexandrine had passed out on the bed and was unable to fetch help when he fell onto the carpet.

Oh! my mother's cry when she learned what had happened but imagined that someone had killed Zola! Her gesture, her arms outstretched, closing around us, her sorrow and ours! I don't know how we lived in that week . . .

Perhaps Jeanne's first thoughts were nearer to the mark than Denise thought. Zola died of carbon monoxide poisoning. On 14 October, two architects dismantled the flue but didn't find enough to suggest that it was blocked.

However, in 1953, the newspaper *Libération* received a letter from one M. Hacquin, claiming that he knew that Zola had been murdered. A friend of his was a stove-fitter and an anti-Dreyfusard. In 1927, this friend had made a confession to him:

> I'll tell you how Zola died ... Zola was deliberately suffocated. I and my men blocked his chimney while doing the repairs on the roof next door. There was a lot of coming and going and we took advantage of the hubbub to locate Zola's chimney and stop it. We unstopped it the next day, very early. No one noticed us.

It seems possible, if not probable, that Zola paid for his courage with his life, just as Jeanne suspected.

On 5 October at Zola's funeral at Montmartre cemetery, Anatole France said: 'Let us envy him. His destiny and his heart reserved for him the most superb of fates: he was a moment in the conscience of mankind'.

At the point when they closed the coffin, someone asked Alexandrine if they ought to put in pictures of his children. 'And one of their mother,' she replied.

Less than two months after Zola's death, she invited the children to come over for a meal. Denise who used to call her 'Bonne Amie', replied 'Chère Amie' ('Dear Friend'), they would be a little late, on account of Jacques being out learning his catechism. Letters passed between Jeanne and Alexandrine for the rest of Jeanne's life – she died before Alexandrine. The letters talked of Dreyfus and, for three years, Jacques's serious illness, osseous tuberculosis.

On the financial side, Alexandrine made sure that Jeanne and the children received 6,000 francs every three months. Given the decline in popularity of Zola's novels post-'J'Accuse', added to the fact that he wasn't alive to write any more, this was some sacrifice on Alexandrine's part. She paid for Denise's private education with Madame Dieterlen. None of this was legally required of her. In the eyes of society at the time, a woman paying for the upkeep of her late husband's mistress and her children was, says Bloch-Dano 'a little unconventional'. After the formal session which discussed the children's livelihoods, Zola's musical collaborator Alfred Bruneau noticed the two women going off down the street side by side.

In letters, Jeanne talked of 'our' two little darlings, 'our' grave (meaning Zola's) and when she placed a bouquet on the grave, 'I united the two of you in my thoughts'. Alexandrine accordingly talked of 'our' two dear treasures, and 'my hand is tied to yours, affectionately sharing the worries you feel . . .' Zola was 'our great and adored friend'.

On 12 July 1906, with all Chambers of the Supreme Court of Appeal sitting jointly, the court revoked the verdict reached by the court martial in Rennes and declared that in reaching the verdict of guilty against Alfred Dreyfus, the court martial was 'in the wrong'. Denise writes:

The rehabilitation of Alfred Dreyfus did not take place until . . . 12 July 1906, so Zola did not experience the great happiness of being able to assist in writing an epilogue to the Affair, which would have been, at one and the same time, his revenge and his triumph.

On 13 July 1906 the Chamber of Deputies passed a law reinstating both Dreyfus and Picquart in the army, Dreyfus with the rank of major and Picquart with that of brigadier general. On the same day, the Chamber passed a bill asking that Zola's ashes be transferred to the Panthéon.

Major Esterhazy (who wrote the *bordereau* used to incriminate Dreyfus) benefited from the Amnesty Law. For safety's sake, though, he moved permanently to England, living with a woman in London, where they were known as Mr and Mrs Fitzgerald. In 1909 they moved to Harpenden, Hertfordshire, successfully posing as Count and Countess de Voilement, while he wrote the occasional anti-semitic article for journals back in France, until his death in 1923 aged seventy-four.

In November 1906 Alexandrine began the legal process of giving the children the surname 'Émile-Zola', all or part of which his descendants have borne ever since. It was a remarkable gesture.

On 3 June 1908 Zola's remains were exhumed from the cemetery in Montmartre, with Alexandrine, Denise, Jacques, Bruneau and Desmoulin present amongst others. A huge crowd greeted the cortège on its way to the Panthéon; the atmosphere was noisy and violent, with both sides shouting at each other; 5,000 anti-Dreyfusards tried to block the way. Alexandrine walked towards the Panthéon, followed by Jeanne, Denise and Jacques, then Alfred and Lucie Dreyfus.

At the ceremony, on the following day, the 'Marseillaise' was played followed by the prelude to 'Messidor' and Beethoven's 'Marche funèbre' while Alexandrine, Jeanne, Denise and Jacques and a number of Zola's closest friends grouped themselves around the tomb. At that point two shots rang out; chaos followed as Mathieu Dreyfus wrestled with a journalist, Louis Grégori, who had fired the shots, wounding Dreyfus in the arm. Later, when Zola's casket was placed next to that of Victor Hugo in the crypt, Alexandrine, Jeanne, Denise and Jacques sat together on their own with the tombs.

In October 1908 Alexandrine Émile-Zola, as she had become, was present at Denise's marriage to Maurice Le Blond. Jeanne died in 1914 at the age of forty-seven from an operation that went wrong. Alexandrine lived till 1925. Among the last people to see her alive were Françoise and Jean-Claude Le Blond, Émile and Jeanne's grand-children.

Postscript

Zola's exile, imposed on him by friends, was not, in the overall run of things, a calamity, nor was it anything like the near-death ordeal experienced by Dreyfus. Yet Zola took it extremely badly, suffering what seems from a modern perspective to be two nervous breakdowns. Balancing the three spheres of his life, political, literary and personal, sometimes overcame him.

In the midst of this, there were delights that he had never experienced before and would never experience again. The summer of 1898 lived on as an idyll, we know, for Zola and Denise and probably for Jeanne and Jacques too. No matter what we might think of the *Quatre Évangiles* today, writing *Fécondité* gave him an immense sense of pleasure and achievement. Difficult and stressful though it was, the three adults' domestic arrangement by the end of the period reached a degree of tranquillity.

We shall never know what Zola would have written or done had he stayed alive for another ten or twenty years. He seemed intent on withdrawing from the political sphere. His writing had taken a utopian turn: it might have carried on, or it might have turned back to its mix of naturalism, social realism and symbolism. What would he have made of the outbreak of hostilities in 1914?

What we do know is that, at a crucial moment in 1897, he

made a brave, unpopular, self-sacrificing decision to support a wrongly convicted man. This decision drew on Zola's awareness of injustice and his sense of the need for truth in governing our affairs. Finding himself in conflict with Left and Right over the matter of anti-semitism, he established a line of argument from outside Judaism, outside the Jewish communities, as to why prejudice, discrimination and persecution were wrong. I don't think that the importance of this can be overestimated. When you trace the statements of French and British socialists leading up to and through the Dreyfus case, it is only when Zola had convinced Jaurès and Jaurès had convinced the French socialists and the French socialists had convinced the British ones that anti-antisemitism became a point of principle.

No matter how egotistical or irritating Zola may appear to us now, as he moans about English boiled potatoes or, we might say, leads what is in effect a bigamous existence, his stand and the sacrifices he made make him a hero in my eyes.

Not that this moment marks a point in which these matters were resolved. Forty years later, events in wartime France were a tragic re-run of the battles that Zola took part in, when the anti-Dreyfus camp and its inheritors found that they had four years or so to show what they could do if they had some real power. The meticulous lists of foreign-born Jews that were handed to Nazi administrators were compiled by the public servants of the Vichy regime. On a personal note, my father's uncles were added to these lists and with some 76,000 others were seized, put on trains and deported to Auschwitz, where they died. One of them, Oscar 'Jeschie' Rosen, was on the same 'convoy', Convoi 62, as Dreyfus's granddaughter Madeleine Dreyfus Lévy. Zola's and Jaurès's words and actions speak to events that have occurred since the 1890s.

In 2014, my wife, Emma-Louise Williams, made a programme for BBC Radio 3 called 'Zola in Norwood', which I presented. We visited Zola's house in Médan, which is now a museum, the Maison Zola. We had an appointment to talk to Madame Martine Le Blond-Zola, the great-granddaughter of Émile Zola. She is the vice-chair of the Association for the Maison Zola–Musée Dreyfus and is responsible for the everyday running of the house, as well as overseeing the building work while the house is being restored. We didn't know that a Dreyfus Museum was being included in the restoration plans, and Madame Le Blond-Zola explained that it will not only be dedicated to the Dreyfus Affair but will also be a place for fighting discrimination: against racism, anti-semitism, homophobia – against all forms of discrimination – and the Dreyfus Affair will be an illustration of that.

We sat in the garden with our two children who were then about the same age as Zola's children in the time frame of this book – not that Zola ever brought them to the house at Médan. You can see the Seine from the house, but between the two runs the railway to Paris. The suburban grandeur of the house and garden was and still is bisected by modernity. In Zola's day, the sight and sound of steam trains chuffing through his garden would have mingled with the lawns and trees. Verneuil, where Jeanne and the children lived when Zola and Alexandrine were in Médan, is nearby but that's in private hands.

We sat on a bench and talked. Madame Le Blond-Zola didn't ever meet her grandmother, Denise, as Denise died before Madame Le Blond-Zola was born. She told us how Denise was remembered through family oral tradition, especially from Madame's father who talked a great deal about Denise, his mother. Denise is also known in the family and beyond for her children's books. In *Les Années Heureuses* ('*The Happy Years*') she wrote what is in effect a disguised memoir of her childhood. One passage talks of 'a good and kind father, older than his wife by some few years, big and strong, greying, very affable, who was adored by his children'.

We see him standing on the steps of a terrace overlooking the garden, listening to the children playing. He creeps up on them, to surprise them.

'That's three times I've been calling for you. What game were you playing that you were so absorbed in? Ah yes, Mummy told me. Come on, come in and have something to eat.'

He took each of them by the hand and laughing and chatting, all three of them went into the dining-room.

Madame Le Blond-Zola talked around the relationships between Alexandrine, Jeanne and the children:

Denise very much respected Madame Zola [Alexandrine] and must have known that Madame Zola had lost a little girl when she was 19. And she was very respectful towards her. Though there were the outings with Madame Zola to the Tuileries gardens on Thursdays, Denise only really got to know Madame Zola after Zola's death. Eventually, the two had a great deal of affection for each other. Madame Zola found in Denise the little girl she had lost and who could have been like Denise. At the same time, Denise was fond of her, thinking that she reminded Madame Zola of her own little girl she had lost.

We talked about Zola's 'engagement' in the Dreyfus case, and Madame pointed out that at the time, there were very few '*intellectuels engagés*' (politically committed intellectuals).

So Zola was an example of courage, citizenship and bravery. That's the reputation he has now, but in his own lifetime, he was hated and people threatened him. People wrote him insulting letters and he was called a '*métèque*' [a racist term for immigrants from the Mediterranean]. He was badly treated in his lifetime but now he's been rehabilitated and that's very impressive, very moving and it feels very good to say so. He is an example of someone who sought justice and truth through a fight against intolerance.

On another level altogether, we talked about Zola's photographs, and Madame said that her father told her that Denise and Jacques would complain about the amount of time their father took making them pose for photos.

That's why we hardly ever see them smiling in the pictures. Back then, you weren't supposed to smile, you had to be very serious, otherwise the photo might end up being blurry, though there's one where Zola put Denise on his bicycle and she was afraid of falling off. She looks very tense, very stressed.

Personally, Madame said, she finds them a bit sad:

The time all four of them were in England was a precious moment for them. Zola was suffering but it was a solace for him and it was the only time when all four of them lived together as a family, night and day. If you think about it, they had about six weeks in all living together out of a lifetime. It's not a lot.

I said that it was as a result of an extraordinary act of generosity on Alexandrine's part. Madame thought so too:

all the more so since she had said to Jeanne, you go and see Zola first. She gave priority to Jeanne. Perhaps it was partly due to the fact that it was the children's holiday, though. If Zola had gone into exile in the autumn, perhaps Madame Zola might have joined him first.

I asked her how she felt about Jeanne, her great-grandmother.

She said she led a life almost as a recluse, rather isolated, under the rule of Madame Zola, who was a very authoritarian figure:

Let's just say that she wasn't very happy. She was a very gentle woman, doubtless very authoritarian in her own way and we can see that by the way she held herself ['*sa stature*']. But she was unhappy because she was under Madame Zola's rule ['*soumise à Madame Zola*'] We shouldn't forget that when Madame Zola received the anonymous letter claiming that Zola had a second family, Madame Zola turned up at Jeanne's house, pushed open the door and broke everything.

Jeanne was very afraid of Alexandrine, very afraid indeed. And you can understand why. So my great-grandmother was unhappy at being ruled in this way.

I said that it was very hard to 'find' Jeanne Rozerot, as her letters don't survive.

Madame said that Jeanne was 'in her':

I feel her. I know her life, and I can imagine it at an intimate level, viscerally, how she could have been. And I think she was a woman who wasn't happy. That's what I'm saying to you. I really feel how she could have been.

Madame confirmed that they didn't have the letters from Jeanne. 'Madame Zola must have destroyed them. She must have sent letters to London but they've disappeared. She kept the letters sent in the other direction, but perhaps Madame Zola ripped up Jeanne's letters.'

Then we came to 'J'Accuse'.

Madame said that she was proud of Zola, but was also someone who admired him for this act of courage, and that she was his descendant:

He was prepared to sacrifice all the comfort that he had enjoyed up till then. That kind of commitment is magnificent. That's why the whole world admires him and he has such a great reputation. It was an exceptional event looked at from that time, no other person would have dared to do it.

I asked her how she thought intellectuals and thinkers had inherited Zola's ideas and what he did.

'J'Accuse' became a kind of leitmotif for intellectuals. On the other hand there were those who were against. When he died it was difficult – and frightening. In his declaration to the jury, Zola said, 'One day, France will be grateful to me.' Well, he was moved to the Panthéon in 1908. But he did what he did to save the Republic, to save France and to get an innocent man back from the penal colony. He couldn't understand why he was condemned to a year in prison and a fine of 3,000 francs . . . and he had to escape, something he didn't want to do. He wanted to go to prison but his lawyer and Clemenceau told him no, you have to leave . . .

Indeed. He had to leave.

Angeline*

Nearly two years ago I was spinning on my bicycle over a deserted road towards Orgeval, above Poissy, when the sudden sight of a wayside house caused me such surprise that I sprang from my machine to take a better look at it. It was a brick-built house, with no marked characteristics, and it stood under the grey November sky, amid the cold wind which was sweeping away the dead leaves, in the centre of spacious grounds planted with old trees. That which rendered it remarkable, which lent it an aspect of fierce, wild, savage strangeness of a nature to oppress the heart, was the frightful abandonment into which it had fallen. And as part of the iron gate was torn away, and a huge notice-board, with lettering half-effaced by the rain, announced that the place was for sale, I entered the garden, yielding to curiosity mingled with uneasiness and anguish.

The house must have been unoccupied for thirty or perhaps forty years. The bricks of the cornices and facings had been disjointed by past winters, and were overgrown with moss and lichen. Cracks, suggestive of precocious wrinkles, scarred the frontage of the building, which looked strong, though no care whatever was now taken of it. The steps below, split by frost, and shut off by nettles and brambles, formed, as it were, a threshold of desolation and death. But the frightful

---

* Or 'The Haunted House', translated by Ernest Vizetelly.

mournfulness of the place came more particularly from its bare, curtainless, glaucous windows, whose panes had been broken by stone-throwing urchins, and which, one and all, revealed the desolate emptiness of the rooms, like dim eyes that had remained wide open in some soulless corpse. Then, too, the spacious garden all around was a scene of devastation; the old flower-beds could scarce be discerned beneath the growth of rank weeds; the paths had disappeared, devoured by hungry plants; the shrubberies had grown to virgin forests; there was all the wild vegetation of some abandoned cemetery in the damp gloom beneath the huge and ancient trees, whose last leaves were that day being swept off by the autumn wind, which ever shrieked its doleful plaint.

Long did I linger there amidst that despairing wail of Nature, for though my heart was oppressed by covert fear, by growing anguish, I was detained by a feeling of ardent pity, a longing to know and to sympathise with all the woe and grief that I felt around me. And when at last I had left the spot and perceived across the road, at a point where the latter forked, a kind of tavern, a hovel where drink was sold, I entered it, fully resolved to question the folks of the neighbourhood.

But I only found there an old woman who sighed and whimpered as she served me a glass of beer. She complained of living on that out-of-the-way road, along which not even a couple of cyclists passed each day. And she talked on interminably, telling me her story, relating that she was called Mother Toussaint, that she and her man had come from Vernon to take that tavern, that things had turned out fairly well at first, but that all had been going from bad to worse since she had become a widow. When, after her rush of words, I began to question her respecting the neighbouring house, she suddenly became circumspect, and glanced at me suspiciously as if she thought that I wished to tear some dread secret from her.

'Ah, yes,' said she, 'La Sauvagiere, the haunted house, as people say hereabouts ... For my part, I know nothing, monsieur, it doesn't date from my time. I shall have only been here thirty years come next Easter, and those things go back to well-nigh forty years now. When we came here the house was already much as you see it. The summers pass, the winters pass, and nothing stirs unless it be the stones that fall.'

'But why,' I asked – 'why is the place not sold, since it is for sale?'

'Ah! why? Why? Can I tell? People say so many things.'

I was doubtless beginning to inspire her with some confidence. Besides, at heart she must have been burning to tell me the many things that people said. She began by relating that not one of the girls of the neighbouring village ever dared to enter La Sauvagiere after twilight, for rumour had it that some poor wandering soul returned thither every night. And, as I expressed astonishment that such a story could still find any credit so near to Paris, she shrugged her shoulders, tried to talk like a strong-minded woman, but finally betrayed by her manner the terror she did not confess.

'There are facts that can't be denied, monsieur. You ask why the place is not sold? I've seen many purchasers arrive, and all have gone off quicker than they came; not one of them has ever put in a second appearance. Well, one matter that's certain is that as soon as a visitor dares venture inside the house some extraordinary things happen. The doors swing to and fro and close by themselves with a bang, as if a hurricane were sweeping past. Cries, moans, and sobs ascend from the cellars, and if the visitor obstinately remains, a heartrending voice raises a continuous cry of "Angeline! Angeline! Angeline!" in such distressful, appealing tones that one's very bones are frozen. I repeat to you that this has been proved, nobody will tell you otherwise.'

I just own that I was now growing impassioned myself, and could feel a little chilly quiver coursing under my skin.

'And this Angeline, who is she?' I asked.

'Ah! monsieur, it would be necessary to tell you all. And once again, for my part I know nothing.'

Nevertheless, the old woman ended by telling me all. Some forty years previously – in or about 1858 – at the time when the triumphant Second Empire was as ever en fête, Monsieur de G., a Tuileries functionary, lost his wife, by whom he had a daughter some ten years old – Angeline, a marvel of beauty, the living portrait of her mother. Two years later, Monsieur de G. married again, espousing another famous beauty, the widow of a general. And it was asserted that, from the very moment of those second nuptials, atrocious jealousy had sprung up between Angeline and her stepmother; the former stricken in the heart at finding her own mother already forgotten, replaced so soon by a stranger; and the other tortured, maddened by always having before her that living portrait of a woman whose memory, she feared, she would never be able to efface. La Sauvagiere was the property of the new Madame de G., and there one evening, on seeing the father passionately embrace his daughter, she, in her jealous madness, it was said, had dealt the child so violent a blow, that the poor girl had fallen to the floor dead, her collar-bone broken. Then the rest was frightful: the distracted father consenting to bury his daughter with his own hands in a cellar of the house in order to save the murderess; the remains lying there for years, whilst the child was said to be living with an aunt; and at last the howls of a dog and its persistent scratching of the ground leading to the discovery of the crime, which was, however, at once hushed up by command of the Tuileries. And now Monsieur and Madame de G. were both dead, while Angeline again returned each night at the call of the heartrending voice that ever cried for her from out of the mysterious spheres beyond the darkness.

'Nobody will contradict me,' concluded Mother Toussaint. 'It is all as true as that two and two make four.'

I had listened to her in bewilderment, resenting certain improbabilities, but won over by the brutal and sombre strangeness of the tragedy. I had heard of this Monsieur de G., and it seemed to me that he had indeed married a second time, and that some family grief had overclouded his life. Was the tale true, then? What a tragical and affecting story! Every human passion stirred up, heightened, exasperated to madness; the most terrifying love tale there could be, a little girl as beautiful as daylight, adored, and yet killed by her stepmother, and buried by her father in the corner of a cellar! There was more here more matter for horror and emotion than one might dare to hope for. I was again about to question and discuss things. Then I asked myself what would be the use of it? Why not carry that frightful story away with me in its flower – such indeed as it had sprouted from popular imagination?

As I again sprang upon my bicycle I gave La Sauvagiere a last glance. The night was falling and the woeful house gazed at me with its dim and empty windows akin to the eyes of a corpse, whilst the wail of the autumn wind still swept through the ancient trees.

Why did this story so fix itself in my brain as to lead to real obsession, perfect torment? This is one of those intellectual problems that are difficult to resolve. In vain I told myself that similar legends overrun the rural districts, and that I had no direct concern in this one. In spite of all, I was haunted by that dead child, that lovely and tragic Angeline, to whom every night for forty years past a desolate voice had called through the empty rooms of the forsaken house.

Thus, during the first two months of the winter, I made researches. It was evident that if anything, however little, had transpired of such a dramatic disappearance, the newspapers of the period must have referred to it. However, I ransacked the collections of the National Library without discovering a line about any such story. Then I questioned contemporaries, men who had formerly had intercourse with Tuileries society; but none could give me a positive reply, I only obtained contradictory information. So much so that, although still and ever tortured by the mystery, I had abandoned all hope of getting to the truth, when chance one morning set me on a fresh track.

Every two or three weeks I paid a visit of goodfellowship, affection, and admiration to the old poet V., who died last

April on the threshold of his seventieth year. Paralysis of the legs had, for many years previous, riveted him to an armchair in his study of the Rue d'Assas whose windows overlooked the Luxembourg gardens. He there peacefully finished a dreamy life, for he had ever lived on imagination, building for himself a palace of ideality, in which he had loved and suffered far away from the real. Who of us does not remember his refined and amiable features, his white hair curly like a child's, his pale blue eyes, which had retained the innocence of youth? One could not say that he invariably told falsehoods. But the truth is that he was prone to invention, in suchwise that one never exactly knew at what point reality ceased to exist for him and at what point dreaming began. He was a very charming old man, long since detached from life, one whose words often filled me with emotion as if indeed they were a vague, discreet revelation of the unknown.

One day, then, I was chatting with him near the window of the little room which a blazing fire ever warmed. It was freezing terribly out of doors. The Luxembourg gardens stretched away white with snow, displaying a broad horizon of immaculate purity. And I know not how, but at last I spoke to him of La Sauvagiere, and of the story that still worried me – that father who had remarried, and that stepmother, jealous of the little girl; then the murder perpetrated in a fit of fury, and the burial in the cellar. V. listened to me with the quiet smile which he retained even in moments of sadness. Then silence fell, his pale blue eyes wandered away over the white immensity of the Luxembourg, whilst a shade of dreaminess, emanating from him, seemed to set a faint quiver all around.

'I knew Monsieur de G. very well,' he said. 'I knew his first wife, whose beauty was superhuman; I knew the second one, who was no less wondrously beautiful; and I myself passionately loved them both without ever telling it. I also knew Angeline, who was yet more beautiful than they, and whom all men a little later would have worshipped on their knees. But things did not happen quite as you say.'

My emotion was profound. Was the unexpected truth that I despaired of at first hand, then? At first I felt no distrust, but said to him, 'Ah! what a service you render me, my friend! I shall at last be able to quiet my poor mind. Make haste to tell me all.'

But he was not listening, his glance still wandered far away. And he began to speak in a dreamy voice, as if creating things and beings in his mind as he proceeded with his narrative.

'At twelve years of age Angeline was one in whom all woman's love, with every impulse of joy and grief, had already flowered. She it was who felt desperately jealous of the new wife whom every day she saw in her father's arms. She suffered from it as from some frightful act of betrayal; it was not her mother only who was insulted by that new union, she herself was tortured, her own heart was pierced. Every night, too, she heard her mother calling her from her tomb, and one night, eager to rejoin her, overcome by excess of suffering and excess of love, this child, who was but twelve years old, thrust a knife into her heart.'

A cry burst from me. 'God of heaven! Is it possible?'

'How great was the fright and horror,' he continued, without hearing me, 'when on the morrow Monsieur and Madame G. found Angeline in her little bed with that knife plunged to its very handle in her breast! They were about to start for Italy; of all their servants, too, there only remained in the house an old nurse who had reared the child. In their terror, fearing that they might be accused of a crime, they induced the woman to help them, and they did indeed bury the body, but in a corner of the conservatory behind the house at the foot of a huge orange-tree. And there she was found on the day when, the parents being dead, the old servant told the story.'

Doubts had come to me while he spoke, and I scrutinised him anxiously, wondering if he had not invented this.

'But,' said I, 'do you also think it possible that Angeline can come back each night in response to the heartrending, mysterious voice that calls her?'

This time he looked at me and smiled indulgently once more.

'Come back, my friend? Why everyone comes back! Why should not the soul of that dear dead child still dwell in the spot where she loved and suffered? If a voice is heard calling her 'tis because life has not yet begun afresh for her. Yet it will begin afresh, be sure of it; for all begins afresh. Nothing is lost, love no more than beauty. Angeline! Angeline! Angeline! She is called, and will be born anew to the sunlight and the flowers.'

Decidedly, neither belief nor tranquillity came to my mind. Indeed, my old friend V., the child-poet, had but increased my torment. He had assuredly been inventing things. And yet, like all visionaries, he could, perhaps, divine the truth.

'Is it all true, what you have been telling me?' I ventured to ask him with a laugh.

He in his turn broke into gentle mirth.

'Why, certainly it is true. Is not the infinite all true?'

That was the last time I saw him, for soon afterwards I had to quit Paris. But I can still picture him, glancing thoughtfully over the white expanse of the Luxembourg, so tranquil in the convictions born of his endless dream, whereas I am consumed by my desire to arrest and for all time determine Truth, which ever and ever flees.

Eighteen months went by. I had been obliged to travel; great trials and great joys had impassioned my life amidst the tempest-gust which carries us all onwards to the Unknown. But at certain moments still I heard the woeful cry, 'Angeline! Angeline! Angeline!' approach from afar and penetrate me. And then I trembled, full of doubt once more, tortured by my desire to know. I could not forget; for me there is no worse hell than uncertainty.

I cannot say how it was that one splendid June evening I again found myself on my bicycle on the lonely road that passes La Sauvagiere. Had I expressly wished to see the place again, or was it mere instinct that had impelled me to quit the highway and turn in that direction? It was nearly eight o'clock, but, those being the longest days of the year, the sky was still radiant with a triumphal sunset, cloudless, all gold and azure. And how light and delicious was the atmosphere, how pleasant was the scent of foliage and grass, how softly and sweetly joyous was the far-stretching peacefulness of the fields!

As on the first occasion, amazement made me spring from my machine in front of La Sauvagiere. I hesitated for a moment. The place was no longer the same. A fine new iron gate glittered in the sunset, the walls had been repaired, and the house, which I could scarce distinguish among the trees, seemed to have regained the smiling gaiety of youth. Was this, then, the predicted resurrection? Had Angeline returned to life at the call of the distant voice?

I had remained on the road, thunderstruck, still gazing, when a halting footfall made me start. I turned and saw Mother Toussaint bringing her cow back from a neighbouring patch of lucerne.

'So those folks were not frightened, eh?' said I, pointing to the house.

She recognised me and stopped her beast.

'Ah, monsieur!' she answered, 'there are people who would tread on God Himself! The place has been sold for more than a year now. But it was a painter who bought it, a painter named B., and those artists, you know, are capable of anything!'

Then she drove on her cow, shaking her head and adding: 'Well, well, we must see how it will all turn out.'

B. the painter, the delicate and skilful artist who had portrayed so many amiable Parisiennes! I knew him a little; we shook hands when we met at theatres and shows, wherever, indeed, people are apt to meet. Thus, all at once, an irresistible longing seized me to go in, make my confession to him, and beg him to tell me what he knew of this Sauvagiere, whose mystery ever haunted me. And without reasoning, without thought even of my dusty cycling suit, which custom, by the way, is now rendering permissible, I opened the gate and rolled my bicycle as far as the mossy trunk of an old tree. At the clear call of the bell affixed to the gate a servant came; I handed him my card and he left me for a moment in the garden.

My surprise increased still more when I glanced around me. The house-front had been repaired, there were no more cracks, no more disjointed bricks; the steps, girt with roses, were once more like a threshold of joyous welcome; and now the living windows smiled and spoke of the happiness behind their snowy curtains. Then, too, there was the garden rid of its nettles and brambles, the flower-bed reviviscent, resembling a huge and fragrant nosegay, and the old trees, standing amid the quietude of centuries, rejuvenated by the golden rain of the summer sun.

When the servant returned he led me to a drawing-room, saying that his master had gone to the neighbouring village, but would soon be home. I would have waited for hours. At first I took patience in examining the room, which was elegantly furnished, with heavy carpets, and window and door curtains of cretonne similar to that which upholstered the large settee and the deep armchairs. The hangings were indeed so full that I felt astonished at the sudden fall of daylight. Then came darkness almost perfect. I know not how long I stayed there; I had been forgotten, no lamp even was brought me. Seated in the gloom, I once again yielded up to my dreams and lived through the whole tragic story. Had Angeline been murdered? Or had she herself thrust a knife into her heart? And I must confess it, in that haunted house, where all had become so black, fear seized up on me – fear which was at the outset but slight uneasiness, a little creeping of the flesh, and which afterwards grew, froze me from head to foot, till I was filled with insane fright.

It seemed to me at first that vague sounds were echoing somewhere. 'Twas doubtless in the depths of the cellars. There were low moans, stifled sobs, footsteps as of some phantom. Then it all ascended and drew nearer, the whole dark house seemed to me full of that frightful anguish. All at once the terrible call arose, 'Angeline! Angeline! Angeline!' with such increasing force that I fancied I could feel a puff of icy breath sweep across my face. A door of the drawing-room was flung open violently, Angeline entered and crossed the room without seeing me. I recognised her in the flash of light which came in with her from the hall, where a lamp was burning. 'Twas really she, the poor dead child, twelve years of age, so marvellously beautiful. Her splendid hair fell over her shoulders, and she was clad in white; she had come all white from the grave, whence every night she rose. Mute, scared, she passed before me, and vanished through another door, whilst again the cry rang out farther away, 'Angeline! Angeline! Angeline!' And I – I remained erect, my brow wet with perspiration, in a state of horror, which made my hair stand on end, beneath the terror-striking blast that had come from the Mysterious.

Almost immediately afterwards, I fancy, at the moment when a servant at last brought a lamp, I became conscious that B., the painter, was beside me, shaking my hand and apologising for having kept me waiting so long. I showed no false pride, but, still quivering with dread, I at once told him my story. And with what astonishment did he not at first listen to me, and then with what kindly laughter did he not seek to reassure me!

'You were doubtless unaware, my dear fellow, that I am a

cousin of the second Madame de G. Poor woman! To accuse her of having murdered that child, she who loved her and wept for her as much as the father himself did! For the only point that is true is that the poor little girl did die here, not, thank heaven! by her own hand, but from a sudden fever which struck her down like a thunderbolt, in suchwise that the parents forsook this house in horror and would never return to it. This explains why it so long remained empty even in their lifetime. After their death came endless lawsuits, which prevented it from being sold. I wished to secure it myself, I watched for it for years, and I assure you that since we have been here we have seen no ghost.'

The little quiver came over me again, and I stammered, 'But Angeline, I have just seen her, here, this moment! The terrible voice was calling her, and she passed by, she crossed this room!'

He looked at me in dismay, fancying that my mind was affected. Then, all at once, he again broke into a sonorous, happy laugh.

'It was my daughter whom you saw. It so happens that Monsieur de G. was her godfather; and in memory of his own dear daughter he chose the name of Angeline. No doubt her mother was calling her just now, and she passed through this room.'

Then he himself opened a door, and once more raised the cry, 'Angeline! Angeline! Angeline!'

The child returned, not dead, but living, sparkling with juvenile gaiety. 'Twas she in her white gown, with her splendid fair hair falling over her shoulders, and so beautiful, so radiant with hope, that she looked like an incarnation of all the springtide of life, bearing in the bud the promise of love and the promise of long years of happiness.

Ah! the dear revenante, the new child that had sprung from the one that was no more! Death was vanquished. My old friend, the poet V., had told no falsehood. Nothing is lost, renascence comes to all, to beauty as well as love. Mothers' voices call them, those lasses of today, those sweethearts of tomorrow, and they live afresh beneath the sun, amid the flowers. And 'twas that awakening of youth that now haunted the house – the house which had once more become young and happy, in the joy at last regained that springs from life the eternal.

J'Accuse*

Sir,

Would you allow me, grateful as I am for the kind reception you once extended to me, to show my concern about maintaining your well-deserved prestige and to point out that your star which, until now, has shone so brightly, risks being dimmed by the most shameful and indelible of stains?

Unscathed by vile slander, you have won the hearts of all. You are radiant in the patriotic glory of our country's alliance with Russia, you are about to preside over the solemn triumph of our World Fair, the jewel that crowns this great century of labour, truth, and freedom. But what filth this wretched Dreyfus affair has cast on your name – I wanted to say 'reign'. A court martial, under orders, has just dared to acquit a certain Esterhazy, a supreme insult to all truth and justice. And now the image of France is sullied by this filth, and history shall record that it was under your presidency that this crime against society was committed.

As they have dared, so shall I dare. Dare to tell the truth, as I have pledged to tell it, in full, since the normal channels of justice have failed to do so. My duty is to speak out; I do not wish to be an accomplice in this travesty. My nights would otherwise be haunted by the spectre of the innocent man, far

---

* By Émile Zola (probably in collaboration with others, especially Georges Clemenceau, editor of *L'Aurore*).

away, suffering the most horrible of tortures for a crime he did not commit.

And it is to you, Sir, that I shall proclaim this truth, with all the force born of the revulsion of an honest man. Knowing your integrity, I am convinced that you do not know the truth. But to whom if not to you, the first magistrate of the country, shall I reveal the vile baseness of the real guilty parties?

The truth, first of all, about Dreyfus's trial and conviction:

At the root of it all is one evil man, Lieutenant Colonel du Paty de Clam, who was at the time a mere major. He is the entire Dreyfus case, and the entirety of it will only come to light when an honest inquiry firmly establishes his actions and responsibilities. He appears to be the shadiest and most complex of creatures, spinning outlandish intrigues, stooping to the deceits of cheap thriller novels, complete with stolen documents, anonymous letters, meetings in deserted spots, mysterious women scurrying around at night, peddling damning evidence. He was the one who came up with the scheme of dictating the text of the *bordereau* to Dreyfus; he was the one who had the idea of observing him in a mirror-lined room. And he was the one that Major Forzinetti caught carrying a shuttered lantern that he planned to throw open on the accused man while he slept, hoping that, jolted awake by the sudden flash of light, Dreyfus would blurt out his guilt.

I need say no more: let us seek and we shall find. I am stating simply that Major du Paty de Clam, as the officer of justice charged with the preliminary investigation of the Dreyfus case, is the first and the most grievous offender in the ghastly miscarriage of justice that has been committed.

The *bordereau* had already been for some time in the hands
of Colonel Sandherr, Head of the Intelligence Office, who
has since died of a paralytic stroke. Information was 'leaked',
papers were disappearing, then as they continue to do to
this day; and, as the search for the author of the *bordereau*
progressed, little by little, an a priori assumption developed
that it could only have come from an officer of the General
Staff, and furthermore, an artillery officer. This interpretation,
wrong on both counts, shows how superficially the *bordereau*
was analysed, for a logical examination shows that it could
only have come from an infantry officer.

So an internal search was conducted. Handwriting samples
were compared, as if this were some family affair, a traitor to
be sniffed out and expelled from within the War Office. And,
although I have no desire to dwell on a story that is only
partly known, Major du Paty de Clam entered on the scene
as soon as the slightest suspicion fell upon Dreyfus. From
that moment on, he was the one who 'invented' Dreyfus the
traitor, the one who orchestrated the whole affair and made
it his own. He boasted that he would confuse him and make
him confess all. Oh, yes, there was of course the Minister of
War, General Mercier, a man of apparently mediocre intellect;
and there were also the Chief of Staff, General de Boisdeffre,
who appears to have yielded to his own religious bigotry, and
the Deputy Chief of Staff, General Gonse, whose conscience
allowed for many accommodations. But, at the end of the
day, it all started with Major du Paty de Clam, who led them
on, hypnotised them, for, as an adept of spiritualism and the
occult, he conversed with spirits. Nobody would ever believe
the experiments to which he subjected the unfortunate

Dreyfus, the traps he set for him, the wild investigations, the monstrous fantasies, the whole demented torture.

Ah, that first trial! What a nightmare it is for all who know it in its true details. Major du Paty de Clam had Dreyfus arrested and placed in solitary confinement. He ran to Madame Dreyfus, terrorised her, telling her that, if she talked, that was it for her husband. Meanwhile, the unfortunate Dreyfus was tearing his hair out and proclaiming his innocence. And this is how the case proceeded, like some fifteenth-century chronicle, shrouded in mystery, swamped in all manner of nasty twists and turns, all stemming from one trumped-up charge, that stupid *bordereau*. This was not only a bit of cheap trickery but also the most outrageous fraud imaginable, for almost all of these notorious secrets turned out in fact to be worthless. I dwell on this, because this is the germ of it all, whence the true crime would emerge, that horrifying miscarriage of justice that has blighted France. I would like to point out how this travesty was made possible, how it sprang out of the machinations of Major du Paty de Clam, how Generals Mercier, de Boisdeffre and Gonse became so ensnared in this falsehood that they would later feel compelled to impose it as holy and indisputable truth. Having set it all in motion merely by carelessness and lack of intelligence, they seem at worst to have given in to the religious bias of their milieu and the prejudices of their class. In the end, they allowed stupidity to prevail.

But now we see Dreyfus appearing before the court martial. Behind the closed doors, the utmost secrecy is demanded. Had a traitor opened the border to the enemy and driven the Kaiser straight to Notre-Dame the measures of secrecy and silence could not have been more stringent. The public was astounded; rumours flew of the most horrible acts, the most monstrous deceptions, lies that were an affront to our history. The public, naturally, was taken in. No punishment could be too harsh. The people clamoured for the traitor to be publicly stripped of his rank and demanded to see him writhing with remorse on his rock of infamy. Could these things be true, these unspeakable acts, these deeds so dangerous that they must be carefully hidden behind closed doors to keep Europe from going up in flames? No! They were nothing but the demented fabrications of Major du Paty de Clam, a cover-up of the most preposterous fantasies imaginable. To be convinced of this one need only read carefully the accusation as it was presented before the court martial.

How flimsy it is! The fact that someone could have been convicted on this charge is the ultimate iniquity. I defy decent men to read it without a stir of indignation in their hearts and a cry of revulsion, at the thought of the undeserved punishment being meted out there on Devil's Island. He knew several languages: a crime! He carried no compromising papers: a crime! He would occasionally visit his country of origin: a crime! He was hard-working, and strove to be well informed: a crime! He did not become confused: a crime! He became confused: a crime! And how childish the language is, how groundless the accusation! We also heard talk of fourteen charges but we found only one, the one about the *bordereau*, and we learn that even there the handwriting experts could not agree. One of them, M. Gobert, faced military pressure when he dared to come to a conclusion other than the desired one. We were told also that twenty-three officers had testified against Dreyfus. We still do not know what questions they were asked, but it is certain that not all of them implicated him. It should be noted, furthermore, that all of them came from the War Office. The whole case had been handled as an internal affair, among insiders. And we must not forget this: members of the General Staff had sought this trial to begin with and had passed judgment. And now they were passing judgment once again.

So all that remained of the case was the *bordereau*, on which the experts had not been able to agree. It is said that within the council chamber the judges were naturally leaning toward acquittal. It becomes clear why, at that point, as justification for the verdict, it became vitally important to turn up some damning evidence, a secret document that, like God, could not be shown, but which explained everything, and was invisible, unknowable, and incontrovertible. I deny the existence of that document. With all my strength, I deny it! Some trivial note, maybe, about some easy women, wherein a certain D... was becoming too insistent, no doubt some demanding husband who felt he wasn't getting a good enough price for the use of his wife. But a document concerning national defence that could not be produced without sparking an immediate declaration of war tomorrow? No! No! It is a lie, all the more odious and cynical in that its perpetrators are getting off free without even admitting it. They stirred up all of France, they hid behind the understandable commotion they had set off, they sealed their lips while troubling our hearts and perverting our spirit. I know of no greater crime against the state.

These, Sir, are the facts that explain how this miscarriage of justice came about. The evidence of Dreyfus's character, his affluence, the lack of motive and his continued affirmation of innocence combine to show that he is the victim of the lurid imagination of Major du Paty de Clam, the religious circles surrounding him, and the 'dirty Jew' obsession that is the scourge of our time.

And now we come to the Esterhazy case. Three years have passed, many consciences remain profoundly troubled, become anxious, investigate, and wind up convinced that Dreyfus is innocent.

I shall not chronicle these doubts and the subsequent conclusion reached by M. Scheurer-Kestner. But, while he was conducting his own investigation, major events were occurring at headquarters. Colonel Sandherr had died and Lieutenant Colonel Picquart had succeeded him as Head of the Intelligence Office. It was in this capacity, in the exercise of his office, that Lieutenant Colonel Picquart came into possession of a telegram addressed to Major Esterhazy by an agent of a foreign power. His express duty was to open an inquiry. What is certain is that he never once acted against the will of his superiors. He thus submitted his suspicions to his hierarchical senior officers, first General Gonse, then General de Boisdeffre, and finally General Billot, who had succeeded General Mercier as Minister of War. That famous much-discussed Picquart file was none other than the Billot file, by which I mean the file created by a subordinate for his minister, which can still probably be found at the War Office. The investigation lasted from May to September 1896, and what must be said loud and clear is that General

Gonse was at that time convinced that Esterhazy was guilty and that Generals de Boisdeffre and Billot had no doubt that the handwriting on the famous *bordereau* was Esterhazy's. This was the definitive conclusion of Lieutenant Colonel Picquart's investigation. But feelings were running high, for the conviction of Esterhazy would inevitably lead to a retrial of Dreyfus, an eventuality that the General Staff wanted at all costs to avoid.

This must have led to a brief moment of psychological anguish. Note that, so far, General Billot was in no way compromised. Newly appointed to his position, he had the authority to bring out the truth. He did not dare, no doubt in terror of public opinion, certainly for fear of implicating the whole General Staff, General de Boisdeffre, and General Gonse, not to mention the subordinates. So he hesitated for a brief moment of struggle between his conscience and what he believed to be the interest of the military. Once that moment passed, it was already too late. He had committed himself and he was compromised. From that point on, his responsibility only grew, he took on the crimes of others, he became as guilty as they, if not more so, for he was in a position to bring about justice and did nothing. Can you understand this: for the last year Generals Billot, Gonse and de Boisdeffre have known that Dreyfus is innocent, and they have kept this terrible knowledge to themselves? And these people sleep at night, and have wives and children they love!

Lieutenant Colonel Picquart had carried out his duty as an honest man. He kept insisting to his superiors in the name of justice. He even begged them, telling them how impolitic it was to temporise in the face of the terrible storm that was brewing and that would break when the truth became known. This was the language that M. Scheurer-Kestner later used with General Billot as well, appealing to his patriotism to take charge of the case so that it would not degenerate into a public disaster. But no! The crime had been committed and the General Staff could no longer admit to it. And so Lieutenant Colonel Picquart was sent away on official duty. He got sent further and further away until he landed in Tunisia, where they tried eventually to reward his courage with an assignment that would certainly have got him massacred, in the very same area where the Marquis de Morès had been killed. He was not in disgrace, indeed: General Gonse even maintained a friendly correspondence with him. It is just that there are certain secrets that are better left alone.

Meanwhile, in Paris, truth was marching on, inevitably, and we know how the long-awaited storm broke. M. Mathieu Dreyfus denounced Major Esterhazy as the real author of the *bordereau* just as M. Scheurer-Kestner was handing over to the Minister of Justice a request for the revision of the trial. This is where Major Esterhazy comes in. Witnesses say that he was at first in a panic, on the verge of suicide or running away. Then all of a sudden, emboldened, he amazed Paris by the violence of his attitude. Rescue had come, in the form of an anonymous letter warning of enemy actions, and a mysterious woman had even gone to the trouble one night of slipping him a paper, stolen from headquarters, that would save him. Here I cannot help seeing the handiwork of Lieutenant Colonel du Paty de Clam, with the trademark fruits of his fertile imagination. His achievement, Dreyfus's conviction, was in danger, and he surely was determined to protect it. A retrial would mean that this whole extraordinary saga, so extravagant, so tragic, with its denouement on Devil's Island, would fall apart! This he could not allow to happen. From then on, it became a duel between Lieutenant Colonel Picquart and Lieutenant Colonel du Paty de Clam, one with his face visible, the other masked. The next step would take them both to civil court. It came down, once again, to the General Staff protecting itself, not wanting to admit its crime, an abomination that has been growing by the minute.

In disbelief, people wondered who Major Esterhazy's protectors were. First of all, behind the scenes, Lieutenant Colonel du Paty de Clam was the one who had concocted the whole story, who kept it going, tipping his hand with his outrageous methods. Next General de Boisdeffre, then General Gonse, and finally, General Billot himself were all pulled into the effort to get the major acquitted, for acknowledging Dreyfus's innocence would make the War Office collapse under the weight of public contempt. And the astounding outcome of this appalling situation was that the one decent man involved, Lieutenant Colonel Picquart who, alone, had done his duty, was to become the victim, the one who got ridiculed and punished. O justice, what horrible despair grips our hearts? It was even claimed that he himself was the forger, that he had fabricated the letter-telegram in order to destroy Esterhazy. But, good God, why? To what end? Find me a motive. Was he, too, being paid off by the Jews? The best part of it is that Picquart was himself an anti-semite. Yes! We have before us the ignoble spectacle of men who are sunken in debts and crimes being hailed as innocent, whereas the honour of a man whose life is spotless is being vilely attacked: a society that sinks to that level has fallen into decay.

The Esterhazy affair, thus, M. Président, comes down to this: a guilty man is being passed off as innocent. For almost two months we have been following this nasty business hour by hour. I am being brief, for this is but the abridged version of a story whose sordid pages will some day be written out in full. And so we have seen General de Pellieux, and then Major Ravary conduct an outrageous inquiry from which criminals emerge glorified and honest people sullied. And then a court martial was convened.

How could anyone expect a court martial to undo what another court martial had done?

I am not even talking about the way the judges were hand-picked. Doesn't the overriding idea of discipline, which is the lifeblood of these soldiers, itself undercut their capacity for fairness? Discipline means obedience. When the Minister of War, the commander in chief, proclaims, in public and to the acclamation of the nation's representatives, the absolute authority of a previous verdict, how can you expect a court martial to rule against him? It is a hierarchical impossibility. General Billot directed the judges in his preliminary remarks, and they proceeded to judgment as they would to battle, unquestioningly. The preconceived opinion they brought to the bench was obviously the following: 'Dreyfus was found guilty for the crime of treason by a court martial; he therefore is guilty and we, a court martial, cannot declare him innocent. On the other hand, we know that acknowledging Esterhazy's guilt would be tantamount to proclaiming Dreyfus innocent.' There was no way for them to escape this rationale.

So they rendered an iniquitous verdict that will forever weigh upon our courts martial and will henceforth cast a shadow of suspicion on all their decrees. The first court martial was perhaps unintelligent; the second one is inescapably criminal. Their excuse, I repeat, is that the supreme chief had spoken, declaring the previous judgment incontrovertible, holy and above mere mortals. How, then, could subordinates contradict it? We are told of the honour of the army; we are supposed to love and respect it. Ah, yes, of course, an army that would rise to the first threat, that would defend French soil, that army is the nation itself, and for that army we have nothing but devotion and respect. But this is not about that army, whose dignity we are seeking, in our cry for justice. What is at stake is the sword, the master that will one day, perhaps, be forced upon us. Bow and scrape before that sword, that god? No!

As I have shown, the Dreyfus case was a matter internal to the War Office: an officer of the General Staff, denounced by his co-officers of the General Staff, sentenced under pressure by the Chiefs of Staff. Once again, he could not be found innocent without the entire General Staff being guilty. And so, by all means imaginable, by press campaigns, by official communications, by influence, the War Office covered up for Esterhazy only to condemn Dreyfus once again. Ah, what a good sweeping out the government of this Republic should give to that Jesuit-lair, as General Billot himself calls it. Where is that truly strong, judiciously patriotic administration that will dare to clean house and start afresh? How many people I know who, faced with the possibility of war, tremble in anguish knowing to what hands we are entrusting our nation's defence! And what a nest of vile intrigues, gossip, and destruction that sacred sanctuary that decides the nation's fate has become! We are horrified by the terrible light the Dreyfus affair has cast upon it all, this human sacrifice of an unfortunate man, a 'dirty Jew'. Ah, what a cesspool of folly and foolishness, what preposterous fantasies, what corrupt police tactics, what inquisitorial, tyrannical practices! What petty whims of a few higher-ups trampling the nation under their boots, ramming back down their throats the people's cries for truth and justice, with the travesty of state security as a pretext.

Indeed, it is a crime to have relied on the most squalid elements of the press, and to have entrusted Esterhazy's defence to the vermin of Paris, who are now gloating over the defeat of justice and plain truth. It is a crime that those people who wish to see a generous France take her place as leader of all the free and just nations are being accused of fomenting turmoil in the country, denounced by the very plotters who are conniving so shamelessly to foist this miscarriage of justice on the entire world. It is a crime to lie to the public, to twist public opinion to insane lengths in the service of the vilest death-dealing machinations. It is a crime to poison the minds of the meek and the humble, to stoke the passions of reactionism and intolerance, by appealing to that odious anti-semitism that, unchecked, will destroy the freedom-loving France of the Rights of Man. It is a crime to exploit patriotism in the service of hatred, and it is, finally, a crime to ensconce the sword as the modern god, whereas all science is toiling to achieve the coming era of truth and justice.

Truth and justice, so ardently longed for! How terrible it is to see them trampled, unrecognised and ignored! I can feel M. Scheurer-Kestner's soul withering and I believe that one day he will even feel sorry for having failed, when questioned by the Senate, to spill all and lay out the whole mess. A man of honour, as he had been all his life, he believed that the truth would speak for itself, especially since it appeared to him plain as day. Why stir up trouble, especially since the sun would soon shine? It is for this serene trust that he is now being so cruelly punished. The same goes for Lieutenant Colonel Picquart, who, guided by the highest sentiment of dignity, did not wish to publish General Gonse's correspondence. These scruples are all the more honourable since he remained mindful of discipline, while his superiors were dragging his name through the mud and casting suspicion on him, in the most astounding and outrageous ways. There are two victims, two decent men, two simple hearts, who left their fates to God, while the devil was taking charge. Regarding Lieutenant Colonel Picquart, even this despicable deed was perpetrated: a French tribunal allowed the statement of the case to become a public indictment of one of the witnesses [Picquart], accusing him of all sorts of wrongdoing. It then chose to prosecute the case behind closed doors as soon as that witness was brought in to defend himself. I say this is yet another crime, and this crime will stir consciences everywhere. These military tribunals have, decidedly, a most singular idea of justice.

This is the plain truth, M. Président, and it is terrifying. It will leave an indelible stain on your presidency. I realise that you have no power over this case, that you are limited by the Constitution and your entourage. You have, nonetheless, your duty as a man, which you will recognise and fulfil. As for myself, I have not despaired in the least, of the triumph of right. I repeat with the most vehement conviction: truth is on the march, and nothing will stop it. Today is only the beginning, for it is only today that the positions have become clear: on one side, those who are guilty, who do not want the light to shine forth, on the other, those who seek justice and who will give their lives to attain it. I said it before and I repeat it now: when truth is buried underground, it grows and it builds up so much force that the day it explodes it blasts everything with it. We shall see whether we have been setting ourselves up for the most resounding of disasters, yet to come.

But this letter is long, Sir, and it is time to conclude it.

I accuse Lieutenant Colonel du Paty de Clam of being the diabolical creator of this miscarriage of justice – unwittingly, I would like to believe – and of defending this sorry deed, over the last three years, by all manner of ludicrous and evil machinations.

I accuse General Mercier of complicity, at least by mental weakness, in one of the greatest iniquities of the century.

I accuse General Billot of having held in his hands absolute proof of Dreyfus's innocence and covering it up, and making himself guilty of this crime against mankind and justice, as a political expedient and a way for the compromised General Staff to save face.

I accuse General de Boisdeffre and General Gonse of complicity in the same crime, the former, no doubt, out of religious prejudice, the latter perhaps out of that esprit de corps that has transformed the War Office into an unassailable holy ark.

I accuse General de Pellieux and Major Ravary of conducting a villainous inquiry, by which I mean a monstrously biased one, as attested by the latter in a report that is an imperishable monument to naïve impudence.

I accuse the three handwriting experts, Messrs Belhomme, Varinard and Couard, of submitting reports that were deceitful and fraudulent, unless a medical examination finds them to be suffering from a condition that impairs their eyesight and judgement.

I accuse the War Office of using the press, particularly *L'Eclair* and *L'Echo de Paris*, to conduct an abominable campaign to mislead the general public and cover up their own wrongdoing.

Finally, I accuse the first court martial of violating the law by convicting the accused on the basis of a document that was kept secret, and I accuse the second court martial of covering up this illegality, on orders, thus committing the judicial crime of knowingly acquitting a guilty man.

In making these accusations I am aware that I am making myself liable to articles 30 and 31 of the law of 29 July 1881 regarding the press, which make libel a punishable offence. I expose myself to that risk voluntarily.

As for the people I am accusing, I do not know them, I have never seen them, and I bear them neither ill will nor hatred. To me they are mere entities, agents of harm to society. The action I am taking is no more than a radical measure to hasten the explosion of truth and justice.

I have but one passion: to enlighten those who have been

kept in the dark, in the name of humanity which has suffered so much and is entitled to happiness. My fiery protest is simply the cry of my very soul. Let them dare, then, to bring me before a court of law and let the inquiry take place in broad daylight! I am waiting.

> With my deepest respect, Sir.
> Émile Zola,
> 13 January 1898

Note on Sources

The main narrative of the book has been written using the following sources:

Evelyne Bloch-Dano, *Madame Zola*
Denise Le Blond-Zola, *Émile Zola, raconté par sa fille*
Frederick Brown, *Zola: A Life*
Ruth Harris, *The Man on Devil's Island: Alfred Dreyfus and the Affair that Divided France*
Ernest Vizetelly, *With Zola in England: A Story of Exile*
————, *Émile Zola, Novelist and Reformer*
Émile Zola, *The Dreyfus Affair, 'J'accuse' and Other Writings*
————, *Notes from Exile*
————, *Correspondance* Volume IX *Octobre 1897–Septembre 1899 (L'affaire Dreyfus)*
————, *Lettres à Jeanne Rozerot*
————, *Oeuvres Complètes*, Volume 18, *De l'affaire aux Quatre Évangiles (1897–1901)*; Volume 19, *L'Utopie sociale: Les Quatre Évangiles [2] 1901*

The Bibliography gives full publication details for each title.

In addition to the above, sources more specifically related to the various chapters include the following:

Chapter 1
'J'accuse'; *Daily News*; *Pall Mall Gazette*; *The Times*; *Morning Post*

Chapter 2
The Times

Chapter 3
Musée-Galerie de la Seita, *Zola photographe* (exhibition
catalogue)
Brigitte Émile-Zola, *Mes étés à Brienne*
François Émile-Zola and [Robert] Massin, *Zola: Photographer*
Oatlands Park Hotel, *Our History*
Émile Zola, *Doctor Pascal*

Chapter 4
Jonathan Beecher & Richard Bienvenu, *The Utopian Vision of
Charles Fourier*
Maurice Le Blond, 'Les Projets Littéraires d'Émile Zola au
moment de sa mort, d'après des documents et manuscrits
inédits'
Brian Nelson, *The Cambridge Companion to Émile Zola*
Émile Zola, *Fécondité* (*Fruitfulness*)
————, *Travail* (*Work*)
————, *Vérité* (*Truth*)

Chapter 5
Beecher & Bienvenu (as above)
Charles Booth, *Life and Labour of the People in London, 1889–1903*
David Shonfield, 'Battle of Omdurman'
Émile Zola, *Angeline ou la maison hantée* (translated by Ernest
Vizetelly as *Angeline*)
London Standard; *Sunday Observer*

Chapter 6
François Émile-Zola and [Robert] Massin, *Zola: Photographer*

Chapter 7
Colin Burns, 'Le retentissement de l'Affaire Dreyfus dans
la presse britannique en 1898–99: esquisse d'un projet de
recherches futures'
————, 'Le Voyage de Zola à Londres en 1893'
Daily Graphic; *The Times*

Chapter 9
Beecher & Bienvenu (as above)
Joseph Conrad, *Letters to R. B. Cunninghame Graham*
Michel Dreyfus, *L'Antisémitisme à gauche*
Harvey Goldberg, *The Life of Jean Jaurès*
Jean Jaurès, *Ressources de Jaurès*
Fabian News; *Jewish Socialist*; *La Petite République*; *The Social-Democrat*; *Der Yidisher Expres*

Chapter 10
David Baguley, *Critical Essays on Émile Zola*
George J. Becker, *Documents of Modern Literary Realism*
David Bradshaw & Rachel Potter, *Prudes on the Prowl*
Peter Brooks, *Henry James Goes to Paris*
Alma W. Byrd, *The First Generation Reception of the Novels of Émile Zola*
W. E. Colburn, 'Zola in England'
R. G. Cox, *Thomas Hardy: The Critical Heritage*
Adrian Frazier, *George Moore, 1852–1933*
Donald Mason, 'The Doll of English Fiction, Hardy, Zola and the Politics of Convention'
James G. Nelson, *Publisher to the Decadents*
Eileen R. Pryme, 'Zola's Plays in England'
Nicolas Henricus Gerardus Schoonderwoerd, *J. T. Grein, Ambassador of the Theatre, 1862–1935*
Martin Seymour-Smith, *Hardy*
Robert Sherard, *Émile Zola: A Biographical and Critical Study*
Dorothy Speirs & Yannick Portebois, *Mon cher Maître: Lettres d'Ernest Vizetelly à Émile Zola*
John Addington Symonds, '"La Bête Humaine": A Study of Zola's Idealism'
Émile Zola, *Fécondité* (*Fruitfulness*)
Contemporary Review; *Glasgow Herald*; *Morning Post*; *Pall Mall Gazette*

Chapter 12
George Barlow, *A History of the Dreyfus Case*
Fred. C. Conybeare, *The Dreyfus Case*

Martyn Cornick, 'The Impact of the Dreyfus Affair in Late-
Victorian Britain'
Carmen Mayer-Robin, '"Justice", Zola's Global Utopian Gospel'
David Christie Murray, 'Some Notes on the Zola Case'
Robert Sherard, 'Emile Zola on Anti-Semitism in France'
G. W. Steevens, *The Tragedy of Dreyfus*
Émile Zola, *Verité* (*Truth*)
Daily Chronicle; *Daily Telegraph*; *Jewish Chronicle*; *Manchester
Guardian*; *Punch*; *The Times*; *Westminster Gazette*

Postscript
'Zola in Norwood', radio programme
[Denise Le Blond-Zola], *Les Années Heureuses, histoires d'enfants*
Interviews by the author and Emma-Louise Williams with
Madame Martine Le Blond-Zola

Bibliography

Writings by Émile Zola

Angeline, translated by Ernest Vizetelly; London, London Star, 1899

Correspondance d'Émile Zola, general editor B. H. Bakker, Volume IX, *Octobre 1897–Septembre 1899 (L'affaire Dreyfus),* volume editors Owen Morgan and Alain Pagès; Montréal & Paris, Les Presses Universitaires de l'Université de Montréal & CNRS Editions, 1993

Doctor Pascal, translated by Vladimir Kean; London, Elek Books, 1957

The Dreyfus Affair, 'J'accuse' and Other Writings, edited by Alain Pagès, translated by Eleanor Levieux; New Haven & London, Yale University Press, 1996

Fécondité, first published in Paris in 1899; first published in English as *Fruitfulness* (1900), translated and much abridged by Ernest Vizetelly

'Lettre à M. Félix Faure, Président de la République' ('J'Accuse'). *L'Aurore,* 13 January 1898 (see Appendix 11)

Lettres à Jeanne Rozerot, 1892–1902, edited by Brigitte Émile-Zola and Alain Pagès, Paris, NRF, Gallimard, 2004

Notes from Exile, edited and translated by Dorothy E. Speirs and edited by Yannick Portebois, Toronto, University of Toronto Press, 2003

Oeuvres complètes, Volume 18, *De l'affaire aux Quatre Évangiles (1897–1901),* edited by Alain Pagès; Volume 19, *L'Utopie sociale: Les Quatre Évangiles [2] 1901,* edited by Béatrice Laville; Paris, Nouveau Monde Editions, 2008, 2009

Truth (translated with Preface by Ernest Vizetelly), London, Chatto & Windus, 1903

Work (translated with Preface by Ernest Vizetelly), London,
Chatto & Windus, 1901

First-hand accounts
Alfred Dreyfus (intro. by Nicholas Halasz), *Five Years of My
Life: The Diary of Captain Alfred Dreyfus*, New York, London,
Peebles Press, 1977
Brigitte Émile-Zola, *Mes étés à Brienne*, Agneaux, France,
Éditions du Frisson Esthétique, 2008
Denise Le Blond-Zola, *Émile Zola, raconté par sa fille*, Paris,
Fasquelle Editeurs, 1931
—— [writing as Denise Aubert], *Les Années Heureuses, histoires
d'enfants*, Paris, Librairie Hachette, 1923
Ernest Vizetelly, *With Zola in England: A Story of Exile*, London,
Chatto & Windus, 1899
——, *Émile Zola, Novelist and Reformer: An account of his life
and work*, London, John Lane, Bodley Head, 1904

Contemporary newspapers, magazines and journals
Contemporary Review; *Daily Chronicle*; *Daily Graphic*; *Daily News*;
Daily Telegraph; *Fabian News*; *Glasgow Herald*; *Jewish Chronicle*;
Jewish Socialist; *London Standard*; *Manchester Guardian*; *Morning
Post*; *Pall Mall Gazette*; *La Petite République*; *Punch*; *The Social-
Democrat*; *Sunday Observer*; *The Times*; *Westminster Gazette*; *Der
Yidisher Expres* (or *The Yiddisher Express*)

Photographic works
Musée-Galerie de la Seita, *Zola photographe* (exhibition
catalogue), Paris, 1987
François Émile-Zola & [Robert] Massin, *Zola: Photographer*,
London, Collins, 1988
Norwood Society, *Emile Zola: photographer in Norwood, South
London 1898–1899*, The Norwood Society/London Borough of
Croydon, 1997

Critical works and commentaries
David Baguley, *'Fécondité' d'Émile Zola, roman à thèse, évangile,
mythe*, Toronto, University of Toronto Press, 1973

——— (ed.), *Critical Essays on Émile Zola*, Boston, MA, G. K. Hall & Co., 1986

George Barlow, *A History of the Dreyfus Case, from the arrest of Captain Dreyfus in October 1894 up to the Flight of Esterhazy in September 1898*, London, Simpkin, Marshall, Hamilton, Kent, 1899

George J. Becker (ed.), *Documents of Modern Literary Realism*, Princeton, Princeton University Press, 1963

Karl Beckson, *London in the 1890s: A Cultural History*, New York & London, W. W. Norton, 1992

Jonathan Beecher & Richard Bienvenu (trans., ed. & intro.), *The Utopian Vision of Charles Fourier: Selected texts on work, love and passionate attraction*, London, Jonathan Cape, 1972

Evelyne Bloch-Dano, *Madame Zola*, Paris, Editions Grasset et Fasquelle, 1997

Harold Bloom (ed. & intro.), *Émile Zola*, Broomall, PA, Chelsea House, 2004

Charles Booth, *Life and Labour of the People in London, 1889–1903* (available at http://www.genguide.co.uk/source/life-and-labour-of-the-people-in-london-charles-booth-survey/266)

David Bradshaw & Rachel Potter (eds), *Prudes on the Prowl: Fiction and obscenity in England, 1850 to the present day*, Oxford, Oxford University Press, 2013

Peter Brooks, *Henry James Goes to Paris*, Princeton & Oxford, Princeton University Press, 2007

Frederick Brown, *Zola: A Life*, Baltimore & London, Johns Hopkins University Press, 1996

———, *For the Soul of France, Culture Wars in the Age of Dreyfus*, New York, Alfred E. Knopf, 2010

William I. Brustein & Louisa Roberts, *The Socialism of Fools? Leftist Origins of Modern Anti-Semitism*, Cambridge, Cambridge University Press, 2015

Colin Burns, 'Le retentissement de l'Affaire Dreyfus dans la presse britannique en 1898–99: esquisse d'un projet de recherches futures', *Les Cahiers Naturalistes*, No. 54, Paris, Société Littéraire des Amis d'Émile Zola, 1980

————, 'Le Voyage de Zola à Londres en 1893, "NOTES SUR LONDRES", texte inédit d'Émile Zola', *Les Cahiers Naturalistes*, No. 60, Paris, Société Littéraire des Amis d'Émile Zola, 1986

Michael Burns, *France and the Dreyfus Affair: A Documentary History*, Boston & New York, Bedford/St Martin's, 1999

Frederick Busi, *The Pope of Antisemitism, the career and legacy of Edouard-Adolphe Drumont*, Lanham, MD, University Press of America, 1986

Alma W. Byrd, *The First Generation Reception of the Novels of Émile Zola in Britain: An annotated bibliography of English Language Responses to his work, 1877–1902*, Lewiston, Queenston, Lampeter, Edwin Mellen Press, 2006

Erin G. Carlston, *Double Agents, espionage, literature and liminal citizens*, New York, Columbia University Press, 2013

Lawson A. Carter, *Zola and the Theater*, Westport, CT, Greenwood Press, 1977

William Elliot Colburn, 'Zola in England, 1883–1903', PhD thesis, University of Illinois, 1949

Joseph Conrad (ed. C. T. Watts), *Letters to R. B. Cunninghame Graham*, Cambridge, Cambridge University Press, 2011 (reissue)

Fred. C. Conybeare, *The Dreyfus Case*, London, George Allen, 1899

Martyn Cornick, 'The Impact of the Dreyfus Affair in Late-Victorian Britain', *Franco-British Studies* 22, 1996, pp. 57–82

R. G. Cox (ed.), *Thomas Hardy: The Critical Heritage*, New York, Barnes & Noble, 1970

Laura Deal, 'Zola in England: Controversy and Change in the 1890s', PhD thesis, Washington DC, American University, 2008

Isabelle Delamotte, *Le Roman de Jeanne, à l'ombre de Zola*, Paris, Belfond, 2009

Michel Dreyfus, *L'Antisémitisme à gauche, histoire d'un paradoxe, de 1830 à nos jours*, Paris, Éditions La Découverte, 2009

Adrian Frazier, *George Moore, 1852–1933*, New Haven & London, Yale University Press, 2000

Harvey Goldberg, *The Life of Jean Jaurès*, Madison, Milwaukee, London, University of Wisconsin Press, 1962

Henri Guillemin, *L'Enigme Esterhazy*, Paris, NRF, Gallimard, 1962

Ruth Harris, *The Man on Devil's Island: Alfred Dreyfus and the Affair that Divided France*, London, Allen Lane, 2010

Chris Healey, *Confessions of a Journalist*, London, Chatto & Windus, 1904

F. W. J. Hemmings, *Émile Zola*, Oxford, Oxford University Press, 2nd edn, 1966

———, *The Life and Times of Émile Zola*, London, New Delhi, New York, Sidney, Bloomsbury Reader, 2013

Paul Hyland & Neil Sammells (eds), *Writing and Censorship in Britain*, London, New York, Routledge, 1992

Jean Jaurès, *Les Preuves* (available at http://gallica.bnf.fr/ark:/12148/bpt6k72819h/f4.image)

———, *Ressources de Jaurès* (available at http://www.jaures.eu/ressources/de_jaures/jaures-les-socialistes-et-laffaire-dreyfus-1900)

———, Untitled Article re Zola Visit, *La Petite Republique*, 23 April 1901 (also published in Zola's *Oeuvres complètes*, Vol. 18)

———, 'Work', *The Social-Democrat*, July 1901, pp. 205–6; translated by Jacques Bonhomme

Jewish Socialists Group, 'James Connolly and the Jews', available at www.jewishsocialist.org.uk/features/item/james-connolly-and-the-jews

Graham King, *Garden of Zola: Émile Zola and his Novels for English Readers*, London, Barrie & Jenkins, 1978

Maurice Le Blond, 'Les Projets Littéraires d'Émile Zola au moment de sa mort, d'après des documents et manuscrits inédits', *Mercure de France*, No. 703, 1 October 1927

J. Robert Maguire, *Ceremonies of Bravery: Oscar Wilde, Carlos Blacker and the Dreyfus Affair*, Oxford, Oxford University Press, 2013

Donald Mason, 'The Doll of English Fiction, Hardy, Zola and the Politics of Convention', PhD thesis, McMaster University, 1994

Carmen Mayer-Robin, '"Justice", Zola's Global Utopian Gospel', *Nineteenth-Century French Studies*, 36, Nos 1 & 2, Fall–Winter 2007–8

Elizabeth Carolyn Miller, *Slow Print: Literary Radicalism and*

Late Victorian Print Culture, Stanford, Stanford University
Press, 2013
David Christie Murray, 'Some Notes on the Zola Case',
Contemporary Review, April 1898, pp. 486–7
National Vigilance Association, 'Pernicious Literature', in George
Joseph Becker (ed.), *Documents of Modern Literary Realism*,
Princeton, Princeton University Press, 1963, pp. 350–82
Brian Nelson (ed.), *The Cambridge Companion to Émile Zola*,
Cambridge, Cambridge University Press, 2007
James G. Nelson, *Publisher to the Decadents: Leonard Smithers
in the Careers of Beardsley, Wilde, Dowson*, University Park,
Pennsylvania University Press, 2000

Oatlands Park Hotel, *Our History*, no date or publication details
given
Alain Pagès, *Une Journée dans l'affaire Dreyfus, 13 janvier 1898,
J'accuse . . .*', Paris, Perrin, 2011
———, *Émile Zola de J'accuse' au Panthéon*, Saint-Paul, Lucien
Souny, 2008
Eileen R. Pryme, 'Zola's Plays in England', *French Studies*, XIII,
no. 1 (Jan. 1959), pp. 28–38
Morris U. Schappes, *The Jewish Question and the Left – old and
new, a challenge to the New Left*, New York, Jewish Currents
reprint no 7, 1970
Nicolas Henricus Gerardus Schoonderwoerd, *J. T. Grein,
Ambassador of the Theatre, 1862–1935*, Assen, Van Gorcum and
Company, NV. 1962
Martin Seymour-Smith, *Hardy*, London, Bloomsbury, 1994
Robert Harborough Sherard, *Émile Zola: A Biographical and
Critical Study*, London, Chatto & Windus, 1893
———, 'Emile Zola on Anti-Semitism in France', *The
Humanitarian*, Vol. XII, February 1898, No. 2
Pamela Shields, *Hertfordshire, Secrets and Spies*, Stroud, Amberley
Publishing, 2009
David Shonfield, 'The Battle of Omdurman', *History Today*,
Vol. 48, Issue 9, September 1998 (available at http://www.
historytoday.com/david-shonfield/battle-omdurman#sthash.
rt8r8ZKB.dpuf)

Dorothy E. Speirs & Yannick Portebois (eds), with Lillian Barra, Michel Duquet, Tanya Magnus, Kathy Marek, Nathalie V. Obregon and Nimisha Visram, *Mon cher Maître, Lettres d'Ernest Vizetelly à Émile Zola*, Montréal, Les Presses de l'Université de Montréal, 2001

G. W. Steevens, *The Tragedy of Dreyfus*, London, New York, Harper & Brothers, 1899

John Stokes, *In the Nineties*, Chicago, University of Chicago Press, 1989

John Addington Symonds, '"La Bête Humaine": A Study of Zola's Idealism', *Fortnightly Review*, LVI, October 1891, pp. 453–62

Marcel Thomas, *Esterhazy, ou l'envers de l'affaire Dreyfus*, Paris, Vernal/Philippe Lebaud, 1989

Karl Zieger (ed.), '"Émile Zola, 'J'Accuse . . . !'" Réactions nationales et internationales', *Journée d'études Valenciennes*, Valenciennes, Presses Universitaires de Valenciennes, 1998

'Zola in Norwood', BBC Radio 3 programme, producer Emma-Louise Williams, presenter Michael Rosen, first broadcast 11 January 2015 (available at http://www.bbc.co.uk/programmes/b04xrq3w)

Index

Note: all buildings and locations are in central London unless otherwise specified.